Dear Pussycat

ALSO BY HELEN GURLEY BROWN

Sex and the Single Girl

Helen Gurley Brown's Single Girl Cookbook

Having It All

Sex and the Office

Sex and the New Single Girl

Cosmopolitan's New Etiquette Guide

Helen Gurley Brown's Outrageous Opinions

*The Late Show: A Semiwild But Practical
Survival Plan for Women Over 50*

I'm Wild Again

Dear Pussycat

Mash Notes and Missives from
the Desk of *Cosmopolitan*'s
Legendary Editor

Helen Gurley Brown

St. Martin's Press ✿ New York

www.stmartins.com

ISBN 0-312-31757-3
EAN 978-0312-31757-7

First Edition: April 2004

10 9 8 7 6 5 4 3 2 1

CONTENTS

One day a former <u>Cosmo</u> editor, visiting St. Martin's Press, knowing they had published a book of mine, <u>I'm Wild Again</u>, told them that people who worked for me saved my letters through the years and treasured them. Why did they do that? The letters were flattering, Ellen Tien said—recipient was told he or she was wonderful but they had some special quality. What <u>kind</u> of special quality, St. Martin's wanted to know and subsequently asked if I might borrow back a few of these letters from the recipients and could they also see some of my letters to other people. I borrowed back some staff letters, and Susie, my undauntable elf, pulled up quite a few copies of letters from our computer, sent to the outside world. St. Martin's read them and decided they would like to publish a small book of my correspondence . . . only <u>my</u> part of the correspondence (I don't save other people's letters). To determine which letters to use, Susie pulled up hundreds (or so it seemed) from the computers for the years 1990 to today. Before computers, carbon copies were the only "permanent" record of letters written, and we didn't have any of those. So, from spending just a little under a thousand hours myself, going <u>through</u> all the letters that had been pulled up—the stack actually reached from the floor to three feet <u>up</u>—I chose some I thought might work (they're not all riveting!), put out the word to those who had saved other letters, put them in twenty categories, and here they are, just as originally written. Now, I won't be trying to persuade <u>you</u> to write letters or be asinine enough to suggest how to write them. Either one is a letter writer or one isn't, I feel. Might as well encourage me to learn how to <u>cook</u> . . . finally! I'm mediocre.

Letter writing has been of considerable help in my career, so perhaps that's why I do so much of it and think highly of the skill.

As a secretary at an ad agency in Los Angeles, Foote, Cone & Belding, in the late forties, early fifties, I wrote letters to my boss, the agency head, Don Belding, when he was out of the city, telling him news of the day and particularly how much we missed him. Long-distance phoning was still pretty exotic and expensive at that time and not an option for anyone except big-deal executives. Don's wife, Alice, read the letters and pestered her husband: "Don, your secretary can write. . . . You ought to let her write copy (on one of the agency's accounts)." "Alice, get off the case, she's a secretary. . . . I don't need her writing copy" was along the lines of what he said. So I entered a contest with <u>Glamour</u> magazine—"Ten Girls with Taste"—and, having the taste of an aardvark but writing a good entry form (not unlike a letter), became one of the winners. My answer to one of the questions, "What would you like to become—what is your ambition?" was the Alice Belding idea—copywriter. I had no idea what I wanted to be except to be less hungry and probably to continue to be Alice's husband's secretary.

<u>Glamour</u>'s personnel director, bless her, called Don Belding and said, "Helen wants to write copy, why don't you let her?" and bless him, he did. Writing advertising copy may not be <u>unlike</u> writing letters . . . you're communicating, trying to get <u>through</u> to somebody. Years later I wrote a letter to a small publisher in New York, Bernard Geis, asking if he'd like to see an outline and first chapter of a book I had in mind—David's idea, I wasn't full of gumption then. The letter got a yes answer and, after receiving and reading the material I sent, Berney decided to publish the book <u>Sex and the Single Girl</u>. <u>That</u> changed my life, to put it mildly. Wish I had the letter I wrote Berney, but he's gone, alas, and his files haven't been kept.

To this moment I <u>still</u> prefer writing letters to talking a lot of the time. Dictating a note takes ninety seconds, a phone call ten minutes. You can also revise a letter to make it better. A Neanderthal, I don't do e-mail, the preference for millions of people as the way to communicate in type. My Royal manual typewriter wouldn't <u>like</u> my defecting to this classy new girl in town! Susie and I fax but continue to put correspondence in envelopes and send it through the mail.

My only suggestion about letter writing (I know, I promised!)—would be that a thank-you note should be sent sooner rather than later, then it doesn't have to be so wonderful. And I don't believe in complaining too much in writing . . . better to be angry on the phone or in person than to have people wince and hate you when they open an envelope (though I do make an occasional exception, as you shall see). If you want to turn down a request, I think it's easier to say no in a letter . . . you can be more gracious, explain better why you can't cooperate. The letter that got me started appreciating the art was written at age fifteen to President Franklin D. Roosevelt. I don't have the actual letter but remember exactly what it said and am including it here. That letter got results—I was hooked!

Compulsively writing letters. Guilty!

#

ONE

(You Can <u>Increase</u> the Friendship Circle if You Write)

Aren't a great many of the letters we write throughout our lives (as well as e-mail now, of course) directed to friends? That surely is true for me, though I've also had a prolific business correspondence. I have more copies of friend letters than could possibly be accommodated in a book, and there were plenty of which there <u>are</u> no copies. It took me about three weeks (while holding down a day job) to go through my friend letters and choose a few I thought might be lively enough to keep you awake. No guarantee!

Dear Mr President,

My sister Mary has Polio, just like you do. I know she would love to hear from you. Could you write her a letter? Her address is:

Mary Gurley
Orthopedic Hospital
2400 S. Flower Street
Los Angeles, California

Thank you with all my heart, Mr. President.

President Franklin D. Roosevelt
the White House
Washington, D.C

July 8, 2002

Dear Georgette,

Sorry we didn't have more of a chance to visit on the Forbes yacht but there were lots of intriguing people prowling around and <u>most</u> of them wanted to talk to <u>you</u>! Georgette, there was something I wanted to mention and maybe I have before—you are always doing all the <u>giving</u> and people's houses and lives are enhanced by that! I have Georgette Mosbacher needlepoint pillows from several Christmases, a beautiful Hermès scarf you once bestowed, for whatever reason, and, as I mentioned, the wonderful La Prairie foundation you so generously supplied (I never felt there was anything like it) that I am <u>still</u> a beneficiary of. Have noted that you are now only interested in good-looking, sexy <u>hunks</u> . . . all other needs have been met . . . and if I run into a "worthy," I'll submit his name. I'm so glad we're friends.

Lots of love,

P.S. Georgette, I always enjoy telling people about you on the Randy and Veronica Hearst yacht that we occupied for a few days together. You got all the faxes . . . the U.S. Secretary of State, financial mogul Ezra Zilkha, film producer David Brown hardly heard a squeak from anybody . . . you were conducting an international business on the deck of the ship and <u>everybody</u> had to be in touch with you.

Ms. Georgette Mosbacher
Fifth Avenue
New York, New York 10028

July 1, 1998

Jeffrey dear,

I'm sorry I was so witchy in the elevator this morning. David had just insisted on reading me, comma by comma, the reviews from the New York Times <u>and</u> the Wall Street Journal of ARMAGEDDON, the rival of DEEP IMPACT. Apparently the rivalry isn't going to be intense because Armageddon is so awful, although you may think otherwise. Anyway, I had already been slowed down about twelve minutes with David's dramatic performance and I simply, as they say, lost it in the elevator. I do apologize. Your mommy is difficult but <u>worthy</u> and you are a good son and I shouldn't have been screaming at your attenuated goodbye.

Love and cheers,

Mr. Jeffrey Lyons
West 57th Street
New York, New York 10019

HGB:ss

July 20, 2001

Dear Danny,

Your brother tells me you've been having a pretty rough time these days that you have been fighting back valiantly and trying every possible way to get your health to improve. Maybe some of the things the doctors are working with will have miraculous results. Danny, I wanted to send along something special from me to you. This pen is in a blue Tiffany box although it isn't a Tiffany pen. It is the pen they gave me on the Concorde on my last flight . . . who <u>knew</u> they wouldn't be flying again for a long long time. I'm sending all my love . . . thanks for letting me in your life.

Mr. Danny Leeds
Salem, South Carolina 29676

September 1, 1998

Dear John and Larry,

Can't quite tell which of you got out the last letter but I think it may be John because you mentioned dancing with Ann Miller at a party Gloria Vanderbilt's mother and aunt were given for their birthday "eons ago." That would definitely have been John. I saw Gloria not too long ago—we gave a little wedding celebration for Woody Allen and Soon-Yi, and she was on the short list of people he approved being invited. She's really rather dear and has aged <u>incredibly</u> well . . . she's my role model. John, she does indeed remember your days together and that subject comes up when we see each other. Though it may sound funny, New York is kind of wonderful in the summer. We took a Madison Avenue bus from the tip of Manhattan Saturday afternoon after the theatre and got all the way to 81st Street in about 12 minutes . . . the city is incredible without traffic. I <u>took</u> computer lessons and found out I could handle it but didn't want to! I like to type, pull the paper out of the machine and put it in an envelope. My adorable Susie uses a computer and does all the heavy thinking and organizing and storing that involves. I can't seem to think anything being on-line would <u>bring</u> me. . . . I just want to keep up with the good friends I now have.

I've never ceased to be staggered by the way you've handled the move from Montserrat. Maybe you cursed the hurricane but you certainly didn't complain much to pals. The stock market is down 500 points today in addition to 500 <u>last</u> week which isn't bringing too many smiles to <u>my</u> house but I daresay we will all survive. I used to say I could always be a good executive secretary again but that can't be said anymore because of the subject we already covered—computers. I can book tables at a good restaurant—and be a whole lot more cordial than the people who are doing it <u>now</u>. . . . I get so irritated with snippy ladies on the phone you're trying to get to do something.

Much love. . . .

Let me hear from you,

Mr. Larry Baldwin
Mr. John Clerc-Scott
Petit Bourg
Guadeloupe

March 28, 2002

Edith dear,

This is a fan letter. I just want to tell you once more what beautiful things you did in our apartment and how grateful I am that you did them. We know you spruced up the living room—new blue drapes and cushions and they still look nice. Same thing in the dining room. It wasn't <u>easy</u> to get a new red shade and this one works beautifully. I don't see the studio every day. . . . the steps are steep to get up there unless you have a real purpose but even in the studio you did wonderful touches—went to lots of trouble to get just the right animal-fabric cushions. Then we get to David's den. . . . it's absolutely glorious. . . . STILL! The combination of fabrics is the best there could be—we know how you agonized about putting so many patterns together and you did the perfect thing.

Edith, why am I writing you this letter? You did beautiful work in our apartment and that work has brought pleasure every day or even every hour. I just don't see more decorating right this minute. April 18th, I have twenty-five people coming over for cocktails. A hot-shot writer, Olivier Bernier—is going to interpret and talk to the group about a very wonderful new book. His mother, Rosamond Bernier, takes groups of people through the Metropolitan. This is a reception I was prevailed upon to give by the New York Public Library. I am one of their Conservators and do very little work for them but kicked in when they asked if they could have the party/lecture at my apartment. Well, it is a beautiful apartment and should be <u>seen</u> and, who knows, there might be a some-day client in the assembled group. I'm going to have everything looking frisky fresh with lots of flowers.

David and I love everything that you accomplished for us and I wish I could send you a client or two because <u>you truly deserve</u>, even if the clients aren't us.

Love and hugs,

Ms. Edith Berke
Woodland Avenue
Summit, New Jersey 07901

COSMOPOLITAN

Helen Gurley Brown, Editor-In-Chief

April 28, 2000

Ernest dear,

It irritates me so that some people are making you unhappy about your diary. . . . whose life is it anyway?! Obviously what you wrote was how you recalled things. . . . why would you be making anything up? We know Elizabeth Taylor had drinking problems and others had drug problems of one kind or another. Liz went to Betty Ford, for God's sake—and Richard Burton was not a Sunday school choirboy. That you had to tell TALK you may not have remembered accurately is simply rotten. The diary is not only fascinating because of the people involved and incidents revealed but because you are a writer—I love "I am beginning to feel that the producer cannot win any popularity contests on a picture!" Tina Brown was the smartest person in the world to feature the diary, a wimp to have listened seriously to the complainers. Don't worry your pretty head. . . . it is a fabulous recounting of Virginia Woolf and even makes me want to keep a diary if I had anything half as fascinating to record!

Much love to you and Laurie,

Mr. Ernest Lehman
Chenault
West Los Angeles, CA. 90049

HGB:ss

**This was Ernest Lehman's longtime wife. She died and
Ernest remarried. He kept this letter along with ones I'd
written to <u>him</u>.**

July 21, 1967

Jackie dear,

I'm always touched by your honesty. If you're depressed or
bored you <u>say</u> you are and no nonsesne [sic]. I don't have any
dazzling solutions . . . so much of the happiness thing seems to
be <u>luck</u>. I was so unhappy and faintly melancholy for
<u>years</u> . . . as a young woman . . . and I am happier now . . .
but I worked hard <u>then</u> and <u>tried</u> to get on with it, <u>too</u>. So it
wasn't like getting religion and going STRAIGHT. The luck just
ran better when I got past 35.

I do believe that as you keep putting out little shoots or roots
or whatever you call them, you also keep getting something
<u>back</u> . . . eventually. That you do have <u>some</u> control over your
destiny. Usually the roots and shoots you put out are tiny and
boring and you think oh god, <u>this</u> isn't the answer . . . I need a
<u>big</u> change and a <u>big</u> deliverance.

But then you can only work with what you have to <u>work</u> with
so that is better than nothing.

A man is so intricately interwoven into ones life it's hard to be
happy if there's something unhappy with <u>him</u> or <u>that</u>
relationship. It is very very hard to say "i'm a sovereign
human being and i will make my <u>own</u> happiness." The two
years david was a producer at fox, filling out his contract
under a hostile administration, and the year or so he was in
publishing in newyork i thought i was going to <u>die</u> because he
was unhappy. it simply rubbed off no matter how "sovereign"
I tried to be. "a pall is on this house" I used to tell him. the
fact that all that changed is more luck than anything else . . .

although he never ceased being the kind of person—or worker—to whom the good new situation could happen.

So what will happen to change jackie's pall?! I don't know, dear, but i know you will plant the acorns and "get something in the mail" so that good things can start coming back from these small but noble efforts.

if there's anything you aren't, it's lazy! aside from your terribly busy days with husband, children, house, hostessing, servants, friends and all the rest there must be shoots to send out this summer of 1967 that would grow into trees next fall or next year. since the happiness one wants seems never to be through the people closest to us, it must somehow be through ourselves . . . and this is true of people with the dreamiest, lovingest husbands . . . can they ever really do it for you? . . . you were once studying dance therapy for disturbed children. if it cant be through dance, isnt there some other way of working with people who interest you and whom you can help?

it won't get you a newly loving husband . . . or children who are 2 and 4 again and relatively "painless." . . . but nobody has a loving husband who is always her true companion and playmate. and the men and women who have that relationship make me a little nauseated anyway . . . like the Ronald Reagans (she apparently adores him). these people with their super-perfect man-woman relationship (and i doubt it) tend to isolate other people with their smugness and nobody can stand them! I think at best a marriage can be a friendship where you dont hate the other person too much of the time . . . but you must have other friends . . . i.e. fairly important interests or you bore him or he bores you or both. i feel it incumbant [sic] on you to plant some jackie acorns! (so trees come up.) you're too damn rich and West Los Angeles isnt the place where it happens easily but somewhere out there are some things that must call you . . . daring, inappropriate things . . . always they're inappropriate and people say "that jackie lehman . . . why is she doing that" but i'm thinking of taking some of your money and opening a travel agency, or buying a boutique, or studying law . . . or volunteering to work in a clinic with children or learning italian and french <u>really</u> well or investing in a show maybe ernest would have some ideas. say to ernest "i am unhappy and i must try to find something that will help me use up <u>me</u> . . . where shall i channel this unhappiness so that i can stop feeling resentful toward <u>you</u> and become my own person?"

most men will not know what in god's name you are talking about and yet if you can get a husband who is on your side, he is the one who can help you bring it off.

as you may know, i was a miserable woman when i <u>forced</u> david to think of something i could do. i said "you have helped dozens of other people find themselves and write. i have an intolerable work situation. tell me something to write while i'm waiting to be fired." he already <u>had</u> the idea—had given it to somebody else the week before—for what later became SEX AND THE SINGLE GIRL. but i made him get it back and it proved to be the right thing. but i had to <u>make</u> him think about it.

what knowledge does <u>ernest</u> have that could be turned into something for you? i dont know, love. maybe it must be done without him. <u>most</u> husbands . . . probably cant be wifehelpers.

jackie dear . . . you must take the first babysteps toward making the days too short . . . and for the rest of your life. you are simply not <u>like</u> all the other beautiful cow-girls whom you pal around with. you can do all the things <u>they</u> do. . . . the tennis and the housing and the shopping because those are fun but in that great marvelous city—the 3rd or fourth biggest in the world . . . there are exciting things that need <u>you</u>. and they are found by making the first phone call or first ridiculous attempt toward doing something that may seem utterly inappropriate! but you know it's the right thing

much love,

December 7, 1980

Dear Ernest,

We know what men often think of their best (male) friends'
new wives, girlfriends, secretaries, etc . . . not kindly! In yours
and David's case, you had gone through two <u>previous</u> wives
with David, both of whom I <u>think</u> you kind of <u>liked</u> . . . did we
<u>need</u> another wife? If you <u>didn't</u> need one you never let on,
were cordial, friendly from the first hour. Okay, in David's and
my first <u>year</u> of marriage, Twentieth Century Fox, David's
employer, was in trouble, as you may remember. Production
Chief, Buddy Adler, died, David struggled on—not happily—
with a new studio chief who decided to appoint another head
of the <u>story</u> department (David's domain) and make David an
independent producer. Sounded okay . . . <u>wasn't</u>. David
geared up for production with a few un-noteworthy properties;
suffered the new story chief, Ted Strauss (do you need all
these <u>names</u>?!), to occupy his "new quarters." Before he left,
decorators were in David's office measuring for the carpets,
David's beloved secretary, Pamela Hedley, had been given to
Strauss, David was in a MAJOR funk (one-third sorrow, two-
thirds fury) you wouldn't have wanted to live with that person
at this point. Ernie, I didn't even <u>know</u> you well but I called up
and poured out <u>my</u> sorrow, that it was tragic to live with
someone so unhappy, how could these bastards be doing what
they were to my husband, etc. etc.? You listened carefully, (you
always have), and then told me, "Helen, David is an only child.
He is used to having his way, kind of like a spoiled little
boy . . . you know, empirical . . . he doesn't take
disappointment very well. This will pass." I was <u>floored</u> and
relieved! I didn't have to bludgeon my way on to the lot to kill
somebody after all because they were hurting my baby . . .
maybe he just had to weather the storm.

Ernie, that was my first experience with your "wise-ness" . . .
your understanding and caring about David, possibly at times
more than anybody else on earth. You and David let <u>me</u> into

the loop but I don't think a mere woman could cause a <u>trio</u> . . .
it's still you and David, the grown-up version of a major
childhood friendship—I'm just happy I get the use of you, too!
I've enjoyed every encounter from then to <u>now</u> . . . is it thirty-
seven years? I liked your dropping by 605 Park once in a
while to let me fix you a melted-cheese sandwich and talk . . .
I could do that <u>again</u>. You've always been interested in <u>my</u>
work . . . (books, magazine, or whatever) and keep me all
puffed up with praise. I consider you one of the serious
blessings of <u>my</u> life. Happy birthday.

Love,

Mr. Ernest Lehman
Chenault
West Los Angeles, California 90049

John Clerc-Scott was head of Previews, an international real estate firm, when he retired with a friend to Montserrat. Yes, we kept up very well by mail (forty-five years!) though we never saw each other again.

October 29, 1990

Dear Larry and John,

It's been such a long time since I wrote you—and you wrote back! I'm thrilled you are in your new house—I really think you were a Class Act throughout your long ordeal. Life seems to be <u>about</u> adjusting and I have never liked it one bit! I would adore to have nearly everything going on just as it has before—at least if I have kind of got a fix on it. I cannot <u>imagine</u> what it would be like to have a whole house blown away because I can hardly cope when the walls of the bathroom are buckling—yet once again—from torrential rains.

John always had the best taste of <u>anyone</u> . . . I remember his wearing a silk muffler or I <u>think</u> I remember that—what I definitely remember were the double-breasted business suits when other people were single. I have two or three <u>good</u> pictures. My decorator died suddenly a few weeks ago and I am <u>bereft</u>. He was in his seventies but never had a sick day—massive coronary. I can't hang a picture by myself but am cheap and frequently try to circumvent decorators and Do It Myself. It takes years off my life, furrows my brow and the decorating also takes <u>years</u>—I finally caved in and hired somebody to do a new bathroom light fixture. I happened to drop the old one on the tile floor which shattered it totally, utterly. Not such a bad thing except this was a custom made fixture from the previous owner and absolutely not duplicatable. I am very glad <u>I</u> did it . . . anyone else I would have murdered.

David is in Tokyo—or getting there—it seems to me he has been on the airplane longer than we have been married. We had a nifty visit to Brazil week before last. I had to make a couple of speeches to pay for the trip—David went along as a wife. A few days in the Amazon and that was interesting. Will you pussycats please write to me? I'm hanging out the window. Bring me up to date.

Much love,

Mr. Larry Baldwin
Mr. John Clerc-Scott
Sierra Mar
Plymouth
Montserrat

HGB/rc

COSMOPOLITAN

Helen Gurley Brown, Editor • 224 West 57th Street, New York, New York, 10019, (212) 649-3555

September 14, 1981

Pamela dear,

Those are the most beautiful Siamese kittens I have ever seen and you are right not to separate Victoria and Albert . . . they <u>must</u> be together. I guess they are not going to be together in the Brown household. It's so <u>tempting</u> but we haven't got anybody to care for them when we're out of town and life just gets very complicated when we begin to figure it out. It's so interesting to know where all the brothers and sisters went. I cannot <u>believe</u> that Napoleon "swims across his pool in Malibu" but would Pamela <u>lie</u> to me?! Pamela, you are so dear to give us a chance at the best of the litter and we are probably <u>mad</u> not to become parents again. I know some lucky person is going to be made joyous by these two <u>soon</u> because how can anybody resist them? Keep me posted.

Love,

Ms. Pamela Hedley
N. Kenter Avenue
Los Angeles, California

HGB: jgr

November 16, 2001

Gloria dear,

Thank you so much for telling me where to <u>find</u> the incredible Dream Boxes. I saw them today and thought they were beautifully displayed—only fitting for objects so rare and extraordinary! I have been to see different works of art displayed in different studios around that area but usually they are on an upstairs floor and the impact is never very WOW! Well, your Dream Boxes look as [if] they were <u>born</u> for the space and vice versa. I took a friend with me who was also deeply impressed and we took our time. Kerry was a gracious host and, when I asked how long you had been working on them, he said anyplace from five years to <u>forever</u>! Gloria, the astonishing thing about you, as we all know, is that you do everything <u>once</u>—better than anybody—but frequently are off to conquer a new world. You have certainly conquered <u>this</u> one. I am so thrilled to see what you are doing—always invite me, please!—and I'll try to congratulate you in person one of these days. You looked smashing at the Landmarks' dinner. . . . everybody said so when they were remarking what a super evening it was. I had a few dances with our friend Peter Rogers, but just a tiny few. Although dance music doesn't get any better than Peter Duchin, <u>my</u> Peter shouldn't have been on his feet at <u>all</u>. . . . he has a leg that is almost paralyzed from an infection. One day, I will get Peter recovered and you freed from twenty-eight-hour-a-day commitments and we will all go dancing. Gloria, the purpose of this letter is to tell you that you are gifted—you know that, don't you? and I was blown away by your work this afternoon.

Much love
and Congratulations,

Ms. Gloria Vanderbilt
Beekman Place
New York, New York 10022

HGB:ss

Patty Hearst and I have been friends for a long time—yes, before the kidnapping. I kept in touch with her while she was in prison—never thought she should have been there. Now I give my letters to her husband, Bernard Shaw, chief of security at the Hearst Corporation, and he takes them home to her.

February 2, 2001

Patty dear,

You were so wonderful on the Today Show yesterday morning. Matt Lauer is a good interviewer and asked the questions, I guess, that everybody in the world wants to know but actually already knows the answers . . . do you ever get over an experience like that (no!) and how do you feel about the famous pardon? Telling us about Jimmy Carter reducing the sentence and now the actual pardon is absolutely fascinating to <u>all</u> of us and you handled the interview so elegantly. You have, indeed, put everything behind you except the sometimes-memory and have achieved so much . . . your acting, your writing, a happy marriage and the raising of two wonderful children. I'm not your mommy but have always been <u>seriously</u> proud of you. Patti [<u>sic</u>], I didn't write a condolence letter about your father, which I should have. I absolutely adored him and <u>am</u> sending deepest sympathy. He was much loved by everybody and those genes (and his love of <u>you</u>) is another reason you turned out so well.

> With love, sympathy and
> Congratulations on the
> show yesterday
> . . . can you do all that in
> one letter?!

Berna Linden and I were secretaries together at Music Corporation of America, she twenty, me 23, both fired, subsequently, by the same boss—head of the radio department. We are in touch regularly by phone and letter.

December 4, 1997

Berna dear,

What good does it do to help a pal with her questions and problems when you never get the merest little thank-you?! That was totally everything I needed to know about the place I had once held a job— Warner Hollywood Studio on North Formosa. Only <u>you</u> would have dredged that up and I deeply appreciate your doing so.

Berna, do you care whom I sat next to at dinner the other night? Our old associate, Lew Wasserman! It was at a party Larry King gave to celebrate his new marriage. Lew does have the gumption (and cuteness—did you ever think of Lew as being cute?! of saying "take a letter, Miss Gurley . . . where is your <u>shorthand</u> book?!"). Edie is still perky. I think work was his great love . . . I never heard a smidge of gossip about him of the girlfriend variety. He wasn't <u>rotten</u> to you and me at Music Corporation, possibly because he didn't know we <u>existed</u>! He was 31, I was 22 and you were 19! Your paragraph assessing your work situation I thought very astute: "I feel as though I don't want to give up the sociability of the business—I have many friends—but it is very competitive and I don't want to take on that stress. What comes to me easily I will deal with. I won't fight to hang around." I don't want you to stop too soon, however. You can do what you do, as rough as it is, a long long time.

Berna, I might have mentioned this earlier in my letter. On the exact day that your letter is dated, September 19, 1997, my sister Mary died. She had macular degeneration and could only see blotches, mostly couldn't hear and only could breathe with great difficulty . . . that had been going on for many months so perhaps it was time. She was just two months short of 80, had fought very very hard all her life to do the best she <u>could</u> and I was enormously proud of her—we were close. I still treasure the afternoon we had with <u>your</u> sister (Jewel) and mine . . . we went to the movies. I know you have lost some of your sisters—I surely hope not all.

May I say thanks thousands of times for getting me the studio information and bringing me up to date about your life. Please do the latter <u>again</u>.

Love and hugs,

Ms. Berna Linden
San Vincente #509
Los Angeles, CA. 90049-6128

HGB:ss

September 30, 1999

Dear Jack and Elaine,

<u>Maybe</u> somebody enjoyed a visit more in his or her lifetime than I enjoyed my visit with <u>you</u> last week but I doubt it! I'm so absolutely thrilled that we could get together—what were you going to <u>do</u>. . . . I insisted on tracking you right into your hotel room! You were most generous with your specific advice for <u>me</u> and letting me ask all the questions about <u>you</u> that I wanted. . . . you know I worship at your feet—or waist, shoulders or wherever! Elaine, he must be doing something right because any time a wife will lie down on a glass coffee table top and do what her husband demands, I have to think he is a special person! I'm doing all the exercise you suggested, specifically for <u>me</u>, and instantly went out and got ten-pound dumb bells . . . bye bye seven's! Elaine, I like your moisturizer better than anything ever used and magazine editors are given virtually every beauty product there is to <u>try</u>. Your Lady Elaine Moisture Tone is <u>very</u> special. Elaine, please don't be insulted that I'm sending a little check so you can send me another bottle . . . is that okay? It's a very <u>modest</u> check for a really great product. I hope I get to see you both (you and Mr. Wonderful) soon again.

Love to you both,

Mr. and Mrs. Jack LaLanne
Quintana Road, Suite 151
Morro Bay, CA 93442-1948

September 7, 2000

Gloria Dear,

I'm so happy about your marriage. As I told an interviewer from the Washington Post a few minutes ago, most of the men I knew were in love with you, even if they were already married, but you weren't quite ready to take the leap. As I wrote in my very long-ago book, one doesn't <u>have</u> to be married to have a super life but it's probably an okay thing to do at some <u>time</u> in that life. Your David sounds terrific. . . . I have my own . . . and David Brown and I are both wishing you all the happiness in the world.

Love and cheers,

Ms. Gloria Steinem
Ms. Magazine
Exchange Place—22nd Floor
New York, New York 10005

HGB:ss

December 17, 2001

Dear Hef,

I am so thrilled that you are going to receive the Henry Johnson
Fisher Award. I've talked to numerous people who feel the same
way, that it's high <u>time</u>! I never received many awards when I was a
successful magazine editor (and out-selling at the newsstand all
those other magazines) but I felt the one you are receiving kind of
made up for a few things—I told people I got the Bank of America
Award and smiled all the way to the bank. Hef, I have told you so
often that here we go again—you were <u>wonderful</u> to me as an utterly
inexperienced editor and made life more comfortable (even
<u>possible</u>!). I had never set foot in a magazine office before but you
and Spec shared so much information, the most important category
being writers and what to <u>pay</u> them . . . I don't think I would do that
for any other magazine editor in the world except now, of course,
baby Cosmo editors strewn here and there. I always thought you
treated me like a little sister, though I am older than you, and were
truly rooting for our success. I'm sure I'm right. I'll so look forward
to seeing you in January at the Waldorf.

Love and congratulations,

Mr. Hugh M. Hefner
Beverly Blvd
Beverly Hills, CA 90210

HGB:ss

Robert Evans is a very special friend of David's and mine. We've been through four wives with him, all scrumptious, and expect the fifth to measure right up . . . we'll meet her soon. This letter was written after Bob had had a stroke, following some drug problems. He's fine now with a hit biographical picture, The Kid Stays in the Picture, in his recent past.

June 23, 1998

Robert dear,

I guess the sun quit shining a few weeks ago when you got felled. . . . a rotten thing to happen, particularly to you—the quintessence of joy (at least some of the time), pleasure-providing for friends, the good life (some of the time there, too). Well, medical stuff isn't very selective . . . gets the undeserving along with the ones you think it's probably good it happened. You are one of the joyous people in one's life and that simply leads me to believe you will get beyond this and be back cheering up the rest of us. Robert, as you probably know, I treasure you more than almost anybody because of what you have meant to David, and how loyal you are, never mind how personally fond I am of you and I am. Robert, sifting through my rose leaves, I remember when you visited me at Cosmo 102 years ago and the girls in the office were all a-twitter. My personal assistant, pretty girl named Robin, couldn't get her work done all morning because she knew you were going to pop by after lunch—you took me to a Japanese restaurant, Nippon, on West 56th Street. I'm sure Robin—and lots of others— would still feel the same way. Why don't you come visit me in my new office and Susie can have the privilege. Pussycat, do what they tell you and then some. . . . I'll look forward to a visit.

> Hugs
> and all my love,

Mr. Robert Evans
Woodland Drive
Beverly Hills, CA. 90210

April 20, 1999

Lizzie dear,

Last night was magnificent. <u>You</u> were magnificent. I kept gazing up
into the Vivian Beaumont and thinking "she filled <u>up</u> this place. . . .
they all came <u>out</u> for her." Honey, you <u>are</u> incredible. Getting Rupert
[Murdoch] to accept the honor from Literacy Volunteers was coup of
the century in <u>itself</u>. . . . I even think he had a good time. I thought
the readings (except for Steve Martin) were a <u>trifle</u> long. I would
have everybody (except for Steve) perhaps four minutes but how can
you argue with perfection? How did you get to be the good person
that you are, helping so many people. We don't <u>know</u> but the entire
world is better that you worked out the way you did. The people who
are no longer illiterate are always touching with their remarks. I was
so happy to be part of your night.

All my love
and congratulations,

Liz Smith

August 9, 2001

Lizzie dear,

I'm late writing, but here we go. I guess you got very angry and hurt some people and I <u>also</u> guess you would give anything in the world for it not to have happened. Lizzie, you don't need this letter but I just wanted to tell you we <u>all</u> get angry—out of control—and though the end result may not be quite so dramatic as it was for you, that doesn't mean any of us are always in control. On a recent trip from Los Angeles to New York I crashed a tray of food on the floor of an American Airlines plane. . . . splatter, splatter. . . . dishes and food flew <u>everywhere</u>! (I was pissed at a flight attendant who didn't <u>tell</u> me they were out of what I had ordered and brought a really <u>disagreeable</u> "something else"—it looked like the insides of a scrambled dinosaur egg. I'm usually easy to get along with but the flight attendant had been snippy from our first moment together—and I simply dumped her yucky tray of food on the floor. Yes, it took two flight attendants numerous mops and towels to get things cleaned up.) David (husband) assured me word would be out and we wouldn't be allowed on <u>any</u> airplane the rest of our lives. Didn't happen but I was out of line, of course, and apologizing got me nowhere. Lizzie, this isn't the <u>most</u> riveting story—are you still reading?—but I simply want to mention that <u>somehow</u> I feel the anger that you felt, even if the result was a little destructive. You'll get through this. I know it's been hell already and nothing is finished but you are young, smart and there's lots of time for your new life. Your father is a good friend of mine—I'm crazy about him—and he couldn't <u>have</u> a bad daughter! Lizzie, this is a <u>real</u> four-leaf clover from my sister's house in Shawnee, Oklahoma. I'm not big on "good-luck talismans" but feel this one couldn't <u>hurt</u>. I gave one to Herb Siegel and the government finally decided Rupert Murdoch <u>could</u> buy Chris-Craft, something Herb has been working on for a long time and he says the clover probably helped.

Love and cheers,

Ms. Lizzie Grubman
Lizzie Grubman / Peggy Siegel P.R.
Lafayette Street—Suite 3404
New York, New York 10012

HGB:ss

July 15, 2002

Yvonne dear,

Yvonne, I'm in terrible trouble! John Schooler did, indeed, send the scrapple and when it arrived, Yvonne, I hadn't a clue! Yes, scrapple had been discussed at dinner but possibly more between John and David than others. I remember vaguely the subject coming up but when the package arrived, having never seen scrapple in my life, I didn't know what was <u>there</u>! I started lying! In my letter to John, I thanked him (profusely) for the wonderful pâté, that David and I were both enjoying it to the max and sharing it with a few lucky friends. Yvonne, David and I don't even <u>eat</u> pâté—don't like the liver taste, I guess—so I even took my scrapple-prezzie to a couple of other people in the office (assuming it was pâté) and asking them if they would like and nobody wanted—they didn't recognize scrapple <u>either</u>. This wouldn't all be so bad except that John Schooler came through so magnificently and these are the thanks he gets <u>plus</u> David never got to eat this food he loves so much. . . . I gave it to my assistant Susie and asked her to dispose of somehow. Yvonne, I have already written to John, apologizing my <u>wildest</u> for not thanking him for what he did . . . I mean this person came <u>through</u>!

We're off to Palo Alto next week to do a little lecture at Stanford—we do that every year at their Publisher's Course—but the real reason to enjoy is to spend a few days in San Francisco—favorite Chinese restaurant (Tommy Toy's), Sears Pancake House and a few others. We even stand in line on Sunday morning from 30 to 40 minutes to get inside for the pancakes . . . they are that <u>wonderful</u>.

Yvonne, I'm so proud of both of us, especially you because you are an entrepreneur and created a <u>business</u>. Let me hear from you.

Much love,

Ms. Yvonne Rich
Pinecrest Drive
Altadena, CA. 91001

Helen Gurley Brown, Editor-In-Chief

July 20, 1988

Dear Paul,

Fred Heyman told me at lunch yesterday you were not feeling wonderfully well. That made me sad. I think of you always as the most ebullient, bouncy, energetic of us all. Whatever has taken its toll of your health I hope it STOPS.

I don't think, Mr. Z., that you are the most sentimental of men. I barely know you, of course. I was your secretary for just a few weeks at Loeb & Loeb in 1945 (1945?!!) as I remember—during those weeks Roosevelt died and then the war ended. ANYWAY, it was a trillion years ago and whoever and whatever you were then you may have become someone very different—stuffy or proper or pompous . . . I <u>doubt</u> it but anything is possible! This is by way of saying I'm not really writing my letter to the you you are <u>now</u> necessarily but to remind you, as a loving fan, how you were <u>then</u>.

Are you up to this? Good! You were the most exciting, most charismatic, most dynamic young lawyer in the world. Your partners at Loeb and Loeb didn't know quite what to make of you except to be somewhat uneasy and jealous. The <u>younger</u> partners . . . the older ones knew what they had and managed very well! You <u>did</u> keep people waiting a lot . . . that didn't seem to do them in either. You'd come bounding in and all was forgiven.

Joe Drown bought the Bel Air Hotel while I was with you—how handsome, how swashbuckling he was (or so he seemed to me). Slim Hawks and Howard Hawks came in to make out their will . . . talk about glamorous . . . she was a knockout (and weighs exactly two and a half times as much now . . . shame!). <u>We</u> made out your income tax return, my dear—the short form—and your income was $25,000. It seemed just fine at the time. You took me to lunch at Perino's as a reward.

Now we get personal. Having not gone to college and landing in the secretarial pool at MCA not too long after highschool, I knew <u>nothing</u>. Would you believe—it's true!—you turned me on to Shakespeare and Emerson. You thought Ralph Waldo's essay on self-reliance might do a little something for me but mostly you were mad about his <u>words</u>—"our own ideas come back to us in alien majesty" you read out loud to me. "Isn't that just wonderful!" you would say. And you did Antony's oratory at Caesar's assassination <u>beautifully</u>, explaining that although A. kept telling his peers he had come to <u>bury</u> Caesar, he was actually giving them <u>hell</u>! You also told me practical things like "if somebody wants to know something you really don't want to tell him, just say, 'look, if you absolutely <u>have</u> to know, <u>insist</u> on knowing, i'll tell you but I prefer not' and usually they'll back down. Even <u>more</u> practically, you told me when I asked if you would introduce some very wealthy loeb and loeb client to me so that I could marry for money that I didn't really have the looks! You weren't all <u>that</u> blunt but you explained these men could have just about anybody they fancied and they often fancied actresses or glamour-girls. It probably set me on the road to achieving though I would definitely have played it the other way if you had been more encouraging!

You were a lovely supportive friend . . . when men often <u>weren't</u> friends of women in those days. Women adored you, of course. You gave me ten pounds of bacon—bacon!—when it was rationed and that was a sensational treat for my family. It was accompanied by a Max Factor make-up kit (one of your clients) in a genuine leather box. Once or twice you took me to a meeting with you—unheard of to bring a secretary along in those days.

My darling friend, I hope you get to feeling <u>lots</u> better. Give Mickey my best. Just know what an influence you had on someone's life—and you were also good in bed though I only got to find out <u>once</u>—strong and ardent and caring.

Love,

November 28, 1990

Frances dear,

That was a most interesting article in the New York Times and I thought you came off just fine. I have an announcement to make: I like your <u>white</u> hair. It is so different from everybody else and it's your trademark—it also is very <u>pretty</u>. A brunette Frances is just one of the girls. . . . a silver-halo Frances is something different and special. Would you now like to tell me what you think about my micro-mini-skirts or too-pencilled-in eyebrows or something else unsolicited?!

Love,

Ms. Frances Lear
Lear's Magazine
Park Avenue
New York, New York 10016

HGB/rc

June 20, 1994

Dear Richard,

Those bastards! To say they don't know what they're doing is too understated to be stated . . . obviously we are dealing here with egomaniacal idiocy. <u>You</u> will be better than ever. I've been there with David (Brown) when he left 20th Century Fox <u>twice</u> and never really got going so well as in his 70's. You're a baby and I'm madly looking forward to your next creation of a company or whatever. Richard, your new life really <u>is</u> going to be better than ever.

Love and cheers,

Mr. Richard E. Snyder
Simon and Schuster
Avenue of the Americas
New York, New York 10020

HGB/rc

HELEN GURLEY BROWN
EDITOR-IN-CHIEF
COSMOPOLITAN INTERNATIONAL EDITIONS

November 15, 1997

Nora dear,

You have never admitted, acknowledged, <u>confessed</u> that you are a Cosmo girl . . . someone who loves men and children but doesn't want to live <u>through</u> them . . . thinks love and work are <u>equally</u> important for a woman, etc.etc.etc. but I've always <u>known</u> you were . . . even when we had to strangle you all those years ago to get you to do a "before and after."

It touched me that you were willing to come to my "industry" lunch and I <u>almost</u> was depressed when I heard you <u>could</u> (because I had got nervous and asked your "replacement" when I hadn't heard friday). Then I got "<u>un-depressed</u>" because you said you couldn't make it <u>anyway</u> . . . yippee!

Honey, it's lovely to have you as a friend after all these years.

Love and hugs

Nora, Cosmo t-shirts for washing cars in, doing the laundry, etc. I was not the designer . . . is this a sickly lavender or <u>what</u>????

Nora Ephron
Broadway
New York, New York 10024

David "knew" Alex Birnbaum when she was a bulge in her mother's tummy. Her father, Herbert R. Mayes, was David's boss on <u>Cosmopolitan</u>. Alex and David share a birthday we celebrate together at the Four Seasons.

COSMOPOLITAN

Helen Gurley Brown, Editor-In-Chief International Editions

June 20, 2000

Dear Alex,

What can I do, I'm <u>hooked</u>?! I have to tell you how beautiful THE LONDON I LOVE is and tell you two or three of its loveliest moments – "But near Belgrave Square and on Wilton Crescent the gray stone houses, window boxes, and wrought-iron balconies make me want to wave the Union Jack," "Velvety calf's liver," "accompanied by applesauce to die for," and then the paragraph I love the best – "Not just because of the constantly replenished smoked salmon and egg salad sandwiches, the light-as-air scones served with extra-thick strawberry jam, and the pot of houseblend tea, but for the pianist. When I hear the first bars of 'A Nightingale sang in Berkeley Square,' I'm a goner. I forgive his occasional lapses into Andrew Lloyd Webber, because his repertoire invariably includes Coward and Gershwin. And you ask why I love London?" You turned out not only to be the best travel writer because of <u>information</u> but because of the <u>writing</u>....delicious and <u>almost</u> awesome! I'm so proud of you, she said possessively.

Love....can't wait for the 28th

Ms. Alexandra ~~~~
East 76th Street
New York, New York

HGB:ss

Clane from my sister's house in Shawnee, Oklahoma. then on fairly powerful.

959 8th Avenue, New York, New York, 10019 Tel (212)649-2222 fax (212)245-4518

COSMOPOLITAN

————————————Helen Gurley Brown—

8/29

Anna dear,

I'm WORRIED about you! You left a distressed little note at the apartment and haven't been able to reach you by phone.

please call me when you have a minute—office works, too—

thanks for picking up black jump suit from apartment.

how are we getting on with piano shawl—any hope? If you can't do it, can't be DONE!

let me hear from you—hope you're NOT depressed or feeling schleppy! but it's okay . . . HAPPENS!

> Love and hugs,

my black slacks you fixed really worked on the QE 2—i took wrong clothes and they were the only thing i wore.

HELEN GURLEY BROWN
EDITOR-IN-CHIEF
COSMOPOLITAN INTERNATIONAL EDITIONS

July 24, 1996

Dear Carlotta,

You always like me to send you my "poetry" . . . stuff
composed at night in order to get to sleep. Others count sheep
or take Benadryl but this seems to do it for me. These are a
little naughty . . . can you manage? No need to acknowledge.

Here's to the goddess who sucks your dick
You ought to tell her this little trick
If what spurts out gets on her skin
She'll never need Estée Lauder again!

Of course her pussy enchants you so
But, my son, there's something you ought to know.
Though you rub and you rub and you rub like hell,
You can't get rid of the codfish smell.

You think women weak from wear and tear?
Assimilate this if you're able.
One strand of pubic hair
Is stronger than the Atlantic cable.

What if you learn one day that God
Can save only one from the firing squad?
Your guy has to choose between you and his prick.
I'd suggest you send for the blindfold quick.

How many men before him he'll ask
To answer isn't an easy task

The Fifth Amendment he isn't buying
Say there were none and he knows you're lying

So throw him a number with charm and grace
So he can put you in your place
Somewhere between slut and virginity
The number you want to throw is three.

Love and hugs,

Herbert R. Mayes, once David's boss at <u>Cosmopolitan</u>, created a whole new look for women's magazines in the late fifties, when he was let go from the Hearst Corporation and became editor of <u>McCall's</u>. Everything was bleed pages—no margins—très glamorous and dramatic. The whole industry and particularly advertisers noted.

COSMOPOLITAN

Helen Gurley Brown, Editor-In-Chief

August 18, 1986

Herbert dear,

If you should ever stop to wonder what you <u>did</u> in life, take a look at this magazine. It is pitiful. No, you didn't do <u>that</u> but think how it was when you were its leader. There was never anything quite so glamorous or ravishing in the whole world but you also had strong writing. This is pathetic. Of course, she can't help the smaller page size and I guess the publisher insists on all the advertising inserts but <u>she</u> ought to try to insist on keeping them out of the "well." There <u>is</u> no middle-of-the-book here . . . every four pages there is an ad. Well, I am not sending this along to tell you how bad <u>they</u> are but to tell you how good <u>you</u> are. No one can ever diminish that brilliance or the impact you made on virtually all magazines that existed or came into being after 1959. I know you are feeling like hell but rejoice! One can't do the same things forever. One moves into a new place. I'm a fine one to talk! I go to a shrink to get reminded of this every so often.

You may think I am the only one who remembers and I am <u>not</u>. You are in a tiny group of editors/publishers Who Made A Difference.

All my love,

Mr. Herbert R. Mayes
Third Avenue
New York, New York 10028

April 7, 1994

Dear Bobbi,

Here is the article you wanted plus a previous one that only <u>mentions</u> the Chasin, Park, Citron Agency but doesn't write about them. I don't think Herman was too thrilled with the second piece although it is very friendly. He felt agents should keep a low profile (as he always did) and <u>stars</u> should be interviewed! As we know, he had the <u>biggest</u>—Frank Sinatra, Dean Martin, Alfred Hitchcock, Charlton Heston—I think he brought Shirley MacLaine to Hollywood.

Bobbi, this might be more than you want to know about my relationship with your uncle-by-marriage and I will only tell you a couple of things because they affect your aunt. He adored her and always felt she was the perfect wife. The reason I know this is because he was the love of my life—long before he knew her—and I wanted <u>desperately</u> to marry him. This was when he first came to MCA from New York—he was 36, me 22. He was devoted to me in his own way—telephoned <u>every</u> Friday afternoon until a few weeks before he died . . . what is that, about 40 years of telephoning? But he never felt I was the one to marry. Pity he couldn't have explained it to me a little better because I was in a semi-state of heartbreak for about two and a half years. The point is that he was totally committed to his family—2 sisters, a brother (although he might have died) and a niece and nephew. As you know, he brought his mother and one of the sisters to California every year. Well, he <u>knew</u> I wouldn't be any good with his family who definitely meant more to him than I did. A few years later he met Diana who was absolutely the right mate for him and I <u>think</u> they had a terrific marriage. I never met your aunt though once in a while I saw her at an industry function. Possibly you wouldn't tell her <u>any</u> of this except I know how crazy he was about her because we remained friends all those hundreds of years—through other love affairs for me and through my marriage. He actually represented my husband, David, and his partner Richard Zanuck. Herman got them a fabulous deal at Universal where they made THE STING and JAWS which certainly didn't hurt the family fortunes or reputations.

Bobbi, you sound like an absolutely super person. Psychiatric nursing couldn't be a more important field and probably there should be <u>more</u> of you. Thank you for the nice things you said about me. Hope the article has just the effect you wanted.

Love,

Ms. Bobbi Crow
S.W. 12th Avenue
Albany, Oregon 97321

HGB/rc

Dear Celebrity

I guess we all write to celebrities . . . I've been doing it ever since I learned how to write. I don't think they <u>mind</u> the letters unless we're asking for something ridiculous, in which case someone else probably reads the letter first and they never see it. Here's a smattering of my missives to the well-known, most of whom are now personal friends.

I've written Barbara Walters a million letters—every time she does a special—but I haven't got off the attempted fix-up trail. One of these days she may say enough!

September 21, 1992

Barbara dear,

Would you let me give somebody your number—at the office—and you can see if you wanted to have a drink with him or whatever.

His name is Robert Stephan Cohen and he's a divorce lawyer—one of my close friends. He himself was divorced two years ago, has been with Etan Merrick (David's once-wife) since that time. They have stopped seeing each other and he's <u>out</u> there. He handled Joni Evans' divorce which got her <u>everything</u> (possibly deservedly) from Dick Snyder of Simon and Schuster. He also handled Henry Kravis' case when Heidi came back for more millions a few years later. He won. I recommended to Faith Stewart Gordon who owns the Russian Tea Room and she <u>didn't</u> have to give her non-working husband half the Tea Room when they were divorced although they had been together 15 years, blah, blah, blah.

He's <u>short</u>, alas, but nice-looking, about 52 I think, desperately smart—a liberal. Barbara, don't go a step further if this is something that wouldn't work for you. I haven't given him your phone number—just checking. You know the ground rules: first you see if <u>anything</u> seems possible on the phone, then you have <u>coffee</u>. Whatever you think. I'll look forward to hearing from you.

Best,

Ms. Barbara Walters
ABC
New York, New York 10023

I've been writing Woody Allen letters since he was a stand-up comic at Basin Street East. Somebody had been talking during his performance, and I threw a bread stick at the talker, told Woody about it in a letter. Since then we've become good friends. I gave a dinner party for him and Soon-Yi when they were married . . . she's a wonderful wife for him.

May 20, 2002

Woody, Woody!

Sarah Allentuch is going to disconnect her cell phone if I don't stop calling her to say how fabulous you were at the Cosmo conference! After the fourth call, she has assured me that <u>she</u> gets the message and will give it to <u>you</u>. Woody, the girls were simply crazy about you. You are the dearest, bestest person to have come all the way down to the Tribeca Grand and honor us with a visit when you were barely off the airplane from Paris. You let me ask personal questions as well as professional ones and were altogether a pussycat (my highest praise). I <u>already</u> owe you for all the screenings you have let me have, plus your visit to Cosmo a few years ago and now <u>this</u>! You made me a star to have <u>produced</u> you for the conference last week— seriously, people haven't quit talking about it. Sarah can disconnect her phone but you shouldn't have to stop reading the mail. . . . I'm going to <u>stop</u>!

Love and Cheers,

Mr. Woody Allen
Manhattan Film Center
Park Avenue
New York, New York 10021

HGB:ss

June 19, 2000

Dear Woody,

Do I always do everything you tell me? Always. Have you ever misguided me? Never . . . until just <u>recently</u>. We rented MR. DEATH: THE RISE AND FALL OF FRED. A. LEUCHTER, JR. from the corner video store and I dived in today after lunch. I always watch something in my office (laser disc, DVD, VHS or whatever) while exercising for 40 minutes—you can get lots done that way. Since my friend recommended this selection I was looking forward to it like a schoolgirl to the prom. Woody, have you totally lost your sense of <u>appropriateness</u>?! That is not a movie for a girl who just ran GYPSY (the original with Rosalind Russell, Natalie Wood, Karl Malden) <u>and</u> FIDLER [sic] ON THE ROOF in one two-day stretch! Am returning MR. DEATH to the store today, not all the way watched, and they will be delighted as they say they have a <u>waiting</u> list (what do <u>I</u> know?!). Thank you I <u>think</u>. Anything you believe in I want to have a "<u>go</u> at" regardless of the reaction.

Woody, David is finishing a movie in the U.K. (CHOCOLAT) and will be back in New York July 27, here most of August and September. I'll call your office mid-July to see what night you and Soon-Yi can have dinner with us.

Bestest,

November 21, 2001

Dear Diane,

I've seen you hold everything in your arms but a boa constrictor (and maybe you did that one day when I wasn't tuned in) but the porcupine was a new high! I kept saying to myself "well, at least he didn't try to get in her hair and nest on top of her head." I think I have more respect for Jack Hanna than for Einstein, Albert Schweitzer or any civilization-improving individual. Diane, also loved you last week at the Toys "R" Us location and what are you carrying but a mammoth <u>snake</u>?! I guess you didn't feel quite up to schmoozing with the dinosaur but you may have gone back and petted him after the show. You are a total delight . . . you and Charlie just get cuter together—taunting a little, teasing a lot and both of you laughing at each other and yourselves. Hard to laugh <u>seriously</u> at someone wearing all those beautiful sweaters. . . . I'm not talking about <u>him</u>.

Love and cheers,

Ms. Diane Sawyer
A.B.C.
Columbus Avenue—10th Floor
New York, New York 10023

HGB:ss

May 25, 1994

Dear Hillary,

You were so good to bring all the women's magazine editors together yesterday to hear about health care reform—we all learned a tremendous lot.

One can have read and heard discussions on television but there is nothing like your personal explanation. In terms of what you might do to have people understand you a little better and stop misinterpreting (I had to leave just as that subject came up or I <u>thought</u> that was what was being discussed), you don't have to do <u>nothin'</u> . . . you are absolutely impeccable in your public appearances and discussions. American women have never had such a role model in or out of the White House . . . I just hope your health doesn't break down carrying the responsibilities that you do but you <u>look</u> healthy, not to mention chic. I don't care <u>what</u> they do to your hair, your hair is so <u>good</u> but you don't even have to <u>try</u> anything else.

This is a fan letter—all the women in the room yesterday felt privileged and honored.

All my best wishes,

Mrs. Hillary Rodham Clinton
The White House
Washington, D.C. 20500

HGB/rc

January 17, 2003

Dear President Clinton,

It must be wonderful to be <u>you</u>! A few words uttered by you can bring unbelievable joy to the listener. In your opening remarks at the Hearst Management Conference in Scottsdale last week, you were good enough to say something about me and I've been glowing, smiling, preening, purring, <u>gloating</u> ever since . . . the whole conference had to have noticed. We were all awed, not to mention entertained and informed, by you. People kept talking about your appearance all through the conference. Someone recorded the talk and many of us will hear again.

May I mention that when I was growing up in Arkansas in the 30's, the state was considered a pitiful, tacky, unprepossessing little state. Our only celebrities, Bob Burns and Dick Powell, did the best they could, but the overall take on us was <u>poor</u>! You fixed all that! With your POW/WOW years in the White House, and, before that, as governor of the state, it got spifffy!! Did it <u>ever</u>!! Mr. President, I'll just mention that my father was killed in the State Capitol Building in Little Rock—squashed in an elevator accident before there were safety regulations, so the city and the building have been pretty indelible in my brain (big-time) ever since. I'm glad you were/are <u>ours</u> because Arkansas got <u>better</u>. Now we have the privilege of having you <u>ours</u> in New York . . . yippee.

All my best wishes,

President William Clinton
West 125th Street
New York, New York 10027

HGB:ss

To say I worshiped Rosemary Clooney might not be too strong an overstatement. I miss her dreadfully.

May 2, 2000

Rosie dear,

I thought I was going to pass out with joy last night when you not only sang like an angel—what <u>else</u> is new?!—but you also dedicated "Do You Miss New York" to me. That is a <u>very</u> big deal to have Rosemary Clooney single you out to be dedicated to! You were magnificent last night . . . you even sang "Hey There" which is in my top ten favorite list of songs along with <u>you</u>—nobody else—singing "Have I Stayed Too Long at the Fair" and an Antonio Jobim song that I think is called "Wave." Of course there are a few other Rosie songs (like a <u>hundred</u>!) that don't have to be categorized in my top ten favorite list of songs because almost <u>anything</u> you sing is in my top ten list. Dante was dear to come over to the table and say hello. He said <u>next</u> time we get to dance. As I told him, I trucked up to room 1906 in the Pierre during dinner to say hello but either you were hiding (I wouldn't blame you!) or you had already come downstairs. Rosie, it was a <u>magnificent</u> evening, basically because you <u>sang</u>, and honoring Tony Bennett wasn't a bad idea either. I hope I'll see you and your delicious husband <u>soon</u>.

Much love,

P.S. David was on a movie location in France which is why he wasn't with us. Like you and me, he thinks folks should keep working.

Mrs. Dante di Paolo
Roxbury Drive
Beverly Hills, CA 90210

HGB:ss

HELEN GURLEY BROWN
EDITOR-IN-CHIEF
COSMOPOLITAN INTERNATIONAL EDITIONS

February 10, 1999

Katie, Katie, Katie!

You've got to read this letter.

Why do you suppose Diane Sawyer is <u>on</u> Good Morning America??? Because of <u>you</u>, kiddo! You and Matt have absolutely mopped <u>up</u> early-morning television and A.B.C. had to <u>do</u> something.

Are you out of your <u>mind</u> . . . jealous, apprehensive, what is she wearing, how is she doing her hair???? Katie, you and Diane are two different people. She's a wonderful person, just like you, in terms of a good soul and all that. I'm sure the last thing she wanted was an early-morning show . . . she DID that already (on CBS years ago). Repeat: she did it for A.B.C. because they had to do something about <u>you</u> so they sent a (very) heavy hitter. I told you already what Barbara Walters said about you three years ago when you both came to a lunch for me. Barbara whispered to me about you . . . "she's a <u>star</u>!"

And this was before you were <u>quite</u> so luminous. Katie, I am going to come over there and strangle you if you don't behave (in your mind). There is <u>always</u> competition . . . it's called Goes With the Territory. Diane and Barbara worked out their rivalry by being friends . . . I think they are <u>almost</u> on the level (honest) though Barbara didn't <u>need</u> the blonde hussy coming to <u>her</u> network . . . . They are both surviving nicely, thank you very much, though they compete for the same guests, etc. etc.

Nobody but NOBODY could detract from your lustre—you are simply the best there is and EVERYBODY says so . . . charm, brains, compassion, looks, sweetness . . . you're you and absolutely golden . . . repeat: I am going to come over there and kill you if you don't A. appreciate who you are B. appreciate what you <u>have</u> C. accept that nobody ain't going to take it away from you even if the other show gains a few points by having its <u>own</u> star. Losing Jay was intolerable. This is simply not anything more than business as usual in the broadcast business, brought on, as it were by <u>your</u> being so sensational. . . . .THERE!

love,

August 28, 1990

Dear Emilio,

You are going to get weary of these thousands of letters from me but I can't resist. Attached is a picture of me in my 25 year old Pucci (atop the Mercedes Benz the Hearst Corp. gave me for my 25th anniversary with Cosmo) and under that is my newest Pucci that I wore in Tokyo celebrating Cosmo's 10th anniversary there.

Yousef Karsh is going to do my portrait (photography) week after next and if he likes the older Pucci, that's what I'm going to wear.

Is Laudomia bringing some fringed evening dresses to New York? I'm perishing to have one of those.

Much love,

Mr. Emilio Pucci
Palazzo Pucci
Firenze, Via de Pucci 6

HGB:ss

This letter actually started a friendship with the mayor before he was. After receiving it, he invited David and me to his house to dinner, and we've been there since the election. Why anybody would want to be mayor of New York City, particularly when they're doing well elsewhere, is a puzzlement—all that work and all that abuse—but he wanted it badly, didn't surprise me that he won. <u>Some</u> of us think he's doing a fantastic job against terrible odds!

January 20, 1997

Dear Mike,

That was an absolutely wonderful talk at the Hearst editor/publisher conference this week . . . We all hear lots of talks and I try to see how many words I can make out of the word Hearst later on in the meeting (actually 37—would you believe that from 6 little letters) but when <u>you</u> started to talk, I didn't tune-out for 15 seconds . . . maybe you know that not only is <u>your</u> time valuable but so is everybody else's . . . some speakers never quite get the hang of that. You also said wonderful things . . . if you are a minnow, you don't start trying to swallow big fish . . . i.e. don't compete, think of something new they haven't thought of yet. It seems so wise but I never heard anybody say that before. Thanks for such a really inspiring, informative and <u>interesting</u> 20 minutes. If you know where you are going to do that the next time, I may show up again!

All my very best wishes,

Mr. Michael R. Bloomberg
Bloomberg Financial Markets
Park Avenue
New York, New York 10022

June 22, 1999

Michael, Michael!

In the history of the world, no one ever created more pleasure for a few favored friends . . . launching all of us at Ascot must have been only slightly less complex than getting the ships to shore during the Normandy Invasion (not that the purposes were similar) but you did your launching with incredible skill and energy and one even felt you kind of enjoyed the whole thing! I would certainly hope so since your investment was mammoth and I don't see how you could have got anything else done for several weeks prior to the launch (although I was quite knocked out with your explanation of how Bloomberg works . . . give everybody not only responsibility but authority and they do lots of things competently instead of the boss being involved!). We had dinner with David Frost Friday night and he and Lady Carina were utterly bamboozled, not to mention jealous, because you had got all of us to the Royal Enclosure by helicopter. Apparently they go often but never transported in that particular way. Michael, it was a magical day, like you don't run into too many of those in a lifetime. Thank you from the bottom of our deeply pitty-patting little hearts. We'll look forward to seeing you soon.

Bestest,

Mr. Michael R. Bloomberg
President & CEO
Bloomberg Financial Markets
Park Avenue
New York, New York 10022

HGB:ss

April 7, 2002

Gene, Gene, Gene!

I interrupted David in the middle of the Mets/Yankees' game today with a burning question: "Why does Gene do it? What motivates him to do what he does?" David said you mean the grapefruit? Yes, David, the grapefruit. It is such a big shipment . . . about 30 big ruby red grapefruit that will create "Gene Shalit's" (grapefruit juice, gin, ice) and breakfast joy longer than most happiness lasts. We have this system where I do the squeezing, David does the quaffing, I get all the rinds for me—not as pitiful as it sounds—to scoop out all the membrane and pulp and become probably even healthier than David. To get to his response, he said, "because he knows it makes us happy." But such generosity, I am pummeling David. Other people may want you to be happy but they don't do anything so lavish and they don't do it on and on. Don't you realize Gene is different, says my husband. If he wants something, he goes about making it happen. Okay, yes, and all that but I am once yet again almost mortally flabbergasted by your giving-ness. Thank you, my dear loving friend. Maybe some day I will hatch a plan to "get even," but no breath-holding . . . I have too far to go.

Kisses, love and hugs,

Mr. Gene Shalit
R.F.D. #2
West Stockbridge, Mass. 01266

July 9, 1990

Dear Madonna,

That is a simply lovely bustier (expensive!) and you are a lovely girl
to have sent it along with the peach sachets and the basket of
blossoms. Everything simply stopped the show—not quite the way
you would have had you been there but I always believed you would
come if you could and a concert did sort of rule that out. I know you
were magnificent . . . and I have played MADONNA—I'M
BREATHLESS about 100,000 times. HANKY PANKY is my
favorite but everything is splendid.

Stephen Sondheim is the luckiest composer in the world to have
you singing his songs. They work but this is a totally new flower in
his collection. To finish with my omnibus praise-letter, just let me
say you are ravishing in DICK TRACY—one never doubted you
would be.

Madonna, thank you for making my anniversary party at the
Rainbow Room so special—that took thoughtfulness on your part
with lots of other things on your mind and I absolutely adore the
bustier . . . I'm wearing it with a tiny black silk skirt and blazer and a
hundred other things.

Love,

Madonna Ciccone
c/o Liz Rosenberg
Time/Warner, Inc.
Rockefeller Plaza
New York, New York 10019

HGB/rc

June 11, 1973

Julie dear,

Do you need this letter? I don't think so but nothing can restrain me. I've been listening to a Burton Lane C.D. for several days—actually by the <u>hour</u> because I'm nutty about him and don't think he ever got the recognition deserved, possibly because of writing with so many <u>different</u> lyricists so he couldn't be a Rodgers and Hart or Lerner and Loewe. Anyway, before you quit reading, unless you already <u>have</u>!—the most wonderful thing on the tape is ONE MORE WALK AROUND THE GARDEN sung by the enchantress. I put up with Finian's Rainbow and Royal Wedding (though they aren't bad) just to get <u>back</u> to your beautiful singing of this song. I don't know who the lyricist was but he must have had you in mind when he wrote. . . . your diction is so exquisite but there also is that soaring soprano.

Julie, I don't know whether you have got all the way through this letter but I will stop right this minute before you get really discouraged!

> Love and Happiness to you
> and Blake,

Mrs. Blake Edwards
San Vicente Boulevard
Suite 840
Los Angeles, CA. 90049

HGB:ss

November 20, 1998

Dear John,

Speaking of editor's personal columns, yours in the December issue is whammo. . . . .I love "Clinton, at least, recognizes that power is, by nature, expansive and imposes itself upon events." You are never angry but always persuasive. The "GEORGE POWER 50" is the best compilation of 50, for any cause you would ever want to run into— now I absolutely know who is who. "What would America think if our passion-starved president happened to be. . . . a woman?"—those eight pages are absolutely glorious as is the concept. John, don't acknowledge this letter—it isn't necessary—and I promise not to write more than every four or five years. . . . some people write more often than they should but I loved chatting with you last week and thought one more person should tell you that your magazine is wonderful.

All my best wishes,

Mr. John F. Kennedy, Jr.
George Magazine
Broadway, 41st Floor
New York, New York 10019

HGB:ss

November 22, 1994

Dear Joyce,

People are still talking about your performance at the Friars' tribute to Tony Bennett. I never saw a room so collapsed in laughter and some of the people weren't <u>necessarily</u> show-biz types who respond happily to performances by their pals, some were more traditional New York society—for lack of better description—and that crowd, too, was collapsed with glee. The joke about Paula Jones recognizing the President's genitalia in a photograph whereas most women couldn't manage that recognition of a loved one in a police lineup is possibly one of the three funniest jokes ever told—seriously! You and I are longtime friends and it thrilled me—although I love Alan King—to see you capture that very high profile room the other night.

Love and cheers,

Ms. Joyce Behar
℅ Brian Reardon
J. Michael Bloom
Park Avenue South, 10th floor
New York, New York 10003

HGB/rc*

David and his partner Richard Zanuck gave Steven Spielberg his first feature film—Sugarland Express—and we've been friends ever since. He is the most unspoiled superstar director you could ever hope to meet.

January 14, 1994

Dear Steven,

I was sitting in the darkened theatre last night (Regency Cinema at 67th and Broadway) waiting for SCHINDLER'S LIST to begin and thinking about your astonishing life. The theatre was jammed—I had a hard time getting even one seat (David had seen the movie in Toronto) but everybody was kind of orderly and nice and there was an anticipatory feeling. Isn't it astonishing, I thought, that this recently post-teenager David and I had dinner with (and Jennings Lang) about 21 years ago, nose pressed to the glass, telling us the difference between a film and cinema, should be the cause of this <u>vast</u> excitement tonight in this theatre and dozens of others. That was <u>before</u> the movie began. Steven, everybody has said everything he could think of to say about this extraordinary happening. From the first few frames when Schindler is picking up his accoutrements—mostly money—from a drawer to go out on the town, the acting, the cinematography, the words that people are saying, the tension, and even the <u>music</u> are so different from anything anybody has ever heard before, one is groping for words to try to describe the experience.

Steven, you are a little <u>busy</u> these days and I'm going to stop. I'm so much looking forward to seeing you at the New York Film Critics Circle Awards on Sunday so I can tell you in person how much your masterpiece moved me. Like everyone else, I was weeping at the end.

Love

Mr. Steven Spielberg
Amblin Productions

HGB/rc

**Tony Bennett I've kept in touch with through letters
after his performances—I never miss one—and they
must do good. . . . I'm always able to get into the next one
however booked. He sketched me one night at a charity
dinner . . . it's framed in my office . . . and I have one of
his seriously good oil paintings. The friendship started—
and goes on—through letter writing (mine!) I'd say.**

February 10, 2003

Tony dear,

MAGIC!

There was the <u>instant</u> standing ovation because people love you,
then several more after that for the voice and the music, <u>but</u> I
would like to put in a good word for the LOOKS! You seem more
trim, more handsome than ever . . . absolutely astonishing!

Folding kd lang into the show as you did was perfect . . . she
wasn't on too long and never left your side . . . just right!
Didn't hurt that you sang two of my favorite Tony Bennett
songs . . . ALL THE WORLD TO ME and OL' DEVIL MOON but
<u>everything</u>—voice, looks, charm—were the best they've ever
been . . . is that possible?! Yes! All David's and my love and
thanks for such an incredible night.

COSMOPOLITAN

Helen Gurley Brown, Editor-In-Chief

April 25, 2001

Michael dear,

Was Friday night at Carnegie Hall one of the most thrilling nights of my life? May sound as though I haven't been <u>thrilled</u> much but that wouldn't be accurate . . . it was MAGIC! I kept glancing up to the highest balcony . . . filled! . . . hundreds up there transported just like us lower below. We saw Irving Berlin's daughter last night and tried hard to tell her about ALWAYS (made me cry) <u>and</u> I LOVE A PIANO . . . we're sputtering praise for our beloved talented friend. Michael, the show is so well-produced that even civilians who know nothing about show production can be in awe. You are at the piano <u>just</u> often enough to please the rigid ones (me) who swoon at <u>both</u> your gifts but keep the whole room entranced by <u>just singing</u> ravishingly on both sides of the stage. Every composer honored, including the not-here ones, must have been smiling from <u>wherever</u>. Loved seeing your father . . . <u>he</u> was smiling hard!

Michael, this clover, from my sister's house in Shawnee, Oklahoma, is <u>supposed</u> to be effective. I've never thought luck has much to do with <u>your</u> success . . . great talent and barge-lifting, bail-toting hard <u>work</u> are what does it but let me send along and you can apply where you wish.

Thank you for such a happy night. Hope to see you <u>soon</u>!

Love,

Mr. Michael Feinstein
Kingswell Avenue #110
Los Angeles, California 90027

HELEN GURLEY BROWN
EDITOR-IN-CHIEF
COSMOPOLITAN INTERNATIONAL EDITIONS

October 8, 1999

Kathie Lee, dear,

You don't hear from me often though we know I write letters like others sneeze but I just want you to know I am always thinking about you. I get to see 10 minutes of the show every day and then have to scram to the office. Rarely does anybody mention this but you are about the best television co-host - or host - there is...totally informed about the work of your guests, sometimes friends, and always funny with - but supportive of - Regis. Think how many there were before you. I think your deep affection for each other - along with the nifty put-downs - shines clearly through.

Kathie Lee, I don't pay any attention to the ridiculous stuff that is sometimes scribbled about you. The jealousy is so raging - because you have everything - people can't control themselves. You are one of the ten finest people I have ever met - and I'm not sure who are the other nine! Character doesn't get any better than yours - along with the talent and the beauty. I'd better stop before I get jealous! The people who know you all feel the same way and that even includes millions who see you on television. Honey, just keep doing everything perfectly as you always have. David and I are just back from Lanei...wherever that is - I think Hawaii - where we celebrated our 40th. Like me, you're a third wife, and I could highly recommend the place when the time comes.
Honey, much love from both of us. Don't worry about a rendezvous but I'm thinking about - and applauding you - ALWAYS.

MEMO FROM

COSMOPOLITAN

959 EIGHTH AVENUE, NEW YORK, NEW YORK 10019 (212) 649-2222

Doesn't sound very frisky or original to say you have worshiped Frank Sinatra all your grown-up life, still swoon to (and play regularly) his music, but I'm saying it. After he left us, I continued to be in touch with one of his daughters, Tina.

November 10, 2000

Tina, Tina!

What an unbelievably wonderful book! I almost couldn't bear for it to be finished because I enjoyed every word. I worshipped your father, like a few hundred million other people, a little past teen-age when he was at the Paramount and the bobbie soxers became delirious but I do have 78's, 33-⅓ albums that stack up from the floor to the top of a table, and now my beloved D.V.D.'s which embrace almost his whole career. When WNEW used to have a whole Thanksgiving week-end that embraced nothing but Sinatra, I was close to being the winner once or twice by calling in the selection they <u>hadn't</u> played . . . it was a joyous way to spend a week-end. Tina, this letter is so far all about <u>me</u> but it's hard not to write about one's relationship with your father. He brings such joy to this very moment with his musicianship but I had the privilege of knowing him just a <u>little</u>. As a secretary at Music Corporation of America around 1942, I used to take the payroll checks over to his radio show at C.B.S. and he would sign all of them for the musicians on his show. Once I sneaked in a gorgeous 11 × 14 photograph of him that I asked him to sign and he wrote, "Dear Helen, thanks for <u>everything</u>!" I tried to persuade my girlfriends the "everything" referred to memorable moments! A hundred years later David and I got to spend an evening with your father at Jilly's. I don't know quite how it was arranged but just your father, Richard Zanuck and his wife Linda, David and me and we were together for a couple of hours. I guess David and Dick were involved with him at Twentieth Century Fox. He said to <u>me</u>, "Oh Helen, what you've done with that magazine!" I guess he kept track of everything. Not nearly often enough I got to see him in concert—Radio City Music Hall, Carnegie Hall, Westbury and visit backstage. I once sent him a collection of the lyrics of virtually all popular songs published from 1928 to about 1940. Don't know how valuable that would have been but my sister Mary had contracted Polio and one of her pleasures, sitting in her wheelchair, was writing down the words to all the popular music of the day from the radio . . . it was quite a collection and, I felt, could jog his memory about something he would like to sing, the music of which he might not have seen recently. His office <u>did</u> acknowledge the prezzie.

Tina, now shall we get to you? The book is absolutely superb and I feel I am qualified to write about writing, regardless of the subject. Surely Jeff Coplon is the right collaborator. Everything moves so gracefully, reasonably swiftly so there isn't a too-prolonged moment but everything is <u>there</u>. Tina, I love these lines: "User-friendly olive tree for climbing." "Tossing on the tinsel with something less than martial precision." "He put out this tremendous energy, and we all felt more alive around him. When he was with you, he was really <u>with</u> you." "I don't think it's just Dad's phrasing, or his timbre, or his flawless musicality." "But as we've seen, Dad was the marrying kind." "Mia was more of a day person while the only dawns my father saw were on the back end of hard day's night." "He knew that the marriage should never have happened and that the responsible party was wincing at him in the mirror." And so many more. Tina, your book is a masterpiece! The cover photograph of you as a little girl looking up adoringly at <u>him</u> has to be the best cover photograph there ever <u>was</u>. Tina, I'm so proud of you.

Love,

Ms. Tina Sinatra
Lloydcrest Drive
Beverly Hills, CA. 90210

HGB:ss

December 21, 2001

Jane dear,

Everyone has a memory of what he or she was doing the morning of Tuesday, September 11. What I was doing was watching one of my favorite people on television deliver the news and weather at 8:55. Yes—vous—very smooth and creamy and then you switched subjects in the middle of the sentence and said you have just had a bulletin the World Trade Center building had been hit by an airplane on some of the top floors. You were aghast but smooth . . . maybe you couldn't believe what you were saying like the <u>rest</u> of us couldn't believe what you were saying. Those moments are very firmly entrenched in my brain. You are always so smooth and credible—I guess we would call it professional and you look eight million dollars. I have stopped commenting on your hair because <u>whatever</u> it does, elegant and pretty are the results (doesn't hurt to have good hair to begin with). Jane, you must please have the happiest New Year. I will trust you not to deliver anymore breath-stopping news bulletins!

Love and Cheers,

Ms. Jane Hansen
The Today Show
NBC
Rockefeller Plaza
New York, New York 10012

HGB:ss

March 2, 1995

Tony dear,

You are such a really wonderful person to say you will come to my party by yourself Tuesday, April 18.

I can imagine what it must feel like to be invited as a <u>hunk</u> instead of a couple. You can imagine how <u>I</u> feel when people ask us as a <u>couple</u> and, if I can't produce Mr. Wonderful because he is in Australia or some place, then the invitation is rather quietly rescinded. If you have to be asked for <u>something</u>, I think I would rather be asked for me than as part of a twosome but, never mind, don't mean to vitiate my <u>thanks</u> . . . I do need you that evening just by yourself but will do something with your very special friend another time. Is that the pussycat girl I met in the elevator last night? Never mind that she's pretty and personable, she also seems very <u>nice</u> . . . I surely would wish no less for you. If you want any love advice, I assume you will call me—I have got people married, unmarried, fixed up on New Year's Eve, you <u>name</u> it.

Love,

Mr. Tony Randall
West 81st Street
New York, New York 10024

HGB/rc

THREE

Thank You, Friend

Friend thank-you letters go in a separate category, I think, because some people will only <u>write</u> a friend a thank-you note, not big on any other kind of friend correspondence. The notes can be pretty effective . . . putting it in writing means you really do take what they did <u>seriously</u>.

Is this me at my most shameless asking? Possibly, but how can I quit shameless-asking when the letters get such good results? Yes, the pass came through.

January 8, 1993

Dear Alan,

I used up my entire repertoire of pleading, charm, cajolery, nostalgia and other assorted qualities <u>last</u> year in asking for my Loew's pass. You graciously sent me one. This year I presume you have <u>had</u> it—I don't even need to <u>presume</u> . . . if the pass didn't arrive, that means I'm off the list.

Do you know what that is <u>doing</u> to me? I used it possibly three times last year (at Loew's 84th) but I just adore <u>having</u> it. It makes me feel like a big shot and has to do with my permanent crush on movies—I wrote you that the last time! David has two winners this year—THE PLAYER and A FEW GOOD MEN.

We strolled by Loew's 84th Saturday afternoon and <u>would</u> have popped in to count the house but how <u>could</u> I . . . no pass! All I can tell you is that I <u>won't</u> write a letter in 1994 (promise!) if the pass never materializes in 1993 but—<u>again</u>!—I just wanted to tell you what it means in my life. Oh well!

All my best wishes,

Mr. Alan Friedberg
Loew's Theatres
Plaza Drive
Secaucus, New Jersey 07094

HGB/rc

February 24, 1993

Dear Robert,

There is no way in the world you could possibly know how thrilled I am with my Loews Theatre pass. Ever since I wrote to Alan Friedberg early in the year I have been semi watching the mailbox and the week hasn't gone by when I haven't (resignedly) said to my husband David, "well I guess it's over . . . it's wonderful they did that for such a long time and they know I can buy my own tickets, still . . ." Every time I pass [sic] Loews 84th, I got heartsick again! Well, here is my beautiful prezzie and I will use it with such pleasure, <u>guaranteeing</u> that I will go to the theatre occasionally and Spend Money like a good person. Thank you ever and ever so much.

All my best wishes,

Mr. Robert F. Smerling
President
Loews Theatre Management Corporation
Plaza Drive
Secaucus, New Jersey 07094

HGB:ss

December 15, 1997

Dear Ann and Gil,

I'm still kind of smiling from my <u>last</u> fix and now a scrumptious new Christmas offering! As I have tried to tell you so many times, Ann, people don't <u>make</u> this ambrosial mix like you do. I once tried a recipe I got from Tom Brokaw but it didn't work and I've really never tried since to do it myself nor have I run into anybody <u>else's</u> granola that entranced and along came YOU! Since it's Christmas, maybe I'll let David have a <u>smidge</u>. Am taking it home tonight, putting it in the refrigerator for freshness-keeping and maybe I'll give David a bowl tomorrow morning before he goes off to California. I do tend to carry on (as if you hadn't experienced this already) about this lovely treat but you've done it again and I'm so very very pleased to be on what I kind of think is a short <u>list</u>.

All my thanks
and Happy Christmas,

Mr. and Ms. Gilbert C. Maurer
E. 58th Street
New York, New York 10022

Me at my pushiest. I asked this man I didn't know, well-known in New York, to help David and me on a planned trip to Morocco . . . what should we see, how would we get to the places? Courtesy of his boss, the king, my "unknown" friend provided two cars (one for us, one for the luggage), an itinerary in three cities, plus the Atlas Mountains, where the cars subsequently, uncomplainingly took us. The man deserved a better thank-you than a letter. Perhaps they were fostering American goodwill. They surely got <u>mine</u>!

October 4, 1991

Dear Jaidi,

David and I came tearing into the party Wednesday night at the Plaza about 9:15, hoping to see you and your illustrious guest, the King of Morocco. Alas, we were too late. People told us you were there for a long time but had already left. David and I were doing a network radio show together that had been booked many weeks in advance and it just happened to be between 8 and 9 p.m. live—we came over as fast as we could. Jaidi, someday we will get to extend our grateful thanks to the King, who made our visit to Morocco three years ago so outstanding with his generous contribution of two cars and drivers. Of course we know <u>you</u> told him he should do that but you may both share the credit for having introduced us to your beautiful country, which we hope to return to again and again. Jaidi, thank you for inviting us to the reception—I hope there will be another one.

All my best wishes,

Ambassador Abdeslam Jaidi
Consul General of Morocco
Fifth Avenue
New York, New York 10016

HGB/rc

May 23, 2000

Dear Tita,

I don't feel you got nearly enough credit for that fabulous evening
you put together when Michael Feinstein sang Sammy Cahn. I am a
Feinstein addict—he could have sung <u>all</u> the songs, as far as I was
concerned, but the other singers were more than competent and no
one can not be enchanting with a Sammy Cahn lyric. Hard to pick
favorites but I FALL IN LOVE TOO EASILY and BUT
BEAUTIFUL are surely in my top ten. You were dear to take all of
us to dinner at Elaine's. I wouldn't want that dinner tab but then
that's <u>you</u>. Tita, I don't lunch very much, am out of the city on
Cosmo business in other countries quite a lot but I will surely look
forward to our next visit. David and I would love to take you to
dinner when we're all in New York at the same time.

Love and hugs,

Ms. Tita Cahn
North Canon Drive
Beverly Hills, CA. 90210

HGB:ss

March 18, 1992

Dear Alfred,

I promise to let you up off the mat and stop bothering you but one more bulletin. A man sitting at our table at the Sarafin party at the Museum last week, Dr. Paul Marks, executive and chief officer of Sloan-Kettering, was <u>also</u> taken with your laser pen and told me if <u>I</u> got one, I must tell him about it so that he could acquire. Okay, my wonderful pen came in nicely gift wrapped from Sharper Image so I called over there to see if they had another one Dr. Marks could buy. Yes, they said. How much, I asked. Two forty-nine, they said. Two dollars and forty-nine cents, I asked? Two hundred and forty-nine dollars, they said!!!! Alfred, I feel like the biggest golddigger of the Western World!!! I will try not to get my heart set on anything so expensive next time—the way you are behaving I could get to be a real <u>burden</u>! Just know how much pleasure I am having from the pen <u>and</u> the laser beam.

Love and cheers,

Mr. Alfred Taubman
The Taubman Company
Fifth Avenue
New York, New York 10021

HGB/rc

October 29, 1998

Dear Myrna,

I am just thrilled speechless to be one of the Ladies' Home Journal's 100 Most Important Women of the 20th Century . . . wow! I don't know whether it's more major to be there with Eleanor Roosevelt and Mother Teresa or Marilyn Monroe and Lucille Ball but I'll take it, I'll <u>take</u> it! Myrna, some editors are not very wonderful to other editors but you are not one of <u>those</u>. . . . you have always been caring and encouraging and, if I may, objective . . . I think I deserved to be one of your hundred but not <u>everybody</u> agrees! Of course, we have to remember that you started as a Cosmo writer and that made you a very wise and sensible person. Honey, all my thanks. . . . thousands and thousands of times.

Love,

Ms. Myrna Blyth
Editor-in-Chief
   & Publishing Director
Ladies' Home Journal
Park Avenue
New York, New York 10017-5529

HGB:ss

November 11, 2002

Jerry dear,

You'll never get your work done if I don't stop writing you notes but this I had to share. When I was all spiffy and dressed up for the New York Landmarks Conservancy dinner at the Plaza last week, Mike Wallace took one look at my shoes and said, "Helen, those are fuck-me-shoes if I ever saw any!" He's right. People kept exclaiming about them all night and do you know they are even danceable without breaking your neck? They are in the top ten happiest purchases I ever made in my life. Enough! I'll hope to see you soon.

All my best wishes,

Mr. Jerry Janko
Shoes
GUCCI
Fifth Avenue
New York, New York 10022

HGB:ss

This gracious lady rummaged through archives of the Little Rock State Capitol to find documents concerning my father, who had once worked there as a state representative. He was going to run for <u>her</u> office the year he was killed—<u>in</u> the State Capitol Building yet!

October 23, 2000

Dear Sharon,

I'm still reeling . . . I don't think that's too strong a word . . . from the reception at the State Capitol Building Friday afternoon and the incredible documents you have given me. The copies of the two acts sponsored by my father in 1919 are beyond belief! The photographs of my father from the 42nd, 43rd, 44th, 45th, 46th General Assembly [<u>sic</u>] of the State of Arkansas House are simply awesome. . . . who ever expected to have <u>those</u>? The work you must have gone to leaves me a little reeling. Sharon, I think you are my new best friend and I didn't mind that you produced the Governor for me on the steps of the State Capitol Building. Governor Huckabee couldn't have been more gracious considering that he didn't know he was going to be descended on but I have a feeling he might think you're <u>special</u>. Sharon, I will be talking about that meeting and your warm hospitality and the beautiful offerings probably for the rest of my life. I'm supposed to be a writer and okay with words but I'm almost failed for this occasion. . . . thank you, thank you. I hope you will stay in my life.

All my best wishes,

Ms. Sharon Priest
Secretary of State
State Capitol
Little Rock, Arkansas 72201

Dear Sandra,

I watched our show Friday night when I got back to New York and, you know what? I wasn't even self-conscious being three feet away from Cindy Crawford all night long. . . . she looked great—what else can she <u>do</u>?! but I looked beautiful also. We know you worked like a crazygirl for over an hour but it <u>showed</u>. Of course, if somebody else had worked that long, it wouldn't have been as good. . . . you are <u>gifted</u>! I'll look forward to our next visit.

Love,

Sandra Soleiman
Make-Up Artist
Politically Incorrect
Beverly Boulevard
Los Angeles, CA. 90036

HGB:ss

April 29, 1998

Dear Tom,

You were so wonderful to help me with the money exchange week before last. As I wrote Colleen, it's a little embarrassing to see your hoarding and miserly instincts so exposed but I felt I was with friends. You even took in my three coins from sixteen countries collection and said you would get them identified with your foreign currency department . . . they probably aren't used to such big transactions! Tom, thank you for being so helpful . . . I will consider you a good new friend.

All my best wishes,

Mr. Tom Roberts
Bank of New York
Fifth Avenue—3rd Floor
New York, New York 10036

HGB:ss

August 29, 1994

Dear Dr. Hinsley,

I think you must be the best doctor in the world! You were so good to go out to see my sister Mary Alford <u>twice</u> to put two of her animals to sleep . . . a very old kitty cat and a doggie. She tells me your staff also sent a sympathy card. I'm glad you're in our lives. I can't think of anybody doing anything more meaningful.

With love
and appreciation,

Dr. James Hinsley
West Independence and Kennedy
Shawnee, Oklahoma 74801

HGB/rc

 Laudomia is Emilio Pucci's daughter.

May 10, 1991

Laudomia dear,

Here's the write-up about the evening at the Metropolitan. I still remember it as a thriller! Would you show this to your father?

I am <u>adoring</u> my new fringed dress. . . . it is absolutely stop-traffic drop dead! Wore it to a dinner for the UN Secretary General Javier Perez de Cuellar and I had the feeling nobody was concentrating on the guest of honor!

Much love . . .

please come back and visit soon. . . . .
a bear hug for your father. . . .

Ms. Laudomia Pucci
Palazzo Pucci Firenze
Via di Pucci
Firenze, Italy

HGB:ss

Steve Ross died soon after this letter was written and received.

November 24, 1992

Dear Courtney and Steve,

The giant turkey has arrived and I will <u>attempt</u> to do justice by it. The cook-housekeeper has Thanksgiving off and <u>because</u> your turkey comes to grace our lives every year, that's the time <u>I</u> cook up a storm—usually just for David and me but the turkey is so enormous the feast goes on all week.

Steve, Courtney, I have always loved people who do things when they don't <u>have</u> to and that has been the story of your lives for a long, long time. You give and give and <u>GIVE</u>! I know this is a different kind of Thanksgiving for you because you've just gone through serious surgery but perhaps this latest procedure will prove <u>miraculous</u>. I'm among a mere <u>hoard</u> of people who expect that to be the case. David and I are sending <u>all</u> our love and thinking of you all the time.

Mr. and Mrs. Steven J. Ross
East 71st Street, 12th floor
New York, New York 10021

HGB/rc

Trying to Help Somebody

Doesn't it make sense to put requests on behalf of a friend (or <u>anybody</u>) in writing because you can make a more outstanding presentation that way and the person being requested from has information to refer back to? Yes! A magazine editor is in a position to try to help folks, and I tried. . . . Here's a smattering of the letters. Attempts at friend fix-ups weren't my most memorable successes, but I'm still at it! Not enough men to go around for my deserving girlfriends. . . . How can I resist?!

August 15, 1991

Dear Barbra,

We are so thrilled with our interview with you in October Cosmo.
Joe Morgenstern did a wonderful profile, as you knew he would, and
this story will enhance our lives. I am waiting breathlessly to see
THE PRINCE OF TIDES. Barbra, when you come to New York,
there is someone I thought you might have a drink with. Single,
wealthy, just divorced, still a Wall Street <u>mogul,</u> funny and brilliant
but not Tom Cruise in the looks dept.—he's 44. David and I could
take you to dinner and we could bring him along or he could buy you
a drink alone or whatever.

I have in mind one or two other people although <u>nobody</u> is good
enough (but, then, whoever <u>is</u> when you start comparing women and
men, etc. etc.)

Barbra, thank you for making us so happy. The VANITY FAIR
article and cover are also sensational.

Love,

Ms. Barbra Streisand
N. Carolwood Drive
Los Angeles, California 90077

HGB/rc

COSMOPOLITAN

Helen Gurley Brown, Editor-In-Chief International Editions

September 22, 1998

Dear Warren,

You'll either do this or you won't.
If you won't, we're still friends...you owe me positively
nothing but that doesn't keep me from being pushy!

Call up a very good friend of mine and buy
her a drink to see if you like her...maybe you can even
tell on the telephone.   Dinner probably wouldn't be
the worst because she is charming, man-appreciating, pretty,
sense of humor, good listener but A. She might not be
quite as young a woman as you should have B. She doesn't
move in your circles...I think of you as very Park Avenue
(maybe because you live and work there but you are Park
Avenue.; she isn't in that world. Was previously
public relations director of the Hearst Corporation,
hasn't held that job for awhile. The girl is a widow,
needs to go out with somebody who isn't gay, even if
just for a drink.   Warren, you aren't in the
philanthropy business and may feel like being only
 with creme de la creme even for a cocktail...life is short.
I feel a little yucky not calling her creme de la creme...
she's my friend..I'm only thinking of the fact

you could have Barbara Walters in the achievement/fame
department, Cameron Diaz in the glamour department.
I have to feel this is a <u>bit</u> of a "kindness" act for you -
on the other hand she is kind of terrific and surely part
of my life, not a loser.   You are going to do
<u>exactly</u> what seems right to you which may be <u>nothing</u>!

Charlotte Veal

E. 54th Street

New York, New York 10022   Apt. 5-E

I'm going to tell her there's only the <u>remotest</u> chance you'll
call but I know she'd be thrilled if you did.

P.S. your totally <u>ignoring</u> letter is not guaranteed
to keep me off your case forever!

                                        Best,

Charlotte is out of New York City
until Monday, September 28 -
has voice mail.

959 8th Avenue, New York, New York, 10019 Tel. (212)649-2222 fax (212)245-4518

October 6, 1994

Dear Billy,

My avowed goal in life is to drive you totally <u>crazy</u> with my pushiness in terms of Cosmo's beauty director, Andrea Pomerantz, whom I want you to have <u>coffee</u> with. Your mother told me somebody had told you something not wonderful about her and that turned you off. I frequently listen to <u>my</u> friends, too, but think about all the divorced people . . . do you suppose any exes ever say anything fabulous about somebody they got divorced from . . . I don't mean that Andrea and your friend are in that position but I'm just saying people have different <u>versions</u> of people and maybe his (your friend's) isn't the <u>only</u> accurate one. Did I or did I not say I would drop this whole thing when we said hello to each other at Cipriani? I <u>did</u> but now I am reneging. Why don't you have coffee and tell her you're doing it because Helen Brown won't leave you alone. If you do that, then I promise to come up with somebody <u>else</u> though it probably can't ever be a Cosmo cover girl because I don't know them and can't deliver. If you still say no we are still friends, okay? I really mean it!

Love,

P.S. This isn't the hardest-up girl in the city . . . my <u>pride</u> is at stake! That was a great looking girl you were lunching with.

Mr. William Siegel
Chris-Craft Industries, Inc.
Madison Avenue—25th floor
New York, New York 10022

HGB/rc

February 28, 2002

Gil dear,

I don't mean to be so pushy but I <u>am</u>! Absolutely loved sitting next to you at dinner last night—nice party. The girl I want to meet you is: Jill Cassidy

New York: East 52nd Street, Apt. 8-E

Paris: Rue Guisarde, 75006 Paris France

She owns the apartment in Paris, goes there April 1st for a month, then comes back here. As I mentioned, her husband owned a lingerie company (Lily of France) and left her quite well fixed. He had lymphoma and she really took good care of him as long as he could last. She skis, speaks fluent French and Italian, <u>may</u> be a little old for you—52—but she's an absolute knock-out in person. If you're busy and don't want girls being pushed at you (I imagine it happens all the time!) I won't be mad. You are just too kind of special for one not to want one of her friends to have the use of you. Jill sees lots of plays, movies, operas, entertains nicely—the fireplace is always lit and the champagne is cold—why don't I stop before you get <u>seriously</u> bored. The picture was made in my office.

Bestest,

Mr. Gil Shiva
The Dakota
West 72nd Street
New York, New York 10023

HGB:ss

I sent this letter to fifteen friends in the Los Angeles area . . . didn't produce results I had hoped for . . . worthy cause.

January 31, 2001

Dear Cathy and Ken,

Do you <u>need</u> this letter? Certainly not but that isn't going to save you! I just want to mention someone in Los Angeles who does wonderful Shiatsu massage if you should ever care. When David and I were in Los Angeles for two days for the Golden Globes—CHOCOLAT didn't win anything—I was screaming with tiredness and called my old friend Robert Dolce, who used to book on the Tonight Show and, after Jay Leno came in, decided to go into another trade. He studied like a maniac and he's <u>good</u>. David and I have a fine Japanese Shiatsu lady in New York so we sort of know good from bad and I was quite impressed. Bob will come to your house with his table and it's a $125.00 or you could go to his house if you prefer. Cathy, Ken, this may be the last thing either of you are interested in but it doesn't hurt me to tell an old friend about <u>another</u> old friend who might bring some kind of tension-release into his/her life. I'm afraid he's a little bit into Chinese medicine and has me drinking more water and eschewing Equal and other unpleasant assignments but such discussions don't have to be part of the visit. Once again, I'm not <u>pushing</u> . . . just told Bob I would tell a few friends about him in case you were interested.

All my best wishes,

Mr. and Mrs. Ken Kragen
Aubrey Road
Beverly Hills, CA 90210

HGB:ss

May 6, 1993

Dear Sandy,

You are an absolute Dream Person to send over my make-up chart. I should have had the guts to tell you I wanted to <u>learn</u> when we booked the appointment. This is perfect for me and I will follow instructions and work hard.

Sandy, if you should <u>want</u> to tell anyone where to go for eyebrow tattooing, it would be Joe Kaplan, Big Joe's, 27 Mount Vernon, Mount Vernon, New York 10550. I <u>doubt</u> there is anybody eyebrow tattooing in the city. A very wealthy and glamorous New York matron told me about him and I have been happy with my eyebrows. Obviously, whenever you or I send anybody off for any kind of work, we can't be <u>responsible</u> . . . this is just someone who has had thousands of years experience in tattoo work.

I'll look forward to our next visit.

Love,

Ms. Sandy Linter
East 52nd Street
New York, New York 10022

HGB:ss

May 2, 1997

Dear Rosalind,

It was so nice to see you at the party at M.O.M.A. Wednesday night. We didn't get to see <u>Hillary</u> because David had an appointment and we had to leave . . . at least I got to visit with <u>you</u> and my beloved pal (Norman and I are now "25 years old"). Rosalind, nobody <u>asked</u> but I wanted to tell you about this wonderful person who makes really great Chanel-type suits . . . little knit suits, silk blouses. I found her because my favorite designer was ADOLFO and he went out of business a couple of years ago . . . she kind of took up the slack. Her things are <u>not</u> real expensive or expensive at all. Rosalind, you didn't <u>ask</u> but I am so fond of her and crazy about the things she does (I was wearing one the other night) and I just thought a Chanel-girl like you ought to know about her. You won't abandon one for the other but, being the busybody of the entire <u>world</u>, I'm going to jot down her name and address:

> Margot Green
> East 80th Street
> Apartment 18-J

Hope I see you again before <u>another</u> seven years!

Best,

Mrs. Norman Orentreich
East 72nd Street
New York, New York 10021

HGB:ss

Magazine editors receive presents. Not bribes exactly, but manufacturers hope you will feature their products in your pages. Not quite sure why I went to bat for this little tennis-ball-size plastic blob with horns sticking up (roll your foot around on it, bear down hard, and tension goes bye-bye!), but I liked it and offered to send to girlfriends in high-anxiety places.

May 5, 1999

Dear David,

We are never going to make any money <u>this</u> way giving all the product away to Helen Brown, not that she isn't thrilled to have her grubby little hands on every single item! In addition to the high-powered ladies I originally requested ULTIMATE STRESS RELIEF <u>for</u>, I have lots of other worthy candidates, some of them equally high-powered. It would be my pleasure to send this genius-creation to them. I <u>know</u> how hard it is to market a new product but how can we miss with <u>this</u> one. Let's float them out there, relieve a lot of stress and see what happens.

<u>All</u> my thanks
and best wishes,

Mr. David Forbes
President
Quality of Life Products, Inc.
Colorado Street, Suite 2106
Austin, Texas 78701

HGB:ss

These people don't advertise in <u>Cosmo</u>, why am I helping? After sampling the product in a hotel room, I wrote the company to see where it could be bought in the United States. They said the hotel was discontinuing freebies to guests, could I tell the hotel how much I liked their stuff? Decided I could.

June 9, 1993

Dear Mr. Fahmy,

My friends at Gilchrist & Soames tell me that you are about to stop your arrangement with them to supply samples of their shampoo at the Watergate. It's not the <u>most</u> pressing concern of my life but, as indicated in the attached xerox, I <u>discovered</u> Gilchrist & Soames at the Watergate and have been addicted ever since. You have to do what is right for your hotel but I can't help feeling this wonderful <u>product</u> is right for your hotel and I hope you will continue to provide it for your guests. I travel a great deal and you can't <u>believe</u> the shampoos you run into in hotel rooms even in <u>good</u> hotels. It was such a pleasure to have this classy product in my clutches and on my head—discovered at the Watergate—that I had been using it ever since. Don't move too <u>swiftly</u> not to still supply this treasure to your guests!

All my best wishes,

Mr. Ibrahim Fahmy
General Manager
Watergate Hotel
Virginia Avenue N.W.
Washington, D.C. 20037

HGB:ss

January 20, 1994

Barbara,

The wig-maker I think you might buy a little hairpiece from is:

Nicholas Piazza
E. 57th Street
New York, New York 10022

Barbara, I bought one of the same hairpieces you did—it is called a spaceball and you pull your hair through holes—and it didn't work at <u>all</u>. He finally filled it all in and made a regular fall for me. Never mind that mistake, I have bought four hairpieces from him after that, two regular wigs and two so-called hairpieces that you plop on top of your own hair when it is getting a little skimpy between shampoos. I think you should have a regular wig—not one that fits down like a shower cap but one you just plop on top of your hair. It can be done without bangs and you just pull a little bit of your own hair in front over the join line. Absolutely up to you. You <u>have</u> nice hair but these are handy for parties or whatever with no hairdresser around. Barbara, <u>tell</u> him you didn't like your spaceball and would only go into something new if he can figure out <u>exactly</u> what will be helpful in your life.

Ms. Barbara Walters
ABC
Columbus Avenue, 10th floor
New York, New York 10023

HGB/rc

This may be the only time in history a face-lift from a major surgeon was acquired by somebody who didn't pay. I didn't search out a surgeon to ask for free for an aging, penniless, deserving friend but, after realizing <u>Cosmo</u> had assigned a major article on cosmetic surgery featuring this particular doctor, I asked our beauty editor to ask the doctor if she might <u>consider</u> helping my friend. Doctor said yes if she could be assured the article featuring her was going to run—she didn't want it yanked after her task was completed. I said we were in business!

June 10, 1994

Dear Dr. Colen,

Thank you for talking to me on the phone yesterday afternoon. I give you my total guarantee that your article, CHANGE YOUR FACE, CHANGE YOUR LIFE, will run in the October 1994 issue of Cosmopolitan. The magazine will be on the newsstands September 20th. We will be able to show you an advance copy of the magazine as early as the first week in September, no later than September 20th. You will continue to try to supply us a before and after picture of an eye operation as well as a total face lift if that is feasible. As you know, I am fervently pushing for the surgery date for my friend for anytime between August 9 and your departure date August 19th.

All my best wishes,

Helen Colen, M.D.
Park Avenue
New York, New York 10021

HGB/rc

January 24, 2002

Dear Jackie,

I have meant to write you for such a long time to congratulate you and the Digest for making you the editor. I'm not the last word on who appoints whom on a magazine but A. I know your work at Family Circle and other places and B. I am the next thing to worshipful of Reader's Digest! I think you deserve each other. For many long years as U.S. editor of Cosmo, I subscribed to a copy of the Digest for every editor who had anything to do with text—about eight—and suggested they read it thoroughly every month because the Digest had the best material but much of it was abridged and it was a great art to know what to leave in and what to take out of an article that is too long, not to mention editing along the way. Jackie, one of my dearest friends, Charlotte Veal, who also knows you, has written an article she and I both think might work in the Digest. David (husband) and I both think it might be a Digest article, not because we're in it but because it is kind of okay— written about somebody well-known—though he isn't still here—David Selznick. Perhaps you'll be good enough to have somebody on your staff read the article and report to you, yes or no, and then you will tell me. Jackie, I deeply appreciate this and am happy for my sake that you are now the editor of my favorite magazine. I'll look forward to hearing from you.

All my best wishes,

Ms. Jacqueline Leo
Reader's Digest Road
Pleasantville, New York 10570

HGB:ss

November 6, 2001

Dear Sherrie,

I'm glad you're sending the article to Cosmo, Redbook and Glamour—it belongs in all three of them.

Sherrie, when we have our Cosmo Conference with <u>all</u> our editors after the first of the year, I'll mention The Rules being published in 27 countries. The things you write are the kind of material they don't have nearly enough of—let's just see. Thrilled your column will be in the November issue of Cosmogirl—yippee, yippee! Sherrie, in addition to the biotin, I slam on a lot of Crisco before I go to bed at night or when I get up during the night. I just don't think it hurts to have something rich and greasy soaking into your nails and it doesn't really hurt the bedclothes. My husband says he can put up with the Crisco since I've given up Mentholatum kisses. More than you want to know!

All my best wishes,

Ms. Sherrie Schneider
"The Rules"
FDR Station
New York, New York 10150

HGB:ss

August 20, 1993

Dear Judge Kram,

I know sentencing for Edward R. Downe, Jr. will be coming
September 15th and, if I may, I would like to say a word in his
behalf. Ed and I have been business and personal friends for 25 years
and my dealings with him have always been first rate. He is
honorable, delivers whatever he has promised and is responsible in
every way. He was an early—maybe the <u>earliest</u> feminist—in the
magazine publishing world, being the first publisher to hire women
to sell advertising. He has always been a minority-advocate and I
think ran the first black woman on the cover of a major woman's
magazine (Ladies' Home Journal)—Naomi Sims in 1968. An editor
deals with a great many people in business and my dealings with Ed
Downe have been some of the most satisfactory and rewarding.
Thank you for reading this letter.

All my best wishes,

The Honorable Shirley Wohl Kram
United States Courthouse
Foley Square
New York, New York 10007

HGB/rc

FIVE

Will You Do Something for Me?

No explanations needed! I'm asking somebody to do something for me (via letter) just about every fifteen (five?) minutes of my life.

January 13, 1995

Dear Norman,

Do you want to do something for me—ask your client, Brooke Shields, if she would be one of the roasters at a luncheon the Advertising Women of New York are giving for me at the Waldorf Starlight Room Tuesday, March 21 at lunch. Other roasters are: Diane Sawyer, Barbara Walters, Liz Smith, Beverly Sills, Gene Shalit and maybe one or two others. She would speak for 2 or 3 minutes. Norman, you and Brooke are probably not feeling too friendly toward me or Cosmo because we didn't use the cover you wanted us to. Brooke was wearing a long glove in the photograph and it just didn't seem right to me although there is no such thing as a not beautiful picture of Brooke Shields. We have, as you know, been honored by Brooke on our cover many times and were, up to the point of not using this picture, I think, good friends.

Norman, the people giving the luncheon have asked me to ask you about Brooke because they want someone <u>young</u> to balance this group of women who are somewhat older (although Diane Sawyer would not like being referred to that way!). And, of course, because she is a star. You don't need <u>us</u>, that's for sure.

Norman, being in a hit show doesn't give one much time or energy to do anything <u>else</u> but I would adore her to do this. If you feel she <u>could</u> would you have someone call and let me know. She could come just in time for her little presentation and leave quickly—it wouldn't have to be a whole lunch.

All my thanks
and best wishes,

Mr. Norman Brokaw
William Morris Agency
Avenue of the Americas
New York, New York 10019

HGB/rc

January 7, 2000

Dear Joan,

You were darling with Kathie Lee Gifford Tuesday morning—you should have been co-host all <u>week</u>.

New subject: What has Joan Rivers done for Helen Brown <u>lately</u>?! It has been all of three weeks since you gave St. Martin's Press and me the wonderful quote for my book, "I'm Wild Again." That meant <u>everything</u> to us. . . . it looks great on the jacket.

Joan, it's too soon to even mention a <u>new</u> request but Cosmetic Executive Women (big trade organization) are creating a journal for their CEW Achiever Award 2000 Dinner May 24th and want someone to write about each of the women they've honored through the years. They suggested <u>you</u>. I told them I can't go near you for another hundred years but here I am. . . . attached letter explains their request. To make this task "easier" (???) I wrote a little something I thought you <u>might</u> say if you wanted to. Your giving me the wig is a true story. So is the Tonight Show incident though you might not have seen me the night I looked scalped. Attached picture of you and me would probably run.

Joan, can you do this? If so, I will owe you a major piece of jewelry. If you can't, I'll only owe you a floor-length lynx. . . . you've done an awful lot <u>already</u>. Could Jocelyn let me know?

Love and Happiest <u>whatever</u>
you want for the New Year,

Ms. Joan Rivers
East 62nd Street
New York, New York 10021

THE LITTLE SOMETHING ABOUT ME I WHIPPED UP
FOR JOAN RIVERS

I think Helen Brown has always <u>tried</u> to get it right. . . . her work, dealings with other people, her looks. Once when she was booked on The Tonight Show she got her head too close to a faulty heater a couple of days before the show and singed all the hair off the front of her head. She did the show anyway but her hair looked pretty skimpy. Soon as I could I picked up a hooker's wig for her in Atlantic City—about three pounds of ash-brown acrylic hair that cascaded like Niagra. I don't know how often she's worn the wig but that's the kind of friends we are. I think she's terrific. Helen has probably helped a few hundred thousand young women in the past 32 years be more beautiful by telling them in the pages of her magazine that looking good—at least as good as you <u>can</u>—is right up there with being loyal, brave, honest, obedient, optimistic, clean, reverent, true and all those other Girl Scout virtues. With 39 editions of Cosmo all over the world she indeed has had something to do with creating a global beauty industry.

January 5, 1994

Dear Leo and Bob,

Special favor—do you suppose we could probably get my grocery order up to the house by <u>noon</u> every Friday? The last few weeks it has been coming in around 3 p.m. My problem is that the housekeeper gets in at 10 in the morning and she needs to start cooking. If she has to wait 5 hours for the groceries, it isn't wonderful. As you may know—though it isn't number one priority in your life—I was a customer of Grenoble for over 20 years and we had this neat arrangement where I always got the groceries by 12 noon. Things are going fine with Regent Food <u>except</u> for this little glitch. Is there anyone you could talk to so the groceries arrive by noon every Friday? I place the order by telephone Thursday afternoon. The account is: David Brown, West 81st Street, New York 10024. Thanks ever so much.

Sincerely,

Messrs. Leo and Bob Shapiro
Regent Food
Third Avenue
New York, New York 10028

HGB/rc

January 12, 1995

Dear Bruno,

David Brown and I have a reservation at Daniel for Monday, February 6 for four people at, I hope, 8 o'clock. I believe you said nothing would be available until 8:30 p.m. but perhaps you will change your mind. We would like very much to be with you and 8:30 is going to be a little late. Having been a magazine editor for a long time, I'm spoiled and can hardly think of anyplace I can't get into at a time that's convenient for us—usually 8 p.m. We are talking Lutèce, La Grenouille, Le Cirque, well it is a long list and I can't believe you want anybody running around feeling as "gruesome" as I do this afternoon after being on the telephone with your restaurant. I was put on the recorded session three different times, left on the phone about ten minutes twice, finally told the reservation could only be at 8:30.

Repeat—I haven't had a "restaurant experience" like this in the last twenty years that I can remember and I just don't think you want me feeling like this. The last time we were in you made a tremendous fuss—champagne, warm greetings. Have we fallen out of grace with Daniel? Of course, we should come in oftener but I wouldn't be real encouraged to do that after having such a not-wonderful experience this afternoon on the phone. My husband, David Brown, is a nice person—just like me! He produces movies, tips insanely and I can't think you want to make him unhappy either. Okay . . . enough! You have probably stopped reading. I am going to call a little closer to February 6 to see if you can take care of us at 8 p.m.

All my best wishes,

Bruno
Daniel
East 76th Street
New York, New York 10021

HGB/rc

June 9, 1997

Dear Jim,

How are you?

Please glance at this note and tell me if anybody in the world would be interested in pursuing a television series based on the lives of some flight attendants. I can't remember one but it seems such a standard subject, surely there must have been. There is this flight attendant on American Airlines to whom everything has happened and I thought the experiences of four flight attendants sharing a flat in Chicago, New York, Denver, Atlanta or wherever—what happens to them in the air and on the ground would be kind of a natural. Jim, I can't put a show together by myself but could come up with the flight attendant, have tons of ideas and help if anyone were interested in pursuing this particular background and group of characters for a show. You're busy and don't need this aggravation but maybe somebody could call or write me and say no, it's the worst idea you ever heard or yes, they would be interested in talking to me a little further. Whatever you say.

All my best wishes,

Mr. Jim Griffin
William Morris Agency
Avenue of the Americas
New York, New York 10019

October 9, 2001

Dear Gurley's

Are you going to be wonderful and send me six more cans of GURLEY'S HONEY ROAST PEANUTS? I don't mean them to be <u>free</u>—you were wildly generous the last time—I want to <u>pay</u>. These are about the best nuts there are in the whole world and I can't find them in New York. I would be so happy to hear from you.

All my thanks
and best wishes,

P.S. You don't hear the name GURLEY very often. I have never run into a single one in New York and my relatives are all conking out in Arkansas. I'm glad <u>you're</u> there.

Gurley's Foods
P.O. Box
Willmar, Minnesota 56201

HGB:ss

March 30, 2000

Dear John,

Are you going to be a wonderful friend, as you have always been, and see if you can find my dress around there? After Tina Brown's tremendous party at the Statue of Liberty to celebrate the launch of TALK, I brought a dress in to you to see if you could find a swatch of fabric that had fallen off the dress under the statue the night before. You didn't throw me out of the salon and said you might be able to go to work on it. I don't have to have the missing swatch—am sure the fabric is no longer alive—you were thinking about something in another fabric or color but I <u>would</u> love to have the dress back. Cosmo is having a major convention of its editors from all around the world May the 7th and I want to bring the dress along. It was strapless, heavy cotton in a red/green/black design. Are you going to take a real prowl around there and see if you can find it. John, thank you so very much.

All my best wishes,

Mr. John Lindsey
Sales Director
Bill Blass Ltd.
Seventh Avenue
New York, New York 10018

HGB:ss

The cosmetics company almost doesn't exist that doesn't succumb to a friendly editor-request. This one, along with rivals, is a pussycat. Securing pages of advertising is something else!

August 9, 1990

Dear Dan,

What have you done for me <u>lately</u>?!

Could you tell me if Revlon still makes Norell lipstick? It is the best lipstick ever invented because it is lush and thick and highly pigmented. Most lipstick now is thin and slippy-slidy . . . really full-bodied lipsticks seem to have gone bye bye but Norell was the best. If you don't any longer make it, could you tell me what else from the Revlon line might be <u>closest</u> to that formula?

I always feel one should go to the top to really get things done.

Best,

Mr. Dan Moriarty
Revlon
Madison Avenue
New York, New York 10022

HGB/rc

Yes, sometimes I get turned down. I never heard from anybody on this one.

January 6, 1994

Dear David,

I'd love to appear on your show—your guests always seem to be having a good time and, since I'm just a few blocks away I wouldn't require much advance notice if you suddenly found yourself with a last-minute dropout.

You might think about Valentine's Day, or I'd be happy to suggest some topics I think would be fun, like: JUST HOW SEXUALLY LIBERATED ARE YOU? ARE YOU THE OFFICE PILL? DO YOU HAVE ANIMAL MAGNETISM? TEST YOUR PARTY PANACHE, FEELINGS: ARE YOU IN TOUCH WITH YOURS? WHAT DO YOUR LEGS SAY ABOUT YOUR RELATIONSHIP WITH MEN? and HOW WELL DO YOU KNOW YOURSELF?

David, Cosmo is the biggest selling women's magazine in the world (27 international editions)—for the past 13 years we've been the biggest seller at college campus book stores and according to The Hollywood Reporter I ranked tenth in the alltime Tonight Show appearances, so I'm comfortable thinking the two of us could come up with something your fans would find entertaining.

I look forward to hearing from you or Robert Morton.

Best,

Mr. David Letterman
The David Letterman Show
Broadway
New York, New York 10019

HGB/rc

June 13, 1991

Dear Nancy,

Do you <u>need</u> this kind of request?! The answer is no but I'm requesting anyway.

Cosmo has a special issue in October focused on WOMEN IN LOVE—women in love with men, with their work, with children, with the environment, with worthy causes, etc. etc. I would love just a few lines from you on what it is like to be in love with a powerful man.

This sounds like a cliché idea and nothing you would want to be connected with but it won't really <u>destroy</u> you and I need you to do this! It can just be a few lines . . . they can be irreverent or practical or funny . . . you can always get a reservation at the last minute at any restaurant in town. You could say you've had to change your phone number 18 times since being married. You could say it's just as easy to love a powerful man as a wimp.

Nancy, I <u>know</u> you (well, a little bit) and you <u>talk</u> so good I know you can say something just right. I am only getting quotes from a few people whose powerful husbands are <u>worth</u> being married to—in my biased opinion!

Nancy, our writer, Ralph Gardner, has left a call I believe or perhaps he has written you a note. I wish you would call him—or you can call <u>me</u> if you prefer. Don't <u>not</u> call!

All my best wishes,

Mrs. Henry Kissinger
East 52nd Street
New York, New York 10022

HGB/rc

Success again, and this was a biggie. Sometimes going right to the top doesn't hurt.

April 27, 1993

Barry dear,

William Morrow & Company has tried hard to interest QVC in taking on my new book, <u>THE LATE SHOW: A Semiwild But Practical Survival Plan For Women Over 50</u>—so I can be on QVC and <u>sell</u> it; so far, they have resisted. It's <u>possible</u> that QVC, reaching mid-America as they do (along with everybody else in the country) may feel that I am a little controversial for them. There <u>is</u> a chapter on sex (suggesting that older people should not let it slip away) but there are twelve <u>other</u> chapters that really have good, moral uplifting and <u>practical</u> advice . . . I <u>think</u>, pretty inspiring stuff. Add to that I <u>am</u> a midwestern girl, grew up in Little Rock, was for a long time a member of the Presbyterian Church in both Little Rock and Los Angeles, and my principal message is that you get out what you put in—you can <u>make</u> your own happiness and health.

Barry, this is an outright, unabashed request for you to put in a "good word" with your people at QVC on behalf of their taking on my book—I'll be very good at <u>selling</u> it. If you don't, can't or won't, I expect us to go on being pals as we always have been. Alas, it always seems to be <u>I</u> who am asking for something—to let me photograph you in your bath robe, to come to my 20th anniversary party, whatever . . . Here I am still at it but how am I to resist when this means so much to me?!

Love,

Mr. Barry Diller
Coldwater Canyon
Beverly Hills, California 90210

SIX

I Can't Do What You Want

Make the speech, join the committee, attend the function, find you a publisher or agent for your book, give you a quote. Anyone with a little influence—a magazine editor is in that category—is asked to do a lot of things he or she can't. I've found it easier to say no in a letter (in response to one from them) than on the phone. Who has time for phone chats—them <u>or</u> you—when saying no to a request? And this way you can be a little gracious while delivering the news they don't want to hear.

I get plenty of requests to help find somebody a publisher or agent. I'm sure all authors get such requests—you got your book published, how about pitching in for a worthy stranger?! Afraid I haven't helped yet! (Are they crazy?!)

January 20, 1998

Dear Monique,

Thanks for your most interesting letter and the outline of CHINA NIGHTS. I remember our flight with you on Pan Am's service to the People's Republic of China . . . it's one of the most exciting adventures I've ever had. Monique, I hate to be such a cop-out but I couldn't begin to offer "help in matching this story to the right publisher." I really don't know which publisher publishes what particular kind of material. All one can do, I think, is look in the book stalls at Barnes and Noble, Borders or whoever, look at books that seem to you to do the kind of thing you are doing with CHINA NIGHTS. You can try sending the outline of your book to that publisher. If no publisher particularly creates the right "feeling" for your particular material, you would just pick a big publishing house and plunge. Publishers are not big on reading unsolicited material but, if it looks absolutely intriguing, they occasionally will. Monique, I couldn't get my sister, brother or childhood friend to "the right publisher"—it just isn't information that I have. I do wish you the bestest with your wonderful project. I will surely try to pop into the Nardin Gallery and see your work. I know it's wonderful. Thanks for thinking of me and lots and lots of good luck with your book.

All my best wishes,

Ms. Monique Seyler
Colonial Drive
Katonah, New York 10536

HGB:ss

> **I get about a dozen of these requests a year—<u>any</u> well-known person does—have almost <u>never</u> been able to comply.**

November 11, 1997

Dear Bill,

Thanks so much for sending me THOSE WHO TRESPASS. I love people who do what they say they are going to and here we are . . . it looks absolutely terrific! Bill, in all my years as a magazine editor, I have never given the <u>first</u> quote for a book. Everybody I know writes books (not that it's that easy to do) and all the writers who work and worked for Cosmo have written books and I couldn't do one testimonial and not do the others so I never did <u>any</u> . . . not one single one in thirty-two years. The book is going to do gorgeously <u>without</u> me. I shall so look forward to reading . . . congratulations!

All my best wishes,

Mr. Bill O'Reilly
Fox News
Avenue of the Americas
New York, New York 10036

HGB:ss

July 6, 1992

Dear Dr. Chopra,

The visit with you last week was a thriller . . . nice to meet someone that you have heard so much about (raves!). That is really an incredible invitation to visit you in Lancaster "for a week's rejuvenation." There isn't any question I could <u>use</u> it! I so rarely <u>can</u> spend a week doing <u>anything</u> away from Cosmo that we probably can't plan on this happening tomorrow but I will tuck the invitation into my file of things to look forward to. If I can't spend a whole week, at least I could visit you and see what you do up there. You were wonderful to send the books. Courtney [Ross] had sent me two of them and these I shared with my sister in Oklahoma who has been in a wheelchair for many years, having been invalid-ed by Polio before there was a Salk vaccine.

She, too, is interested in and impressed by your work. Maybe I will share some of the new books with her after I have studied carefully. Doctor, we will be new friends—thank you for responding so generously to our "new friendship" and I <u>will</u> look forward to a visit at some point.

All my best wishes,

Deepak Chopra, M.D.
P.O. Box
So. Lancaster, Maine 01561

HGB/rc

January 18, 1993

Iris dear,

Your Annual Dachshund Party sounds so glorious as I know they have all been in the past. David and I are not able to be with you but will be woofing and barking for you and Liz the Lionhearted and all your guests and celebrators.

Love,

Ms. Iris Love
East 38th Street
New York, New York 10016
Suite 26-A

HGB:ss

March 3, 1993

Dear Anna,

Anything you are connected with is a first-class operation. Thank you so much for asking me to be on the committee for the American Suicide Foundation Lifesavers Dinner honoring Tina Brown, James Brady and others. Anna, I am not a very helpful committee member. I can't attend <u>meetings</u> nor guarantee a table. The Hearst Corporation decides which charities we will be involved with and buy tables for and we get so many requests I don't try to influence them one way or the other although, as you know, Hearst does frequently participate in whatever philanthropy. I think, Anna, just to use my name as a committee member is "cheating" because you won't really be <u>getting</u> anything from me. I'm deeply honored to have been asked.

All my best wishes,

Ms. Anna Wintour
Vogue
Condé Nast Publications, Inc.
Madison Avenue
New York, New York 10017

HGB/rc

October 28, 1998

Steve dear,

I'm not responding to the Steve Forbes address in Alexandria, Virginia, because I wanted to write you personally. I am such an enthusiast for <u>you</u>, proud of everything you have achieved, seriously impressed that you were a candidate for president of the United States. Steve, I can't be part of Americans for Hope, Growth and Opportunity Chairman's Council because I am simply not <u>for</u> the flat tax. Thank you for your very thoughtful letter and solicitation. Maybe we are not <u>quite</u> on the same side but, again, I find you and your work so impressive.

All my best wishes,

Mr. Steve Forbes
Forbes Magazine
Fifth Avenue
New York, New York 10019

HGB:ss

November 22, 2000

Dear Mr. Isaacson,

I am a genuine fraud and must write you this letter before I get any <u>more</u> fraudulent! You have written the most reasonable and comprehensive letter outlining the four major categories that CUNY TV needs to develop as part of the process of writing a multi-year plan for growth and expansion (I'm quoting your words), but I must be brave and strong and explain that I <u>shouldn't</u> be on the Advisory Committee because, knowing me, I <u>won't</u> be participating and helpful. Sometimes I have been a guest on a CUNY television show and I so much respect who you are and what you are doing but this is a cause I know I can't devote real energy and intelligence to. There virtually are no causes that I <u>can</u> because I am busier than ever as international editor of Cosmopolitan (we have 41 editions all over the world and keep opening new ones) and I virtually don't do <u>anything</u> extracurricular. I got carried away because you <u>asked</u> me and CUNY is so worthy. Maybe someday there will be <u>something</u> I can do to be helpful . . . thanks for the original invitation and putting up with this long, pesky letter!

All my best wishes,

Mr. Robert Isaacson
Executive Director
CUNY TV
City University Graduate Center
Fifth Avenue, Suite 1400
New York, New York 10016

HGB:ss

July 8, 2002

Dear Jim,

What a beautiful offering . . . the actual desk used by Dr. Norman Vincent Peale from 1932–1984. Not only The Real Thing but a beautiful piece of furniture. Jim, my husband is 86, I am 80 and we are simply trying to decide what to do with all the stuff we already have, not acquire anything "new." We don't have children to leave things to so the beneficiaries in our will are going to get lots of furniture and other artifacts. Your offering particularly interests me because my mother <u>worshipped</u> Dr. Peale and, though she lived in Arkansas, mercifully got to hear him at the Marble Collegiate Church when she visited David and me in New York. Some fortunate person is going to acquire this beautiful antique . . . I'm just glad it's <u>there</u>.

All my best wishes,

Mr. Jim Bickford
American Dreams
Koval Lane
Las Vegas, NV 89109

HGB:ss

April 16, 2001

Dear Zarela,

I surely do remember our meeting and talking at Judy Green's Christmas party and the restaurant you talked about, Danzon, sounds wonderful and exciting. It's good to know that things you have heard about are <u>really going to happen</u>. Zarela, I'm in such trouble! Why did I offer a pair of nifty high-heel shoes to be on display at the restaurant when whatever decent ones I <u>have</u>, I am <u>wearing</u>! Naturally, I don't want something scruffy and expendable—I can live without them—to be on display with my name. The beautiful and expensive Manolo Blahnik shoes I am <u>wearing</u> and would be appropriate, I feel I can't let go. I assume this is a pretty permanent exhibit. Zarela, someone who helps me get organized with my clothes, once in spring/summer, once in fall/winter is coming over in two or three weeks to get me fixed up for summer. As we go through everything, let me see if there is a pair of decent shoes I might contribute. Please don't count on me because I think I was a little off-the-wall to make an offer. I <u>am</u> excited that the restaurant is going to <u>happen</u>. . . . congratulations, congratulations!

All my best wishes,

Ms. Zarela Martinez
East 53rd Street
New York, New York 10022

HGB:ss

September 24, 2001

Ms. Sarah Sheffer,

It's very flattering that you have given me credit for the saying on your birthday card—"Good Girls Go To Heaven, Bad Girls Go Everywhere." Sarah, there is no <u>way</u> I can give you official permission to use this particular saying. It appears on a needlepoint pillow someone gave me at least fifteen years ago. The people who created this and other pillows have been out of business for many years so there is no way of checking with them. We don't know <u>who</u> created the saying, I just know that when anybody ever comes to my office to photograph or do a t.v. interview, they usually have the pillow in the picture—that is why the pillow is associated with me. Your letter is so flattering and so reassuring but there isn't any <u>way</u> I can give official permission for the quote to be on a greeting card since I didn't create it and don't know who <u>did</u>. . . . let's hope you don't get into too much trouble. Your other cards are terrific—I'm so glad you sent them to me.

All my best wishes,

Doc Milo Productions
The Barn at Eagle Village
Park Road
Eagle, PA 19480

HGB:ss

SEVEN

Dear Doctor, Please Get Me Fixed

(And Thank You for What You Already Did!)

I've found doctors more responsive to letters and faxes from me than to phone calls, provided I don't have a chicken bone stuck in my throat! I've found they <u>will</u> call if you ask a question by fax, whereas sometimes a phone call is not returned. (Maybe your doctors are not as big-deal, high-powered—can a doctor <u>be</u> a mogul?— as mine.)

May 5, 1997

Dear Dr. Daly,

Am I your favorite patient? Well, if you don't want to go quite <u>that</u> far, am I a patient you would like to help with something? Good!

Doctor, we did my surgery last June 27, as I remember, and it was magnificent! Here's my problem: my tummy is as hard as a football and <u>resembles</u> one. . . . no matter how I exercise or how little I eat it is pooching out there, I guess, because we had to cut muscle and now the tummy exercises don't do a whole lot of good. If I starve enough to weigh only 100 pounds, the poochiness goes down a bit—not all the way—but I am more comfortable weighing 104 and eating like a somewhat normal person.

Are you still reading? There isn't such a thing as surgery to remove scar tissue, is there? I suppose it would be called cosmetic surgery and, since we were in there the last time working with scar tissue that had wrapped itself around an intestine, you may not want to even <u>think</u> about scar tissue again! Doctor, whatever you say. I try so hard to fight age and do it rather successfully, for the most part, but here is this sticking-out stomach that is <u>depressing</u> me! If you ever have a moment, would you telephone and give me your opinion. I won't keep you on the phone more than 4 minutes, I promise.

> All my thanks
> and best wishes,

Dr. John M. Daly
Department of Surgery
New York Hospital
East 68th Street
New York, New York 10021

September 3, 2002

Dr. Harvey Klein

Dear Dr. Klein,

Would you consider advising me about something
on the telephone?   If not, I'll come in though you aren't
crazy about pippy-poo appointments!

I have arthritis in one shoulder, diagnosed
a couple of years ago by somebody you sent me to - arthritis/
bursitis.   Have had many sessions sith Elizabeth Burgholtz
(your suggestion) and she's terrifid but what they do is
get/you to use the aching joint - don't let it sit there
and just get worse which it will.   I have workouts with her
and assiduously do them twice a day away from her - I couldn't
be more disciplined.   Problem: I hurt.   The pain isn't
horrendous...mostly quite mild unless I am doing the exercises
but who wants to hurt?!   Do you recommend at all something
like Celebrex (over-the-counter arthritis remedy) or Aleve?
Some "sufferers" pick up a concoction called GLUCOSAMINE
SULPHATE at the drug store. Used to have to be brougnt in
from Mexico or Switzerland but now it's here.   I'm not in enough
pain to be going up the walls or anything but it woudd be nice
not to hurt.   Could I hear your thoughts about this? I don't

do anything you don't say is okay. Maybe Celebrex side effects
aren't good and I'm not eager to add to my daily pills.

My bestest thanks -

Helen

January 9, 2001

Norman dear,

Thank you so much for sending the fascinating information about the effects of nutrition and metabolism on aging. I have read it with such interest and will indeed check with my internist, Harvey Klein, about having the Glucose/Insulin Tolerance Test. I had it once with Bob Atkins, the Diet Revolution doctor and I was inculcating too much sugar but that was many years ago. I'd like to try again.

Norman, you haven't seen me for a month or two and I miss you though I order supplies from your office. It seemed to me during my last three visits—several months apart—silicone wasn't being very effective in my somewhat rippled skin—upper lip and chin. Lots of little tiny craters and peaks in that area which are hard to smooth out. That's what laserbrasion is all about but we couldn't very well do that again. I'm using my rehabilitation cream and when I wake up in the morning—after a nifty eight hours—the skin is smoother. . . . it puckers up again during the day.

Norman, more than you want to know but you are always a good listener! I'll check in one of these days. David's movie— CHOCOLAT—which you meant to see but couldn't, is being a big success and I'm so pleased for David. He took it to the White House Saturday night at their request and Bill said he liked it. . . . good! Hope you got through your birthday just fine. . . . it's much too close to Christmas—that was naughty of your folks!

Love and hugs. . . .

this is important work, as always, that you are doing and I'm sure you're on to something,

Dr. Norman Orentreich
Orentreich Foundation for the Advancement Of Science
Fifth Avenue
New York, New York 10021

February 2, 2001

Dear Dr. Aston,

You were <u>wonderful</u> with Katie Couric on The Today Show. I was getting bored with your patient, although she looks wonderful!—but then finally <u>you</u> got on and answered questions <u>everybody</u> wants answered. Now, of course, there will be a line clear down to 57th Street of people trying to get into your office but, never mind. . . . I know you will always fit in special friends. Hillary Clinton looks so good that Ann Siegel and I decided it had to be <u>you</u>. When I approached Muffie with this question at a party last week she said, "Helen, if I answered questions like that I'd be in divorce court!" I don't know whether that constitutes a yes or a no but A. Hillary looks fine B. Muffie has integrity C. I was so proud of you on the show this morning. See you soon.

Best,

Dr. Sherrell Aston
Park Avenue
New York, New York 10021

HGB:ss

July 6, 1999

Dear Dr. Pritchett,

You have to do something for David and me the next time you see each other. I want you to write a prescription for him that will somehow take the place of the pyribenzamine which I have been ordering for years but they don't make it anymore—recent decision. This drug was prescribed for me about forty years ago because I used to break out in terrible hives after major physical activity. . . . winning Charleston contests and things like that. It had such a soothing effect, I eventually started using it as a sleeping potion—just one-half or a quarter of a tablet. To get David persuaded not to use anything really <u>serious</u> in the way of a sleeping potion, I suggested he try the pyribenzamine and it has worked for him for several years—he takes a whole tablet. Can you think of anything that might be in that category? Obviously it is an antihistamine and I don't know why they quit making but you are a genius and will think of a replacement.

All my thanks. . . . love,

Dr. Rees Pritchett
East 68th Street
New York, New York 10021

HGB:ss

This doctor, head of surgery at the hospital, was taking a lot of press abuse for having been on the golf course when needed for an emergency. Should a doctor <u>never</u> play golf on the chance he might be needed back at the ranch? He was right at the hospital the morning we needed him for <u>me</u>.

March 20, 1997

Dear Dr. Daly,

You've been getting some gruesome press lately but you mustn't worry your beautiful head—it will go. . . . .newspapers are always after anything that will make a seemingly scandalous story and we've all been hit. I want you to remember all day long and all the time that you are a <u>surgeon</u>. . . . probably in the top ten of anybody in the world. You do exquisite work, save lives and make people's life after you <u>better</u>. That's what happened with me and I never tire of telling people how brilliant you are and also how kind. We have to remember your pro bono work also—what you are doing for women with breast cancer and others to prevent their having it. Please please be of good cheer.

With love and hugs,

Dr. John M. Daly
Department of Surgery
New York Hospital
East 68th Street
New York, New York 10021

HGB:ss

COSMOPOLITAN

Helen Gurley Brown, Editor-In-Chief

November 7, 1998

Dear Dr. Borgen,

Would you like to know how I am (since you performed the exquisite surgery on me in July?) I'm fine and should have told you sooner.

I had six weeks of radiation, supervised by Dr. McCormick whom I saw every week. Three weeks ago I saw Dr. Norton who says I'm tippy-top. He prescribed Tamoxifen—two tablets a day. I have another appointment with him in February. I will never be able to tell you how grateful I am that you actually saved my bosom—only the most modest part cut out—and <u>probably</u> saved my life. (slightly more important)! I'm writing about my experience with you in a book but we're probably a year away from publication so no holding our breath. Doctor, thank you sounds a little weak but thank you just the same for being a wonderful surgeon, for always being so kind and explaining everything and, furthermore, for being <u>fast</u>! From the moment of our first appointment it was only thirteen days 'till surgery. "Wonderful" doesn't quite do it . . . I should have said <u>fantastic</u> surgeon!

> With deep gratitude and all
> my best wishes,

EIGHT

So What Do You Think?

Compiling material for a book, article, speech, advising students, perhaps just to cheer themselves up, people ask for input on various subjects. Hard not to kick right in and show off (or pontificate!).

How should you behave in order to be successful? I get lots of these letters. Yes, I guess we could say I have <u>been</u> that, but I can be pretty pontifical!

January 9, 1998

Dear Dr. Good,

Older people can sound very pompous and boring to your young students but maybe you learn a <u>few</u> things as life goes on that can be passed along. I certainly had the least outstanding prospects as a young person and you <u>can</u> survive (and do very, very well!) if you just try hard. That sounds very cliché but what it means is that you don't have your head in the clouds and your dreams so unrealistic that they may or may not ever be realized. . . . what you do is get up every day and do the stuff that is out there that you <u>can</u> do—the rotten assignments, the self-discipline in terms of exercise and the food you put into your body, try some new stuff that isn't comfortable and nobody asked you to do it but give it a shot. . . . I think it's called initiative. Before I <u>do</u> get boring just let me suggest that everyone—that includes all your students!—has the potential for doing <u>something</u> meaningful and satisfying. If you start when you are very young just doing the best you can and trying to get a little further, it's going to turn out okay. It started happening to me around age 30 but it <u>can</u> happen sooner.

All my best wishes,

Dr. N. Stanford Good
Lancaster Bible College
Eden Road
Lancaster, PA. 17601

Mr. Jim Adams
Assistant Editor
Esquire

I guess I don't believe in "best ideas." I believe in simply <u>doing</u> your best every day and the consistent effort will generate good. Does this sound a little fatuous? Sorry! I've just found that life turns not so much on breakthrough ideas as on the steady wearing down of obstacles and barriers. Keep moving, don't wait for the flashing light, ringing bell, screaming siren . . . the good stuff is in there happening.

July 13, 2000

Dear Dana,

I guess my most heartfelt piece of advice is that you don't have to
know <u>exactly</u> where you are going when you are only seventeen years
old or even a few years older. During that period you begin to find out
what you are good at or what you like doing a whole lot and later that
may become a career but at this stage in your life I think you just
plunge into whatever is out there—your school work, summer or
week-end job, play and, for sure, <u>friendship</u>. It's hard to think of this
period of your life as a big adventure when you feel kind of scared
and shaky, but it <u>is</u> a time to reach out because nothing is set in
cement. Hope you'll be involved in lots of activities, lots of friendship
and pour a lot into everything . . . there's plenty of time to specialize!

All my best wishes,

Ms. Dana Gottlieb
East 73rd Street
New York, New York 10021

HGB:ss

May 5, 1994

Dear Jim,

In my experience, success comes <u>slowly</u>. You aren't thinking success, success, success 16 hours every day as you are growing up and becoming an adult person. You don't do that <u>after</u> you grow up either.

Perhaps my own experience is not typical but, having started work right after high school, I held 17 secretarial jobs and got fired from numerous ones until I finally got a copywriting job at age 33. I didn't get to Cosmo until I was <u>43</u>. I've been sailing along ever since—well paid, successful and producer of a successful product—but I'm just saying I think these things come when you "put the time in." That means you do everything every day to the best of your ability even if it is mental. I didn't start on this philosophy until I was around 30— before that I was just busy being young and <u>not</u> very successful but, gradually, if you give it your best shot nearly every time you can't <u>help</u> but have a success on your hands. This advice is a little <u>general</u> but what I'm saying is that you don't need to be a big shot <u>early</u> . . . just get on with the tasks that are there and gradually the tasks get more important and the so-called success comes.

All my best wishes,

Mr. Jim Kenyon
Worcester Central School
Main Street
RR 1
Worcester, New York 12197

HGB/rc

January 18, 1995

Dear Mr. Warren,

I didn't really <u>receive</u> much advice about my profession as an editor . . . I was just plopped in as a grown up (age 43) and let paddle around and try to stay afloat. Having been working in an office since I was 18 years old, I had learned a <u>few</u> things on my own about working hard and trying to get along with other people and not being a total pain in the neck. Once <u>on</u> the job I did pick up some good advice from another woman executive although she wasn't very high up the ladder herself. I was having trouble getting the courage to fire somebody who absolutely had to go. She said, "Helen, remember that right is on your side. You <u>cannot</u> let this person stay and do right by the rest of your employees. If she/he <u>stays</u>, sure, it helps that person's feelings and finances and morale . . . nobody likes to get <u>fired</u> but, you will be ignoring the rest of the office who are going to be brought down by this person's staying (the employee in question was absolutely not good at the job and, since we had very few employees, the ones we had had to be really satisfactory). Are you going to think 'kindheartedly' about this one person and be Miss Sympathetic or are you going to think about what's good for the entire staff and the magazine you work for?" That has helped me with whomever I have had to fire ever since—and there haven't been <u>that</u> many but you absolutely cannot know somebody's worth until they have worked for you for a while. I just get it in my head that "right is on my side" and do what I have to do.

All my best wishes,

Mr. Dennis Warren
Gilleland Road
Huntsville, Alabama 35803

HGB/rc

April 30, 1998

Dear Mr. Renaud,

I'd <u>like</u> to respond to your request for ideas on getting things done faster and being more organized at work or home but it just seems to be indigenous to me—in my DNA or something—and I've never had to figure out how to do it faster or more-organized. . . . I just <u>am</u> organized so don't know what to pass along. In an article I wrote for Fortune Magazine last year, I suggested that a boss should always go to his or her co-workers' offices rather than letting them come to yours because you can leave when you want to, also that you ask people what they want to talk to you about before you make an appointment by telephone with somebody outside the company— maybe they've got the wrong person in the first place and shouldn't be paying you a visit. Obviously you do the most difficult and yukky things first every day and get them over with—otherwise you might not get them done <u>altogether</u>. Sorry I can't be more helpful.

All my best wishes,

P.S. I have major flaws—never mind that flailing around disorganized hasn't ever been one of them!

Mr. R. Brian Renaud
Cherrywood Road
Louisville, KY 40207

HGB:ss

January 22, 2002

Dear Eileen,

I was very touched by your letter and are those wonderful grandchildren or not?! Wonderful picture. Eileen, my mother died several years ago at age 80. I didn't deal with it well at all but sobbed my brains out all the way from New York to Shawnee, Oklahoma, for her funeral. After I quit sobbing, I started writing—just for myself, nobody else—how I was feeling about her and the life we had had together. It was <u>anything</u> but tranquil but I loved her, I think, as much as she did me so there was no disparity about where we were coming from. She always felt I was a slave to other people (including my husband!). The doctors were using me as a guinea pig when all they were trying to do was get my incurable acne arrested and occasionally tried out new formulas, etc., etc. So I wrote all of that—I wrote and wrote and wrote. I was never proud of her because she was a mouse but I think, long before she died, she knew that I appreciated who she really <u>was</u>. . . . .a troubled person from her childhood on but always doing the best she could which included caring for an invalid child (in a wheelchair) for 64 years. Eileen, you don't need me to tell you any more about <u>my</u> mother except that she sacrificed so much for me—maybe that's where some of the sobs were coming from. When we were all living together in California, she got on a train and took my sister back to the Ozark Mountains in Arkansas to live with <u>her</u> relatives so I wouldn't be burdened with an invalid in <u>my</u> grown-up life, possibly never to marry and things like that. Okay, that's <u>enough</u> about Cleo. I think it's okay to concentrate <u>hard</u> on what they did for us but also to be realistic. . . . a mommy can be pretty aggravating sometimes and you lose your temper. I'm sure you were a <u>wonderful</u> daughter or you wouldn't miss your mother quite so much <u>now</u>. I think you just keep going over things you did together and even writing about some of them, if you want to. I always find writing somewhat gets it out of your system. I loved hearing from you and am crazy about my photograph.

All my best wishes,

P.S. You will just get through this grief period like other unhappy times in life . . . it's called one day at a time. But, since there isn't any other solution, you just plan to do it better than other people because it's <u>you</u>!

Ms. Eileen M. O'Shea
Brian Lane
East Northport, New York 11731

HGB:ss

February 26, 2002

Dear Tina and James,

I think the best advice was from my mother—occasionally they <u>do</u>
know something!—she said when I was about eight years old, "Use
your brain." In those days girls were only supposed to use their <u>looks</u>
and possibly mommy didn't think my looks were quite going to be
adequate to be of much help but throughout the years she helped
with the homework, encouraged me to get good grades, try out for
the debating society, enter contests that required slogans—smiled up
a storm when there seemed to be evidence my brain was <u>working</u>.
Other mothers weren't concentrating on daughters' brains.

Sincerely,

Ms. Tina Gourlay
Mr. James Paterson
West 50th Street
Apartment 19-F
New York, New York 10019

HGB:ss

Many people have written to ask about school experiences and what ideas could be passed along to help students <u>now</u>. They often ask about specific teachers.

January 15, 1999

Dear Rick:

It's kind of wild around here and I won't write <u>lengthily</u> but, indeed, I did spend 2 years at John H. Francis Polytechnic High School and 1 year before that at Belmont High. I'm afraid Poly High doesn't exist any longer, not even the building, but it was a memorable time in my life and, in many ways, the beginning of whatever it was I became. I had wonderful teachers . . . They <u>cared</u>. . . . And whatever I put in, I seem to have gotten out . . . Ran for office, got elected, was class valedictorian, etc., etc. I was a little girl from Little Rock with a deep southern drawl and perhaps you can imagine what it was like for this twerp to be running into black people on equal footing for the first time in my twerpy life . . . Well, we got along <u>fine</u>! The men were great dancers and the women forgave me for being so lousy at basketball . . . Nobody wanted me on her team but they put up with me. I can't think of a more wonderful place to have gone to high school . . . Maybe someday I will see if I can get Poly High rebuilt.

All my best wishes,

Rick Obrand
Carson Street Elementary School
E. Carson Street
Carson, CA 90745

July 1, 1997

Dear Linda,

The teacher who influenced my life would be Mrs. Oates in Pulaski Heights grammar school. She was my <u>first</u> teacher—me age 6—and she told my mother I had special performing talent. She made me Mother Goose in the class play and I was the <u>star</u> whereas Jack and the Beanstalk, Little Miss Muffet, Jack Sprat and others only reported to me—I was in every <u>scene</u>! I went on writing and performing <u>in</u> little grammar school and junior high projects from that moment. In senior high, a really splendid English teacher—mousey, ancient (she must have been all of 50) not popular with other students—thought I had a <u>little</u> writing ability but, more than that, she thought <u>everybody</u> should learn the rules of grammar and appreciate good <u>writing</u>. Another who helped with the <u>performing</u> arts—Ms. Ethel McGee . . . when I entered a debating contest, she coached as she continued to do through my valedictory address graduation night. My <u>mother</u> was a school teacher and she helped too. What interests me is that all these women were <u>mousey</u> but they got it out of others!

All my best wishes,

Ms. Linda Evanchyk
Journalism Teacher
Choctawhatchee Senior High School
Racetrack Road, N.W.

HGB:ss

Many letters have asked what a public library meant to me. I should have created one answer and used it through the years but kept creating new ones. Here's <u>one</u>.

November 3, 1994

Dear Ms. Thompson,

I <u>am</u> "one of the millions who have benefitted from our nation's libraries and librarians." In Little Rock, Arkansas, when I was growing up during the Depression, there <u>weren't</u> so many places you could go to spend hours <u>free</u> (no admission charge) and I got addicted to the library from about age 6, not just because the price was right but because I began to see all the treasures available for the asking and reading. There was no week when my sister Mary and I didn't have at least five books checked out of the library which we returned reasonably efficiently so that we could take out others. Later when we moved to Los Angeles, California, <u>that</u> public library was a treasure trove indeed . . . room after room categorized by fiction, history, art, science, and other specific categories. One joy in going there is that the building was so lovely and posh compared to the very modest house in which we lived . . . it was like visiting a <u>castle</u>! Though I wasn't a great reader or intellectual then or <u>now</u>, I know the hours I spent in both those libraries created the <u>interest</u> in good writing. We know what I experienced was good <u>reading</u>. The New York Public Library is in my will . . . it's a marvel, too.

All my best wishes,

Ms. Sue Ann Thompson
Arizona Library Association
N. 32nd Street, #D-1
Phoenix, Arizona 85032

HGB/rc

March 18, 1994

Dear Mr. Callos,

That is a wonderful class project that you are planning. I happen to be married to a terrifically kind and thoughtful man and we don't have a lot of conflict in our marriage. That is certainly one place where people get carried away with fighting. In my office, there are conflicts <u>daily</u> . . . not always between me and another person but among the people who work here. My own <u>personal</u> method of solving conflict is not to lose your temper if at <u>all</u> possible. For a boss <u>or</u> an employee or just among friends, being out of control in a screaming rage is no way to get anything settled. First, it puts off the settlement, second, people hate and despise you and that is a condition I don't like to deal with. Let's just say that even though one would <u>like</u> to have a temper tantrum, it doesn't work so you don't let yourself have it. That would be true in dealing with almost anybody in the world—salespeople, restaurant helpers, bus drivers, airplane personnel—you can get <u>mad</u> but you will get a lot further if you present them with charm and reasonableness at the same time you ask for what you want. I'm not sure how any of these ideas apply to your students but maybe they will help later on in life.

All my best wishes,

Mr. Thomas P. Callos
Marne Drive
Reno, Nevada 89503

HGB/rc

June 16, 2000

Dear Charmaine,

Thanks for your lovely note. It pleases me that you were once a student at Rutgers in one of Richard Heffner's classes . . . I think he is so super and it's good to think of the two of you together. Charmaine, "schmoozing with complete strangers" is always a challenge for someone who is basically shy but usually people from a magazine are welcome wherever they go because people like their product to be talked about in the magazine. If you see a woman by herself, you could certainly start with her or, <u>two</u> women talking to each other, you could start with them and you might even be ingenuous and say something like "could I join your conversation for just a moment. . . . tell me what you were talking about and I will try not to be intrusive but just <u>listen</u>!" It isn't generally a good idea to interrupt two <u>men</u> who are talking together, let alone three, but you could try the same approach. Sometimes asking a <u>question</u> of whomever you are starting to talk to is not a bad idea. It can be almost any kind of question, about the product at the launch or have they ever seen anything similar or do they go to many such launches, or whatever. Charmaine, just be your basic nice self, very gradually approach your strangers—if it goes with your job, think of it as something you <u>have</u> to do and self-discipline will get you through! You're going to be fine.

All my best wishes,

Ms. Charmaine Lim
79th Avenue #2N
Kew Gardens Hills, NY 11367

HGB:ss

November 15, 2002

Dear Cheryle,

I know your book about "messed up experiences" will be interesting and inspiring! Cheryle, this sounds a little weird but let me tell you the truth: I didn't really ever <u>mess</u> up in my career in anything but a peripheral way. I couldn't <u>afford</u> to—I was supporting a mother and invalid sister and had to have a job at all times. For my 17 secretarial jobs, I was fired once in a while but it was because the company closed down or changed cities . . . I really didn't bring the firing on <u>myself</u>. Having arrogantly said that I never messed up, I could amend that and say not <u>seriously</u>, just pippypoo incidents, not important enough to be asked to leave. These are two:

I worked for an advertising agency, Foote Cone & Belding, and my boss, Don Belding, wanted to send a new product to his mentor, Albert Lasker, who founded Lord & Thomas, which later became Foote Cone & Belding. Okay, we get in our product, the original ball point pen, and send a bunch off to various people who Mr. Belding thought should know what he was doing—acquiring a fantastic new product. I addressed the letter to Mr. Albert Lasker, La Kenta, California. It turns out that La Kenta is spelled "Quinta" and the post office didn't even recognize what city I was trying to reach; all the beautiful new ball point pens came back. Mr. Belding was unhappy but not as unhappy as he was <u>later</u> when I locked a first-edition collector's item book in a file cabinet instead of getting it off to the head of the Union Oil Company as a Christmas present. Mr. Belding had searched long and seriously for a perfect gift for his client and this was it and what happened to me was that I was into zombie-hood during that particular Christmas period, having just broken up with a longtime beau, and I forgot all about sending over the book. Mr. Belding was ready to hang me out the window by my feet when he called the Union Oil mogul to ask how he liked his Christmas present and there was no Christmas present! I was Mr. Belding's secretary for 5 years and <u>didn't</u> get fired though one day when he was making a major speech in Portland, Oregon, I left out a page of the speech in typing—he just had to vamp for what might have been on that particular page.

Cheryle, I don't <u>know</u> how much help and hope can be derived from listening to other people's messed-up stories but <u>grown-up</u>s who have had the experience will enjoy reading about others. Lots of good luck.

All my best wishes,

Ms. Cheryle E. Ackerman
Autry Falls Drive
Alpharetta, GA 30022

HGB:ss

Got any heroes?

June 9, 1997

Dear Mr. Jovich,

Thank you for your most interesting letter. Alas, I just didn't <u>have</u> heroes and heroines, not a single one! Of course there were always celebrities one admired, worshipped from afar, never <u>hoped</u> to emulate because they were too glossy. I would have to say the heroes of my life in terms of helping me achieve were my mother and my husband. I didn't know what my mother was doing at the time and didn't <u>appreciate</u> her effort at getting me educated and encouraging me to use my brain. She was <u>anything</u> but a heroine at the time but she can be that <u>now.</u> I <u>hope</u> I let her know when she was still living. My other "hero" is my husband, who felt I had something to offer and not only thought I should write and edit a magazine but created the idea for both a book and a woman's publication. Can heroes live in your same house? I think so!

All my best wishes,

Mr. John B. Jovich
Olde Stone Lane
Lancaster, New York 14086

HGB:ss

Sometimes people just want general information on a subject. Happy to try to help!

April 12, 2002

Dear Henrietta—may I call you that?

The social history of Valium sounds like a most interesting study and I know your work will be intriguing. In the years I was U.S. editor of Cosmopolitan, we didn't <u>specifically</u> do an article on Valium. It might have been included in an article dealing with depression, stress or other problems Valium might alleviate but I don't remember those possible paragraphs. Sorry I can't be more helpful. At one point, Valium was about as generic as aspirin and you tell me its use is on the rise again. My personal experience was in trying it once or twice and finding that it was <u>too</u> "efficient," if that is the right descriptive word. Taking off for New York from Los Angeles on my honeymoon—December, 1959—I'm doped with Valium, I was addled, left my luggage behind in Pacific Palisades—we had to have it shipped to New York. We are talking about someone who can't even handle a cup of coffee . . . caffeine makes me hyper and Valium had the same effect the other direction. The second time I tried Valium, before a party, again, I was a walking zombie. So much for my personal experiences with the product. Wish I could be more helpful. I know it is going to be a wonderful study.

All my best wishes,
And thanks so much for
being in touch,

Ms. Henrietta Birchenough
Producer "In Pills We Trust"

Patrice dear,

My Siamese cat, Samantha, brought profound pleasure and entertainment for eighteen years. She grew up in the Pacific Palisades area of Los Angeles, where she could go hunting every day, frequently brought me a lizard or mouse. I would get them away from her if they weren't yet dead but forgave her her cannibalism because I rationalized it was "cat nature." She slept on my tummy, ate almost an entire cashmere sweater which I used as a bed jacket—started nibbling the sleeves and just kept going, a little per night. Sometimes she would push the glasses off my face when I was reading so I would pay more attention to <u>her</u> . . . not a problem. She made a tremendous fuss when David and I were out of the city . . . unrolled an entire roll of toilet tissue in two bathrooms to show her pique (when others were taking care of her). She waited until David and I got back from Europe one August, greeted us as usual at the door, couldn't seem to make it to the chair, table or windowsill as she always did a hundred times a day, quietly died the day we returned. I miss her to this very moment.

Pat, when your book gets compiled, if you need a photograph of Samantha and me, I can probably look through the files . . . they're a little voluminous—and pull one out. Lots of good luck with your book—it sounds terrific.

All my best wishes,

Ms. Patrice S. Fox
S.I.H. 35 #1001
Austin, Texas 78741

HGB:ss

August 2, 1994

Dear Meghan,

My favorite childhood recipe was <u>fudge</u>. They didn't know a great deal about sugar being harmful in those days and people ate a lot of it. I'm enclosing the recipe. My mother made fudge for my sister and me until we were about ages 10 and 14 respectively, then we made it ourselves. No, I don't make fudge anymore. Alas, I don't even <u>eat</u> it. I'm glad I enjoyed it so much as a little girl since the fudge days are finished. Mother also made cinnamon toast and hot chocolate—equally lethal—both favorite childhood recipes.

I grew up in Little Rock, Arkansas.

All my best wishes,

Ms. Meghan M. Smith
Wilson Place
Irvington, New Jersey 07111

HGB/rc

CHILDHOOD FUDGE

2 cups granulated sugar
1/2 cup milk
1 teaspoon vanilla extract
1 tablespoon Karo syrup
4 tablespoons cocoa

Mix all these ingredients, bring them to a boil in a saucepan. Cook them until a few drops in a cup of cold water form a soft ball. Take fudge off the stove. If you want to add nuts at this time, you can. Smooth out on a plate. Try to wait until the fudge gets cool before starting to eat.

This writer—heavyweight—had a chapter on me in her book. Glad to be included but felt her work needed a smidge of correcting!

May 5, 1997

Dear Sylvia,

Thanks so much for sending me a transcript of our interview . . . you did <u>good</u>! Reading your interpretation of my early life even helped me understand a few things . . . not bad since we did everything on the telephone and spent a total of perhaps 45 minutes together! Sylvia, I did a little editing. Most of it is just regular copy editing via Cosmo rules! You used the word "she" and then "her" too <u>often</u> . . . it gets boring when a word is repeated over and over in a sentence. You can see what I did because I'm sending along the original manuscript, the one with my pencil editing and, finally, a retyped version. Sylvia, I just rewrote one little section—the last paragraph on page 7. It wouldn't be fair to leave your reader with the idea that I have somehow been irresponsible and encouraged young women to depend too heavily on male attention and to be too preoccupied with their looks. Cosmopolitan was <u>dedicated</u> for 32 years to telling young women that their work-life was just as important as their love-life. We pushed looking as good as possible, being fit and not overweight, for your <u>own</u> sake, not necessarily because of "them." The <u>last</u> thing one ever was trying to do was make young women insecure about their looks or their appeal for men. See if you can live with the paragraph that I wrote because it would be accurate. I'm sure it will be a wonderful book and some day I'll have the pleasure of reading.

All my best wishes,

Sylvia B. Rimm, Ph.D., Director
Family Achievement Clinic
Westlake HealthCare Associates, Suite 500
Westlake, Ohio 44145

NINE

Dear Author, Article Writer, Opinion Purveyor

The purpose of a fan letter is to tell somebody you have enjoyed his or her work, isn't it? You aren't writing out of vanity . . . you want them to know they have brought pleasure into your life. For me reading in bed with a dish of diet Jell-O and a few dried peaches and prunes (or at a room-service table in a good hotel with reading matter propped up, class A breakfast ready to be consumed) is one of life's three top pleasure-givers. Reading <u>without</u> the culinary blandishments isn't bad either. As a writer, I know the pleasure of reading a fan letter (the other kind I don't get into!). I send a <u>lot</u> of fan letters to writers.

November 30, 1999

Lois dear,

I can't remember when I have loved a book so much and I have read a few. . . . MOMMY DRESSING had pure enchantment for me in so many ways. I loved a million sentences—"A little brown jug of custard that appeared from nowhere, like Sleeping Beauty, in a glass casket, awaiting only the kiss of my nickel to release it." "Her breasts released from her punishing D-cup cages, resembled a family of seals sunning themselves on a rock. Great buoyant things, with lives of their own. Dirigibles, sailing." On and on it goes. Perhaps the most astonishing quality of this book is that you have been so scrupulously fair with your mother. She seems unconscionably cruel but you choose only to understand <u>why</u> she was who she was and to forgive. Being slapped by your mother but, worse, being <u>locked</u> in a closet. . . . we don't <u>do</u> that to people who are children. "My nurse quickly shut me up in my closet where Eleanor Powell's tap board, my costumes, my silver shoes, lay in a heap like pets who had to be put down"—as though being locked in a closet were what mommies did or allowed to have happen, to 'bad' little girls." You are so retrospectively tolerant!

The book is a treasure trove of history. You even mention songs I remember well and sang—"Perfidia"—"Bésame Mucho"—"Bei Mir Bist du Schön" and "Mairzy Doats." Your accounts of kissing, necking, a little passing-out from drinking are also part of one's life and I so very much enjoyed the sections in which you explain how career women were not really accepted by their mates for a long time, also how dumb women were trained to be about <u>money</u>. Lois, thank you for so much pleasure. I'm glad you have been in <u>my</u> life both professionally and as a friend and one of those conditions will go right on!

Love and congratulations,

Ms. Lois Gould
Washington, Connecticut

June 16, 1999

Lizzie dear,

WHY GOSSIP IS GOOD FOR US in Brill's Content is just
wonderful! You can't write a bad word—"I think gossip is one of
the great luxuries of a democracy. It is the tawdry jewel in the
crown of free speech and free expression. You don't read gossip
columns in dictatorships. Gossip is for leisure, for fun, for
entertainment, for relaxation. Should the day come when we are
enduring big black headlines about War, Famine, Terrorism, Natural
Disaster—that kind of news will drive gossip underground and out
of sight. Then we won't have gossip to kick around any longer."
That's <u>brilliant</u>! In your Friday column I also liked "A lot of fat-cat
white male Democratic politicians". . . . and later in the column
"Sure, Tom and Nicole were impressed and thrilled by the
legendary Kubrick, but enough to throw away all caution and all
clothes?" The reason <u>your</u> gossip column does well, among other
reasons, is that you can <u>write</u>.

Your Serious Fan,

Ms. Liz Smith
East 38th Street—Apt. 26-A
New York, New York 10016

HGB:ss

June 5, 2000

Gail dear,

Your article on Al Gore on the Op-Ed page this morning is the most wonderful thing I've ever seen! "Why does he plait each sentence as if he were teaching macramé to kindergartners?" "Al Gore likes nothing better than immersing himself in a complex subject like arms control or global warming. You can just see his neurons branching."—Are you a writer or something?! Only the bestest. Gail, with so many people writing so much about the candidates, it seems to me this article is the only one that explains <u>anybody's</u> hesitancy to vote for Gore. I've been thinking and thinking "He's so wonderful, why isn't everybody backing him?" and you've made it quite clear. I hope, hope, he may indeed get to be "an authentic Al Gore" in time to get himself elected.

                                        With great admiration,
                                        As always,

Ms. Gail Sheehy
Central Park South
New York, New York 10019

HGB:ss

August 5, 2002

Margaret dear,

I have dreaded coming to the end of MARY CALLED MAGDALENE for two reasons. One, I knew we were going to have the Crucifixion and that is pretty intolerable stuff. Two, my pleasure at reading this book would be finished because a book some time has to <u>end</u>. Margaret, I find this achievement almost unbelievable (except that it's <u>you</u>!). I can't imagine where you would go to research such a book except the bible and those details are sketchy. What you did was use your incredible imagination and empathy for the heroine to create the most believable account of her life one could possibly hope for. The scenes between Mary and Jesus are so reasonable and right, one can't believe you weren't there taking notes! Mary, being a good little Christian (a baptised Presbyterian at age 9), I found the book especially fascinating because of never having had any real information about these people. Of course, there <u>wasn't</u> any but you have taken care of that. I stopped believing in God many years ago when my father was killed in an elevator accident and my sister contracted Polio (to spend the rest of her life long life in a wheelchair) but I find your book just as meaningful as if I were still a believer. You know how much I enjoyed THE AUTOBIOGRAPHY OF HENRY VIII, MARY QUEEN OF SCOTLAND AND THE ISLES, THE MEMOIRS OF CLEOPATRA, but MARY is their worthy teammate. I think the book jacket copy is almost worthy of the <u>book</u> . . . says everything much better than I have been able to say it in this letter. Margaret, you have given me hours (and hours) of pure pleasure. Thank you, from a very grateful heart.

All my best wishes,

Ms. Margaret George
Harvard Drive
Madison, Wisconsin 53705

HGB:ss

I have been writing Art Buchwald for forty-one years, ever since he wrote favorably, on its publication, about my book <u>Sex and the Single Girl</u> in his syndicated column. They have never made another one like Art.

June 8, 2000

Art dear,

Have I <u>ever</u> enjoyed anything quite as much as STELLA IN HEAVEN? I don't <u>think</u> so unless it was one of your other biographies. This is charming, fresh, fascinating and <u>you</u>. Susie hates me to write letters like this where I quote back things but I just have to mention how delicious some things were/are—"You are not permitted to tip here at all, which is how you know this is truly Heaven," "You can also play golf where the course is designed so that you never hit a bad shot." "When I give to individuals I can hear them say thank you. The American Red Cross or the Anti Defamation League never says thank you. They just say could I give more," "Twoey felt I was playing with fire. I don't know much about your religion, but I am sure a female rabbi can make you more miserable than a male one. Rabbis and priests traffic in sin and guilt." These and so many other creations knocked me out. Art, this book is going to be a total smash—different from anything you've ever done but reflective of your massive talent and sense of humor.

Love and congratulations,

Mr. Art Buchwald
C/O The Regency Hotel
Park Avenue
New York, New York 10021

HGB:ss

August 24, 2000

Arthur, Arthur!

When have I ever enjoyed a book so much as ORIGINAL STORY
BY ARTHUR LAURENTS?! Well, <u>you</u> can't answer that if <u>I</u>
can't . . . maybe it was GONE WITH THE WIND when I was
fifteen. Whatever, this book has charmed, enchanted, educated,
<u>riveted</u> me for several weeks. . . . I read just before going to sleep,
book in hand, a bowl of sugar free Jell-O (one serving from a whole
package so it will be gummy), blob of Dannon Lite on top in the
other, result: pleasure for a brief moment everyday. I preferred
stretching <u>out</u> the joy of your book to gobbling all at once. Joy
started with knowing many or most of the people you wrote about,
certainly knowing the plays and movies, getting acquainted with the
ones I <u>didn't</u> know and, how shall I say this, being utterly bewitched
by your special world. Surely no other book has ever explained or
delineated the feelings/lifestyle of a homosexual like this incredible
book. Aside from these enjoyments—the famous players, learning
the infamous and riveting details of putting together shows one has
loved, there was the <u>writing</u>. Are you going to think I am a total ass
to tell you how lovely <u>that</u> is? Never mind, that isn't going to <u>stop</u>
me! I only let myself mark five or six places that I wanted to
mention. . . . I could have marked every page—"I had thought I had
put it behind me but failure is vengeful and patient." "Better the
worst than nothing." "He was bewildered. He refused to accept my
self-banishment: we had to see each other. That was all the
encouragement I needed. I slowed down, calculated, huskied my
tone, played the strings: told him I couldn't pretend I could just be
his friend because I knew I wasn't capable, I cared too much. All of
it was not entirely true before I said it but as I said it, it all became
true." "Lana Turner telephoned John Garfield before they started
<u>The Postman Always Rings Twice</u>. Both were married, both were
famous, where could they go? They made out in the backseat of a
car in her garage. (Source: Garfield.)" "As writer-director I was
therefore guilty of every crime including the score; the critics
lynched me, crucified me, and just to make sure, burned me at the
stake." "Sadly, I simply didn't care about him one way or the other.

Monsters erode your feelings until you no longer care. He was a brilliant choreographer, he was better at staging a musical than anyone: the ballet would miss him, the theatre would miss him, I wouldn't." "From Tom's pool, you can see into the heart of the park. In summer, we swim laps every day. Often we walk through the park, then sit on that bench, looking at the view. Yesterday, we sat there a little longer than usual, just looking at the changing light, not saying anything. But Tom reads my mind. 'You're going to live twenty more years,' he assured me. 'Maybe even more.' As long as he lives, I will." Loved your experience on page 149 as a virgin trying to become deflowered—never anything on "the loss of" so funny or touching.

Arthur, this letter is apt to go on for two or three weeks if I don't use a little discipline! I long to tell you _my_ experience with a couple of your friends . . . having got Mike Nichols to leave the baby grand Steinway in the apartment when we bought it because I hoped to get Stephen Sondheim to come over and play. I'm so glad you write about him over-the-top enthusiastically because he is the best. I was a Sondheim groupie for years . . . went to every over-a-delicatessen or in-the-back-of-a-garage performance anybody put together with his music (lyrics). Hal Prince even told Ruth Mitchell she had to let me watch from the wings the night I saw FOLLIES the seventh time. . . . I couldn't get enough. Steve and I had a falling out when I wrote him a condolence letter after MERRILY WE ROLL ALONG and said he didn't have to worry about one little flop, the rest of his work made up for _everything!_ He wrote back the most vicious single-spaced letter anyone has ever seen to the effect that I was a total asshole not to realize how hard he had worked on MERRILY and one achievement never compensated for a subsequent tragedy, etc., etc. He was right, of course, but I never read such a letter . . . maybe he heaped all his disappointment, rage, and venom on his not-too-brilliant little fan.

Enough! I must stop before I start telling you about Jule Styne letting me sit on the piano bench beside him and sing "Guess I'll Hang My Tears Out To Dry," "The Party's Over" and anything else I chose without major wincing. He was indulgent and <u>gifted</u>, as you happen to mention!

Arthur, I promised to stop this letter two days ago . . . apologies! Barbara Walters gave ORIGINAL STORY BY ARTHUR LAURENTS to David (my husband) telling him he would love every word. He did and gave it to me. I've virtually gone into mourning because it's over!

Love, congratulations and
deep gratitude,

Mr. Arthur Laurents
St. Luke's Place
New York, New York 10013

November 22, 1991

Dear Katie,

I was thrilled with your Op Ed piece in the New York Times, DATE RAPE HYSTERIA. That has been my viewpoint throughout the past few years—that we mustn't give up the precious sexual freedom and equality so hard won for women. I think trying to scare every woman to death by telling her she is a prime risk for AIDS is another way of hoping to curtail female sexuality although God knows there is a risk if you are sharing a needle with somebody who has got AIDS or having anal sex with that person. Don't let me get off the point! Your article is simply wonderful—I have it at the board at Cosmo.

Hope you don't think I'm presumptuous (or boring!) if I send you <u>my</u> editorial page article in the Wall Street Journal. What a big ruckus <u>that</u> caused but I sort of felt I was saying what you are saying—that grown up girls have healthy sex drives—hallelujah!— and you don't want to let anybody try to obliterate this.

All my best wishes,

Ms. Katie Roiphe
℅ Mr. Mitchell Levitas
New York Times
Op Ed Section
W. 43rd Street
New York, New York 10036

HGB:ss

December 28, 1992

Dear Ellen,

Absolutely loved your Op-Ed article Saturday in the New York Times. I've been saying forever that young women shouldn't have sex until they were older—at least a 20th birthday—but my Cosmo audience is <u>not</u> teenagers and so it isn't a theme I've dwelt on as much as some other themes. Never mind what <u>I've</u> dwelt on, your article was full of incontrovertible evidence that sex when someone is hardly more than a child herself is seriously contra-indicated. It was a pleasure to hear this message from someone not trying to stamp <u>out</u> sexuality in the young—that couldn't/shouldn't be possible—but just to ask for a little postponement as people who postponed <u>know,</u> it is still wonderful when you get there. Maybe your very moving message—Sex is for Grownups—will lead even young people to start thinking that way and to be encouraged by responsible, caring but non-puritanical teachers and parents. It's a wonderful article.

All my best wishes,

Ms. Ellen Hopkins
Rolling Stone
Avenue of the Americas
New York, New York 10019

HGB/rc

September 12, 1994

Robert dear,

I never saw a lovelier inscription for anyone in a book than the one you did for me on the title page of THE KID STAYS IN THE PICTURE . . . I'm flabbergasted and thrilled. Robert, as I think you know, I have loved this book since its earliest, scruffy word-processed pages and Cosmo's book department made an offer. We were told the book was being re-written—which it surely was—and, after that happened, we really never had a chance to acquire though we kept asking. I think you put it in the right places because we couldn't give you a cover, as NEW YORK did, and PREMIERE is the magazine of your industry, but I would love to have had some of it for my own magazine—our loss! Robert, I know what a long, arduous task it was to get the book written—first by somebody who didn't speak in your voice and later by you . . . writing is both satisfying and arduous. Whatever you had to go through brought forth this wonderful story—every page reads like Häagen-Dazs (that's a compliment!)—what I mean is you can't put it down once you get started. I'm so proud of you and thrilled for you and your life, my darling friend, is now starting all over again. I'll be cheering very loudly when the book becomes a best-seller.

All my love and affection,

Mr. Robert Evans
Woodland Drive
Beverly Hills, California 90210

HGB/rc

October 8, 2001

Dear Dennis—May I call you that?

I must have enjoyed <u>something</u> as much as <u>THE LAST MOGUL</u> in the last few years but I can't remember <u>when</u>. I started <u>JOHN ADAMS</u> and read a few pages, put it aside to read <u>your</u> book and never returned. I can't <u>remember</u> a book so conscientiously researched and interestingly reported. Of course, looking at your BIBLIOGRAPHY, several years have to have been spent getting <u>through</u> all the material you researched <u>from</u>. . . . .awesome! Your dedication to telling the <u>entire</u> story is so prevalent throughout the book. . . . .we are talking <u>entire</u>! Your book had a special interest for me—why <u>not</u>?!—because I worked at MCA as a secretary two different times. First I was Larry Barnett's twenty-year-old assistant. . . . sometimes he used to find me in the typing pool with my head on my typewriter, sound asleep, because this <u>was</u> World War II and I might have been dancing at the USO the night before. After I left to be the script girl on Abbott and Costello (an MCA show) I came back to work for Mickey Rockford—sometimes Karl Kramer was in the picture. Being Herman Citron's girlfriend during this period didn't help. I used to scrunch down in the front seat of his car parked at the curb, waiting for him to come out at the end of the day but I don't think I scrunched quite well enough. . . . I <u>did</u> get fired! Agents were not supposed to fraternize with the "help." This is more than you want to know . . . forgive me! This letter is supposed to be about <u>you</u> but I've almost stopped sifting through the rose petals. Herman married somebody else, I didn't marry until fifteen years later but the man called me every Friday afternoon his entire life and later became David Brown's (my husband's) agent. Herman said if we had ever been married, we would have been divorced in fifteen minutes. Probably correct. David and I have been married for forty-two!

Now, back to <u>you</u>! I have to agree <u>totally</u> with Larry King, who says, "About as good a piece of journalism as you'll ever read." I guess I <u>don't</u> agree, with Tony Hillerman, who says, "It is a Tale of incredible evil." They (the MCA agents) somehow don't seem very

<u>evil</u>. . . . just a little beyond the boundaries of opportunism. MCA clients did so <u>well</u>. . . . how bad could it <u>be</u>?! Dennis—I'm being overly familiar again—the book is a masterpiece. Thank you for <u>so</u> much pleasure!

All my best wishes,

Mr. Dennis McDougal
c/o Perseus Books
East 53rd Street
New York, New York 10022

(attn: Ms Rachel Rokicki)

TEN

Dear Airline, Hotel, Restaurant... You're Wonderful!

Don't I have anything better to do than sit around writing letters to people who (a) don't expect them, (b) wouldn't know (or care) if they didn't receive them, and (c) do I or do I not carry on a lot about being too busy in life? . . . No, I <u>can't</u> have lunch with you . . . ever! Well, traveling as much as David and I do, when some special service or food arrives in your life, you want to tell the perpetrators. Maybe my writing these letters is like other people writing authors or actors, but I write them, <u>too</u>!

September 16, 1992

Dear Mr. Crandall,

You do want to know how it all came out, yes? You remember my 15-page letter asking for a little help with David's and my proposed trip to the Great Barrier Reef and Bali using our American Advantage Miles. We were having trouble getting a first-class seat released on the Qantas flight from Sydney to Los Angeles and not to have brought it off would have meant staying overnight in an airport motel. They <u>had</u> the seat, we just couldn't get it away from them . . . that must be where <u>you</u> came in. Joanna Stathopoulos in your Dallas office pleaded with Qantas so long and hard on our behalf they finally did release the seat and off we took for that insane 14-hour non-stop trip from Sydney to Los Angeles, thence to our beloved American Airlines to get back to New York. Have you <u>flown</u> a 747-400? That's like asking if Dwayne Andreas ever ate a Harvest Burger! Of course, the DC-10 wasn't bad either and you do something quite special and charming on all your coast flights I think . . . the warm cookies and milk just before landing . . . really terrific!

Well, before your eyes start glazing <u>again</u>—I'm sure that was the chronic condition with my first letter—just let me say thank you for <u>whatever</u> you did. It's not <u>easy</u> to get to Hayman Island, thence to Bali using American Advantage Miles no matter <u>how</u> many you have but it happened. Only Garuda didn't come through with comp tickets from Sydney to Bali and back again . . . said they didn't believe in that kind of thing. I'm going to fix them in my January column in Cosmo (where I'll talk about the joys of American) when I try to describe getting your leg rests up and your seat <u>back</u> at the same time on their airplane without breaking your arm! I finally worked out a system where you stand in the aisle, press all the levers to make it <u>happen</u>, then take a flying leap into the seat before it changes its mind and reverts to neutral again. Thanks, Mr. Crandall, for <u>whatever</u> you did . . . I seem to think it was <u>something</u> . . . now we've got to start saving miles again. I have in mind Eastern Europe or Angkor Wat.

Obviously that's going to take a little while and you don't have to dread getting another letter <u>soon</u>!

All my best wishes,

Mr. Robert Crandall
President
American Airlines, Inc.
D.F.W. Airport, Texas 75261

April 22, 1992

Dear Mr. Allen,

This is a pretentious letter, written more to please me than it could possibly mean anything to you, but I wanted to tell you how much we enjoyed our flight 97 from Lisbon this afternoon. David and I have been "around the world on a plane" (several planes) to quote a Cole Porter lyric and have always been semi-partial to European carriers because first-class is usually more luxe than anything local though Pan Am did very, very well many years ago. (I told you this was a pretentious letter!) Well, this afternoon we decided our Delta flight was just as wonderful as any travel we had ever experienced—maybe it's because first-class was a little light and they passed the Beluga <u>twice</u> (are they allowed to do that?). If I had been a flight attendant, I would have eaten it myself! Speaking of flight attendants, I wanted to tell you about one on your flight. I never ran into anybody like her before and that is the true truth. Her name is Gerda Jungbaaer (German), a Delta flight supervisor who lives in Connecticut. She was just pure heaven about twice as attentive as the dream girls on China Air—they got the Academy Award before Gerda. A male attendant on that flight loaned my husband his personal copy of SPY—also kind of a special thing to do.

It's 4 a.m. Portuguese time which may be why I'm sounding a little goofy! While I'm at it, I might as well tell you I've been on the Delta Shuttle (to Washington) twice in seven days and <u>it's</u> special too. Congratulations!

All my best wishes,

Mr. Ronald W. Allen
C.E.O.
Delta Airlines
Hartsfield Atlanta International Airport
Atlanta, Georgia 30320

HGB/rc

January 24, 2001

Dear Mr. MacKay,

Having spent my honeymoon in the Swan Suite of the Bel Air Hotel forty-one years ago, I never <u>stayed</u> at another Los Angeles hotel (and I do visit two or three times a year) but last week my husband was with a group of Miramax people who were promoting a new movie—CHOCOLAT (my husband is the producer) and headquarters was the Four Seasons. Wow! Maybe what I loved the most was your swimming pool that really <u>is</u> heated (toasty warm unlike some pools that <u>say</u> they are heated and are about 38 degrees). I also love that it is a <u>lap</u> pool—you can't drown and the length is perfect. While carrying on about this facility, I'll just mention the major massage I had in the spa with a young Greek masseur, Dimitri, and I never <u>had</u> a better experience—this from someone who knows that world fairly well. He was strong, worked like a beaver but also seemed to understand aches and pains and did everything with compassion and skill. There! Are you tired about my carrying on about your spa and about your staff? People in other areas were wonderful as well—waiters, telephone operators, housekeepers, concierge . . . everybody simply first-rate. It was a super experience and I wanted to tell you so.

All my best wishes,

Mr. William MacKay
Regional Vice President
General Manager
Four Seasons Hotel
South Doheny Drive
Los Angeles, California 90048

HGB:ss

May 28, 2002

Dear Mr. Orlando,

Somebody made a brilliant decision to have our Cosmo conference of editors from all over the world at the Tribeca Grand. I can't think of any hotel that could have been more wonderful for us. It's smack in the middle of downtown New York, of course, and the location is what everybody wanted but never mind location, everything <u>works</u> in your hotel! Our breakfast, lunches and coffee breaks were delicious, the auditorium perfect for our collected women (from 43 countries) and the staff always cordial. When housekeeping picked up some stuff from my room, brought from home, even though a hand written note told them not to <u>do</u> that (housekeeper couldn't read English), Jeffrey Felshaw went over to the Gourmet Garage, picked up the dried peaches, apricots and other stuff which had been confiscated and a couple of whole grain candy bars, in addition, to keep me happy. This hotel is a wonderful happening for New York and we'll have to have another conference and bring everybody back.

All my best wishes,

Mr. Brett Orlando
General Manager
Tribeca Grand Hotel
Avenue of the Americas
New York, New York

HGB:ss

July 2, 2001

Dear Steve,

I ran into Pete in the lobby at Claridges a couple of weeks ago
and am yapping at him about the wonderfulness of the hotel—
everything sparkling and fresh, cocktail-tea area like a
Gainsborough painting, chandeliers sparkling, greeted by name
and even shaken <u>hands</u> with by personnel who have known
you. . . . not just the concierge but clerks and elevator men. . . .
<u>very</u> sweet and Pete said, "Helen, stop right here! Everything
you see and like was instigated by Steve. . . . it's <u>his</u> baby. . . .
tell <u>him</u>!" Okay, whoever did it, the hotel has never been so
wonderful. . . . your carpet bill alone would take care of H.M.O.'s
for masses of Americans without any congressional interference.
I'm not quite sure <u>why</u> you bought all those hotels, Steve. . . . we
had a nifty stay at the Savoy in February when Harvey Weinstein
shipped everybody to London for the B.A.F.T.R.A. awards. . . . <u>it</u>
was shiny and nice, <u>too</u>. Whatever motivated you, maybe the need
to buy already good properties and improve them, is in your D.N.A.
I'm glad it's there! I can even find the hairdryer at Claridges now . . .
they used to hide it in the back of a dresser drawer, now it's on <u>top</u>.
I send blessings. We jumped on the QE 2 to come home, not nearly
so sumptuous!

Love,

Mr. Steve Schwarzman
The Blackstone Group
Park Avenue
New York, New York 10154

HGB:ss

March 24, 1994

Dear Mr. Levin,

My longstemmed pink (favorite color) roses are beautiful and bringing such pleasure. You were so nice to send them. I've been staying at the Holiday Inn in Shawnee, Oklahoma, since 1980. We decided to have a family reunion and gather people in from Arkansas, Missouri and Oklahoma, and the Inn seemed like the best place to stash them. We were wonderfully treated and I've been camping there twice a year ever since. It is a wonderful swimming pool—they let me sneak in at 1 or 2 in the morning—it is still heated and I splash very quietly. Thank you so much for the flowers.

All my best wishes,

Mr. Michael Levin
President
Holiday Inn Worldwide
Ravinia Drive, Suite 2000
Atlanta, Georgia 30346

HGB/rc

September 20, 1993

Dear Housekeeping Department,

Let me return these shorts which don't belong to my husband, David Brown. He was staying in room 198 at the Bel Air from Tuesday, September 14, through Saturday the 18th. If anybody happens to have turned in some nice Brooks Brothers shorts, you could send them to us.

All my best wishes,

Bel Air Hotel
Housekeeping Department
Stone Canyon Road
Los Angeles, California 90024

HGB/rc

May 2, 1994

Dear Mr. Klein,

You may think that I have carried on enough already about your opening the pool at the Hotel Kempinski for me the other evening when I checked in after closing time. I will just say again that it meant <u>everything</u> to me . . . I try so hard to stay slender and healthy and, after a giant celebration in Moscow launching our magazine for women, COSMOPOLITAN, I was in perilous shape. I didn't even realize the Kempinski <u>had</u> a pool until someone told me at dinner. What a pool! It is one of the most beautiful I have ever seen and I'm thrilled to have been able to splash around, thanks to your generosity, late Thursday evening. I hope I will be back at the Kempinski soon to swim during regular hours but, meantime, thank you for being so indulgent. We enjoyed our stay <u>tremendously</u> . . . I hardly got any sleep from looking out the window at St. Basil's which stays lighted until midnight . . . what a scene!

All my thanks
and best wishes,

Mr. Moritz Klein
Hotel Baltschug Kempinski Moskau
Ul. Balchug 1
113035 Moscow
Russian Federation

HGB/rc

January 4, 2001

Dear Mr. Volponi,

I am determined to write you this letter though it may or may not get all the way to St. Maarten. My husband and I spent the most incredible time at La Samanna . . . you already <u>know</u> about your glorious resort . . . surely the most beautiful setting in the Caribbean. In case no one has told you in the last ten minutes, I will just remark on the <u>food</u> . . . one doesn't <u>need</u> to go to Paris. We only went into town one night for dinner because everything was too good "at home." Your staff is incredibly cordial—and efficient—and I can only say <u>good</u> except these three things which I insist on telling you about!

1. I would have a clock in one of the rooms. Yes, one is supposed to <u>forget</u> about time at La Samanna but you do get kind of curious about what time are you going to bed, are you late for dinner, should you leave for the airport, etc. etc. I just found it a <u>little</u> inconvenient that I had to go hunt up a wristwatch to find out what time it was.

2. I bet I'm the only person in the world who ever commented about <u>this</u> but your swimming pool is, for my little body, <u>icy</u>! Probably it is just air-temperature but some of us like <u>heated</u> and are a bit spoiled. To mention three really incredible pools that <u>are</u> heated, there is the Bel Air in Los Angeles, California, the Oriental in Bangkok, the Mandarin in Manila. Those places are warm, too, but the pools don't give you cardiac arrest when you jump in. I would go thaw out in a hot bath in bungalow N-12 everyday after my icy swim.

3. This is more serious: some people can sleep with the radio or television blasting in their ear or an eighteen-piece military band marching outside . . . I am not one of those and the crickets nearly drove me <u>mad</u>! They really do yap all night long. When I asked a concierge about them, he simply said "throw water on them!" How do you do <u>that</u>? There is no bucket in any of the rooms. I used the tiny ice bucket several

different times—first I threw out the ice cubes then filled up the bucket with water but there is tall shrubbery on two sides of that bungalow and you couldn't begin to get to all the crickets with the ice bucket. Maybe there should be some arrangements for somebody like me who can't sleep very well if there is interfering noise. Finally we packed me off to the living room and I slept on the couch (because the crickets were not quite so yappity outside <u>that</u> window). Not exactly what we had in mind for a wedding anniversary celebration . . . him in the bedroom, me the living room—(we did that for five straight nights) but still blessed La Samanna for its beauty.

Never mind! The hotel is glorious and you have the best-flushing toilets of any hotel in the entire world. Truth!

All my best wishes,

Mr. John Volponi
La Samanna
St. Maarten

January 2, 1995

Elaine dear,

"We didn't get a Christmas present from Elaine," I said to my spouse.

"Why should we?" he said, "we're not <u>in</u> Elaine's often enough to be one of her best customers although we'd <u>like</u> to be."

"Well, she has sent us presents before," I kept going.

"She still loves you," said my husband, "and don't <u>worry</u> about it!"

Well, the Scottish Smoked Salmon and caviar came in last week . . . quel happiness! Elaine, I would have known you loved us anyway but it was wonderful to receive the sumptuous present. I hope we'll see you often during the New Year.

Much love from
us both,

Ms. Elaine Kaufman
Elaine's
Second Avenue
New York, New York 10021

HGB/rc

August 5, 1999

Dear Lee and Joan,

Are you ready for a fan letter? My husband and I were both lecturing at Stanford (he graduated a few years ago) and decided to treat ourselves to a week-end in San Francisco <u>including</u> a visit to Sears' on Powell Street (as if you didn't know). I hadn't been to Sears' for over ten years but stood in line on the street (Sunday morning) like a good girl until we could get inside. I haven't stood in line for anything anywhere <u>lately</u> that I can remember except getting luggage through the security check at the airport but, though I'm not frequently the waiting type, I knew this was a worthy wait. Voilà! there never were such pancakes nor ever will be again, I imagine. I try to describe those little Swedish pancakes to people who haven't had the pleasure—"chewy" is the word I come up with—not big and flour-y or overbearing. They're <u>almost</u> too good to be true. Our waitress was of the same caliber . . . you people are amazing! I just wanted you to know what a wonderful re-visit I had to your restaurant and it wouldn't surprise me if I scooched back for another visit as fast as it might be worked out. We stay at Camden Place right in the neighborhood—what could be more sensible?! Thank you for all that pleasure.

All my best wishes,

Lee and Joan Boyajian
Sears' Fine Food
Powell Street
San Francisco, California 99410

HGB:ss

February 4, 1999

Sirio dear,

What a fabulous, exquisite dinner! David and I were so happy to be two of your honored guests when you entertained the President . . . it's not bad to have a U.S. President clomping around in your upstairs dining room. Sirio, you are always generous and thoughtful but this went beyond all imagining . . . the dinner was extraordinary—lobster risotto is already my favorite but it's going to have to make room on the list for bass Wellington. I know the night was special for <u>you</u>, though you and the staff were slugging your brains out, but it was surely special for David and me. Deepest, bestest thanks,

Mr. Sirio Maccioni
Le Cirque
Madison Avenue
New York, New York 10022

HGB:ss

May 3, 2002

Dear Alfonso,

You either love me very much or are trying to <u>destroy</u> me! I ate every one of the glorious, freshly-baked Tratoria del Arte chocolate chip cookies <u>before</u> tea time . . . who cannot plunge right in?! You were so dear to send these to me . . . I am touched and smiling like a Cheshire kitty.

Thanks so much . . .
see you soon.

Mr. Alfonso Cacace
Manager
Tratoria del Arte
7th Avenue
New York, New York 10019

HGB:ss

June 23, 2000

Warner dear,

Your staff made such a fuss over me at Tavern on the Green I
thought I must be Queen Noor or somebody! I was met at the door,
taken to the most wonderful window table in the Crystal Room and a
Captain appeared, waiting right <u>at</u> the table while we not only
ordered our drink but the entire luncheon . . . <u>my</u> kind of service!
The Captain was Michelle Villasensor . . . I asked for her name
because things were outstanding . . . the <u>food</u> wasn't bad either!
Portions so big that we had half of my salmon and half of my
guest's salmon put in tin foil so she could use them for lunch and
dinner all week-end. Caesar salad was in the top five I have ever
tasted and the chocolate mousse, don't ask! I have decided to stop
carrying on about the Tavern and tell you that I got almost the same
treatment at the Tea Room this week . . . lovely booth, terrific food—
another nifty Caesar and somebody named Karen was as attentive as
it gets. Okay, do you know what you are doing or <u>not</u>?! You certainly
do in terms of making non-extraordinary people feel <u>extraordinary</u>!
Thanks, pussycat.

All my best wishes,

Mr. Warner LeRoy
Tavern on the Green/Russian Tea Room
LeRoy Adventures, Inc.
Broadway
New York, New York 10023

HGB:ss

December 7, 1994

Dear Brasserie,

If I had any class I would have <u>laundered</u> this napkin that I took away last night from the Danny Frank radio broadcast . . . you graciously brought smoked salmon with endives and I took it away—delicious! You don't really want this napkin back but stealing I usually reserve for something more major than salmon. Thanks for such a happy snack . . . I should have taken <u>more</u>.

Best,

The Brasserie
E. 53rd Street
New York, New York 10022

HGB/rc

ELEVEN

Cosmopolitan

(How It Works)

How many letters can you be interested in that have to do with the running of a magazine? Obviously with <u>me</u> in charge, there were a lot of letters! Not to exhaust your patience, here's just a sampling.

May 27, 1994

Dear Ms. Martinson,

My boss, Frank Bennack, has turned your letter over to me. Having women with a rather ample bosom on the cover of Cosmo is just a hallmark that was established many years ago which I don't think we ought to change. I am small chested myself but that doesn't keep me or, I think, readers of the magazine from enjoying looking at women who are more ample. My experience from dealing with thousands of young women (actually millions) through the magazine and through my own experience is that <u>all</u> teenage women are insecure about something and showing small bosomed women on the cover of a magazine isn't going to remove them from their insecurity—they aren't as pretty as somebody else, as smart, as popular with boys; they don't have the right parents or the right background—it is always <u>something</u>. Cosmo—do you read the magazine?—is about overcoming your "insecurity" by being the best person that you can possibly be—working hard, using all your potential and looking as good as you <u>can</u>. I have no guilt about that philosophy. I do appreciate your writing.

All my best wishes,

Ms. M. Martinson
Kipling Collegiate Institute
The Westway
Etobicoke, Ontario M9R 1H4

HGB:ss

Helen Gurley Brown, Editor · 224 West 57th Street, New York, New York, 10019, (212) 265-7300

August 14, 1972

Dear Eric,

As I mentioned in our telephone conversation, our feeling is
that COSMOPOLITAN is such a self-help magazine in <u>many</u> areas
that it isn't quite true to us to bear down so heavily on sex
in your cover lines. I would hope that you could change at
least fifty per cent of them. The two I object to most are
10 WAYS TO DECORATE YOUR UTERINE WALL and TURN YOUR PERIOD
INTO A DASH. I'm enclosing the September issue of COSMO so
you can see how few of our <u>own</u> cover lines are sexy.

Regarding the cover illustration, as you know, I think it's
just generally not very pretty and won't sell as many magazines
for you as something more attractive would. She looks gloomy,
which is always a put-off and I don't think <u>anybody</u> is going to
be attracted to that bosom! You have told me how expensive it
is to try another cover but I would hope very much that you might
be able to do so. May I hear from you soon?

Mr. S. Eric Rayman
The Harvard Lampoon
Bow Street
Cambridge, Mass. 02138

HGB/s tw

cc: Richard E. Deems

October 2, 1990

Dear Philip,

Thanks so much for your letter and I appreciate your concern about our telling the <u>truth</u> in our beauty editorials. Philip, as a magazine editor, I am always looking for something fresh and frisky that the reader hasn't read five hundred times before, and using a tiny dab of Vaseline to shine the surface of hair is at least <u>new</u>. There are a very few eternal true-truths in the beauty world and if a magazine just kept repeating them over and over again, year after year, it would be terribly boring and all our readers would yawn over the beauty pages (and stop buying the magazine maybe). Beauty is not like fashion or decorating where you have merchandise of interest to the reader to show . . . it has to have tips and ideas and how-to instructions. Also, alas, you can't give readers too much real scientific information involving molecular chemistry etc. because that bores them, too.

The idea of switching shampoos has been in just about every magazine for the last few years and no doubt our beauty editor thinks it is <u>true</u>—makes hair stimulated and even healthy.

Philip, let me look for a way to bring up the subject of switching shampoos again in Cosmo and, at that time, we can say it's a myth that "rotating" shampoos helps your hair. I'll talk to Andrea Lynn, our new beauty editor, about it and perhaps we can incorporate a quote from you in some way. I won't forget. You're always good to <u>care</u>—about Cosmo readers and all <u>other</u> females who want their hair beautiful.

All my best wishes,

Mr. Philip Kingsley
Philip Kingsley Trichological Centre
East 53rd Street
New York, New York 10022

HGB/rc

November 15, 1994

Dear Demille,

Thanks for your most recent letter. We don't have a black model scheduled for the cover but we are doing a major profile on Naomi Campbell if she will see us. I'm also enclosing an article we did on achievements by black women not too long ago. I'm also going to increase our use of black and other non-Caucasian people as fashion models. You are good to keep after me and I appreciate your writing!

All my best wishes,

Ms. Demille J. James
SW 173rd Street
Miami, Florida 33157

HGB/rc

August 23, 1990

Dear Mary Jo,

In response to your letter of August 13th, 1990, I went back over the notes on your "Tall is Terrific" piece, and while it's true that you added the quotes we requested, the problem is, we feel they were not stylish, fresh or funny enough for our needs. In other words, the fact that you <u>added</u> them is not enough; every revise has to work for the editors (including myself) who review each piece, and this one just didn't. Nor did everyone agree, as you say, that the article was basically fine. I notice that in Diane's letter of March 2, 1989, she mentioned that, overall, the piece skimmed the subject matter; that we needed more amusing, touching anecdotes; that the tone was too breezy. All <u>Cosmo</u> editors support their writers, and perhaps Diane was being overly gentle, but I'd think those comments (and there were others) would indicate that a fair amount of effort was needed.

Certainly, I'm sorry that you will never again write for <u>Cosmo</u>. And I can appreciate that you're upset.

But we simply do not pay full fee for pieces that don't work out. Many <u>don't</u>, alas, and this is our standard procedure with anyone who writes for us.

All my best wishes,

Ms. Mary Jo Kaplan
West End Avenue
Apt. 5E
New York, New York 10024

HGB:ss

I didn't do a lot of article assigning. That was done by the managing editor, Guy Flatley; executive editor, Roberta Ashley; and several senior editors. <u>Occasionally</u>, though, I got into the act.

September 27, 1990

Dear Linda,

As we agreed on the phone yesterday, you are going to write a <u>sort</u> of article for Cosmo about two famous women in history and what it was like to them to be in love with the men they were in love with:

CLEOPATRA

JOSEPHINE de BONAPARTE

Each would be written first person giving some of the machinations she had to go through and her feelings about the whole thing— perhaps her fears and anxieties and when it was pure ecstacy and what the "problems" were—just when she thought everything was fantastic, it wasn't—we would throw in a little history.

Linda, I am kind of repeating your own idea but doing it first-person I think would be delicious.

The price is $4,000—approximately 3500 words—definitely not any longer.

Let me repeat that we should throw in a <u>little</u> grounding as Cleopatra explains who she is or who her lineage is and maybe she would just say how could somebody who is the seventh daughter of the sixth king who ruled over the world be having such problems with this man and Josephine will say that she's not really a hooker. Maybe she slept with a few men—things like that—and I thought the gist would be she had Bonaparte exactly where she wanted him and then she kind of threw him away out of carelessness and now she wishes to heaven she could get him back again blah, blah, blah.

Our write-off fee is 15%—one can't see it being invoked with you because we'll adore the article.

These are the groundrules vis-à-vis our foreign rights: First North American periodical rights—with 60 day option to buy all magazine and periodical rights throughout the world for 20% additional fee.

I'm not putting a deadline but do you think we might expect this by December 1 or sooner?

Bobbie will be working with you and she, too, will be so happy that we've got together.

All my best wishes,

Ms. Linda Wolfe
West End Avenue
New York, New York 10024

HGB/rc

August 5, 1992

Dear Norman,

Would you like to write an article for Cosmo on powerful men and their sex drive?

It's always been my belief that men who are driven in business and government are also driven in bed. There may be a few neutrals but one can't think of too many. Maybe Harry Truman is the only one. Even powerful homosexuals probably also are sexually active. Don't know how <u>you</u> feel about this but I can't believe you don't feel the same way! It would be a personal opinion article from you backed up with a few names or incidents. We can't actually invoke Henry Kravis or Ron Perelman, both of whom are heavy players both sexually and professionally I <u>think</u>. We can drop a few presidents or presidential candidates of <u>course</u>. Bill Clinton is highly sexed; even George Bush did <u>something</u>.

Norman, first we have to see if the subject would interest you at <u>all</u>—there is no particular deadline—then we would talk about your fee and how long the article should be. My chances are probably not <u>great</u> but I'm starting at the top . . .

Will you have somebody call me?

                    Best,

Mr. Norman Mailer
Columbia Heights
Brooklyn, New York 11201

HGB/rc

February 12, 1992

Dear Ruth,

You were so wonderful to call me two or three months ago suggesting we might possibly get together on an article. Ruth, we do have one major and one front of book article with a sexual theme every month, are <u>fairly</u> booked up with material but can always think about something extra. I guess what I would need from you is some idea that is hitting you . . . something that you have noticed in your practice or a truth we have all forgotten—some way we should be improving and enjoying our sexual selves. This is putting the burden on <u>you</u>. I assume you have someone who writes with you but, since we have lots of writers who could take one of <u>our</u> ideas and go with it, what I probably need from you is something we haven't <u>thought</u> of that would come from <u>you</u>. Ruth, this isn't a <u>gouge</u> letter but just to tell you I was thrilled to hear from you and if something occurs you think would be right for us, I would love to know about it. The Winter Olympics remind me of our nice visit four years ago at Calgary—too bad so much time goes by and it takes an Olympics to get people together. I <u>do</u> consider us friends regardless how seldom it's face to face.

Best,

Dr. Ruth Westheimer
East 73rd Street
New York, New York 10021

HGB/rc

You remember the <u>Cosmo</u> male nude centerfolds? Not a
bad idea. I thought it up one day while washing
dishes . . . they like to look at <u>us</u> naked, why not us
<u>them</u>? Through the years we had about ten. Nothing ever
caused quite the sensation of Burt Reynolds, bless his
heart. He thought we kept him from being recognized as
an actor. We think we got him the <u>parts</u>! One of our guys
later became the governor of California.

April 17, 1992

Dear Charlotte,

It was thrilling to talk to you yesterday.

Here is a list of the actors who will be on the opposite side of the
poster of Arnold Schwarzenegger: although all are famous, we
picked them, for the most part, because the pictures that we can get
of them are quite gorgeous. That is what we need for this poster.

> <u>Choices</u>
> Dolph Lundgren
> Patrick Swayze
> Brad Pitt
> Kevin Costner
> John F. Kennedy, Jr.
> Jeff Fahey
> Mario Van Peebles
> Marky Mark
>
> <u>Back-Ups</u>
> Michael Douglas
> Jason Priestly
> Rob Lowe

Charlotte, we'll chat about what photograph Arnold will be
comfortable with, whether it is Annie Leibovitz or Herb Ritts or we
can't get them and it is somebody else. I know exactly what he is

thinking about and respect that—he doesn't want to be known ever as just a beautiful body. For our purposes, however, we do need to show that he is masculine and beautiful.

We have Annie Liebovitz book with the terrific picture of Arnold on horseback, it's sensational and I can imagine how much he likes <u>it</u> but that isn't the kind of thing we need, of course. We would need something emphasizing more his body.

Charlotte, I am sure we will work this out. My needs are to be hunky and your needs are to be establishment and "respectable" and I know we will meet someplace in the middle, probably more on your side than mine. Don't you think the arrangement should be that Arnold has total approval of the photograph. If the shooting is a <u>disaster</u>, then Cosmo wouldn't be required to go ahead and run the photograph nor pay the money to Arnold's charity that we agreed on.

We would be stuck with the photography fee, of course. Just thinking about the doomsday script—don't expect any of this to happen.

I'll look forward to hearing from you.

All my best wishes,

Mrs. Charlotte Parker
Parker Public Relations
Olympic Boulevard
Suite 400
Los Angeles, California 90064

HGB:ss

April 1, 1993

Dear Clint,

I don't know <u>anyone</u> who isn't happy that you won those two magnificent Academy Awards, even my husband, who had a picture in the running (A Few Good Men). If <u>somebody</u> had to win besides our crowd, it should have been you. Clint, Cosmo is writing a profile about you with a very responsible writer and researcher who I am sure won't do anything dumb. His name is Michael Segell. It would be <u>enormously</u> wonderful—to put it mildly—if you would just talk to him for just a few minutes on the phone when he calls. I would have preferred an interview <u>with</u> you but I know you don't do very many of these and this is what I am doing instead. He will be calling Marco Barla and I hope you will tell Mr. Barla that you will spend just those few minutes on the phone with our writer.

I haven't been sitting next to you at dinner recently, thus getting dessert lifted right off my plate, and I have subsequently gained four pounds. It's all your fault!

Love and cheers
and congratulations,

Mr. Clint Eastwood
Malpaso Productions
Warner Boulevard
Burbank, California 91522

HGB/rc

Sometimes we had to explain ourselves! This ex-stewardess didn't like our article on flight attendants. <u>Cosmo</u>'s publisher's wife had been a flight attendant, for heaven's sake, and the group were some of our most dedicated readers. I had to explain the article had been <u>written</u> by a flight attendant and she didn't speak for everyone.

June 25, 1992

Dear Tania,

Thank you for your very thoughtful letter. We picked the article, Memories of a Very Frequent Flier, up from Newsday, the Long Island newspaper, and, since it was fairly well written and amusing, we bought. Flight attendants on <u>many</u> airlines are what I would consider Cosmo's best friends—they are our readers—and I certainly wouldn't want to do anything to offend them. Apparently the things that the article writer wrote about really happened to <u>her</u> so we can't gainsay the truth of <u>her</u> life. Regarding Pan Am, I don't regret their demise as much as you do perhaps but I am a serious griever. My husband and I owned a ton of Pan Am stock and held on for years after things were looking bleak because we had such a fondness for the company—first trip around the world, all kinds of trips to specific destinations; in 1979 William Sewell took us, along with other friends, on the re-inauguration of the China Clipper flight to Beijing. I still get seriously irritated seeing somebody else's name (is it Delta?) on the wonderful Pan Am building at JFK. Thank you so much for writing.

All my best wishes,

Ms. Tania Anderson
Rio Drive #715
Falls Church, Virginia 22041

February 1, 1995

Dear Kate,

You made such a fuss when McCall's published a chapter from my
book, THE LATE SHOW. Everyone made me feel like a princess
and you took a wonderful photograph of me and even got in
wonderful Chinese food for me to eat. So now Cosmo has bought a
chapter from WHY GOOD GIRLS DON'T GET AHEAD and you
haven't heard a word from me! Kate, we are thrilled with the book.
Obviously we go through lots and lots of material, as you do, and
<u>everything</u> isn't a sure bet with us whatsoever. I love the particular
part we took about a gutsy girl trusting her <u>instinct</u> . . . that is
something that works for our sex. I think, Kate, you do <u>everything</u>
well . . . write, edit, intuit and you are also a wonderful friend. I'm so
glad we have you in Cosmo.

Love,

Ms. Kate White
Redbook
West 57th Street
New York, New York 10019

HGB/rc

November 11, 1991

Dear Pat,

There isn't anything I can do about Cosmo's reviewer. I took out a <u>few</u> things I didn't like but, finally, had to let the reviewer <u>review</u>. Nolte is on page 150, not that that means anything. On top of everything else, Barbra is going to wonder what is Annette Bening doing on the cover of Cosmo when we don't <u>do</u> movie stars. Well, about once every three years we <u>do</u> and Bening being pregnant by Beatty made this interesting to me. Pat, since Guy Flatley's review of TIDES is not everything I would like it to be, maybe we could do without Barbra even <u>seeing</u> the magazine. In my column in January STEP INTO MY PARLOR, I <u>am</u> recommending Cosmo readers go see THE PRINCE OF TIDES. I don't remember <u>ever</u> having recommended a movie in that space but I thought it was justified!

Love and cheers,

Ms. Pat Newcomb
Century Hill
Los Angeles, California 90067

HGB/rc

Cosmo had a cover format . . . gorgeous girl, friendly, **never** haughty; but in exquisite taste. Our beloved photographer Francesco Scavullo chose the model, knew any exciting new people on the scene. Looking at transparencies on the light box after the shoot, I could reject, rarely did. This letter suggests something daring . . . a **couple** on the cover??

February 1, 1993

Dear Francesco,

If I ever think of a couple I think is <u>good</u> enough for us, we will think about doing them on the cover—you have already said okay. There seems to be something "wrong" with everybody—Juliette Lewis is not quite pretty enough, Cindy and Richard Gere have been done too much and Demi Moore and Bruce Willis live on the west coast—I guess they could come in but I'm not sure I even <u>want</u> them! Anyway, I thought this cover shot from German Cosmo was the kind of thing we probably wanted—they're both <u>gorgeous</u> but don't know when we are going to get two really <u>famous</u> people who look like them. We'll just keep thinking about it, okay?

Love,

Mr. Francesco Scavullo
East 63rd Street
New York, New York 10021

HGB:rc

August 2, 1994

Susan dear,

Most everyone knows (because I have always said so) that my husband does all the Cosmo cover blurbs and has for a hundred years. Well, he reads article after article to determine what those blurbs should be—he long ago quit making up nifty blurbs that would sell magazines but the article didn't correspond. Well, to get to the point, this weekend he was doing blurbs for November and read your article, SEXUAL TRUST—THE GREATEST TURN-ON OF ALL. He said—quote—that is the best article you have ever run. Not bad from a reader who is really <u>fussy</u>. I don't know that I disagree with him. I wish you could <u>only</u> write for Cosmopolitan but I can't afford to have you do that. I'm thrilled you write for us as much as you do.

Love and cheers,

Ms. Susan Jacoby
E. 86th Street, #2-A
New York, New York 10028

HGB/rc

Through the years we had many prominent visitors to Cosmo, all invited by letter. This one captured Janet.

April 14, 1994

Dear Ms. Reno,

You were wonderful on Good Morning America this morning and you were on TODAY about 5 minutes later.

I always like to hear you talk because you are so <u>sensible</u>!

Cosmo has picked you as one of its 8 big time achievers in our special feminist issue (the page is marked). I have this super idea: when you are in New York someday, why don't you come and visit the Cosmo editors for half an hour or so. We ask very few people—only one or two a year—and the staff is very choosey. They would <u>adore</u> to be with you—we have talked about it frequently. Previous visitors have been Mario Cuomo, Ted Turner, Mike Wallace, Sam Donaldson, Steven Spielberg, Rupert Murdoch, Henry Kissinger, Elizabeth Dole, and a few others . . . a rather variegated group! We would ask questions and you would answer—our top editors and creative people, off the record. We would keep you exactly one hour and we are easy to find—just across the street from Carnegie Hall. Please keep this in mind and I will call your office at some point to see if I'm making any headway. Meanwhile, we're all sending our congratulations and very best wishes.

Ms. Janet Reno
United States Attorney General
Department of Justice
Washington, D.C. 20530

HGB/rc

May 16, 1994

Dear Candice,

When you are in New York sometime, can we persuade you to visit Cosmo some afternoon—our top editors and art directors—about twenty people.

We usually meet on Tuesday at 4 o'clock but any afternoon would be fine. For one hour—and we just ask questions—off the record.

Candice, we are so <u>choosey</u>. The staff only seems interested in meeting prominent people and we only ask about two visitors a year. The staff has asked me to produce <u>you</u>. We love you at Cosmo and have been friends and fans since you were a <u>photographer</u>! Have we a chance? I do hope you can say yes—just <u>any</u> time you are in town is fine.

You were wonderful at the Museum of Broadcasting tribute dinner—I don't think <u>anyone</u> could have done what you did—funny and charming and <u>smart</u>. I loved it when you were obviously <u>listening</u> to a speaker and had to be reminded to introduce the <u>next</u> one! You only did that twice. David and I go to most of these and you were simply the best.

Let me hear from you.

Best,

Ms. Candice Bergen
PMK
Broadway, 8th floor
New York, New York 10019

HGB/rc

February 15, 1991

Shelley dear,

What a thrill to have <u>two</u> letters from you. The thought of you seven miles from the Iraqi border on guard duty is absolutely spine-chilling. Hung on every word as you wrote about chasing the man who went to the latrine out of uniform. People can get very crazy! Shelley, do you know how important you are to us? You are our one personal link to the Gulf—what a responsibility for a beautiful, young 21-year-old blonde! I'm sharing your letters with Diane Baroni, Lisa Frantz and Irene Copeland. We cherish every one that you write to us. The news this morning is that Saddam Hussein made a tentative offer by radio to withdraw and everyone is hanging out by the television set. President Bush has just said that it probably was a fluke or a fake. We'll see.

Shelley, here is a picture of the staff that went into our Christmas issue. I guess this is the only one I have of <u>everybody</u>. Obviously we were not really in Hawaii but up on the roof.

Much love and let
us hear from you,

P.S. I sent your grandmother a copy of the Cosmo in which we wrote about you.

SPC S. Mitchell
CCO. 25th Sig. Bn.
APO New York 09739
Operation Desert Shield

HGB/rc

Advertising pays the bills, you knew that! Having spent fifteen years, before becoming an editor, in advertising vineyards, I always felt comfortable with advertisers. Sometimes we need to explain to a potential (and ultraconservative) advertiser just what <u>Cosmo is</u>! Car accounts were never pushovers.

May 29, 1992

Dear Mrs. Ewing,

Cosmo's publisher, Seth Hoyt, has asked me to drop you a note about the letter Mr. Ewing wrote earlier this month. I know Seth has spoken with both of you, has heard you express your feelings, and tells me you understand our point of view, too.

Cosmo is really my brain child, so I wanted to tell you how we feel about what we do. I know you don't have hours to read a long letter and I'll try to be brief. For 27 years, Cosmo has been a magazine for young women who love men and love children, are traditional in many ways, but don't want to live <u>through</u> other people, they want to achieve on their own. This has been such a successful format we haven't felt the need to change. Within that format we deal with many different subjects: careers, health, money, travel, general articles, celebrity profiles, fiction and, of course, food, fashion, beauty and decorating—the staples of many women's magazines. Our strongest material is, however, emotional. Not having children myself, I have usually left that subject to other magazines, concentrating instead on man/woman relationships.

Since most young Cosmo women are involved or hope to be involved in a love relationship, that seems also to be an important subject for us to deal with. We try to bring help and hope to our reader's life while dealing with the real world. Mrs. Ewing, I feel <u>everyone</u> has problems coping at times and that is really our specialty. I feel sex is a wonderful happening and that is <u>another</u> subject we deal with.

We aren't <u>pushing</u>, just discussing because these are healthy, young people and the subject interests them. I don't mean to be too self-serving or tedious with my explanation of what we try to do but just to say what our basic goals are that we have tried to meet throughout all the years. We feel we are a very responsible magazine, that we are trying to <u>enhance</u> the life of our young reader, help her deal with problems—this is the <u>real</u> world—and achieve the very best for herself and her loved ones. Mrs. Ewing, not <u>everyone</u> fits into the same mold—there are lots of different <u>kinds</u> of young women . . . some marry younger, some later, some are divorced, some remain single; people opt to have children early or late or not at all but we are just trying to help this young woman with her life. Having come from there to <u>here</u> myself—no college education, or money, average looks, average I.Q., no family influence (my family are "hillbillies" in the Ozark Mountains in Arkansas), I <u>know</u> one can come a long, long way if you make the <u>effort</u> and that is what we tell our reader. You can't "phone it in," you can't expect other people to bring you rewards and riches, but you can have them yourself with your very own effort. You get <u>exactly</u> out of life what you put in. Regarding Cosmo's photographs and illustrations, they are indeed sexy or at least sensuous. That has been our format for 27 years and since I devoutly believe the human body is wonderful to look at (both men's and women's) if it's in good shape, we continue to show legs and arms and surely bosoms. So does every other woman's magazine. Being small-breasted myself, I don't see why we shouldn't enjoy looking at people better endowed. Cosmo is an intimate magazine for young women—it is not edited for men. I feel we do what we do with great taste and that young women are not fragile creatures who must be protected from the real world.

I'm afraid I have been very subjective here and written longer than I promised but Cosmo is such an <u>honorable</u> magazine, our goals are so serious and important to us, it is hard for me to understand anyone thinking that Cosmo could possibly <u>harm</u> a young woman reader. As you may know, we now have 27 international editions of Cosmo— young women all over the world who want what we want <u>for</u> them . . . a better life through their own efforts while enjoying good relationships with the loved ones in their lives and that includes parents, friends, relatives, bosses, children, a husband or boyfriend.

I'll just mention that although I grew up in Arkansas, I have spent considerable time in Oklahoma the past 40 years! My invalid sister lives in Shawnee and I visit her twice a year—I feel my visits there keep me in touch with different worlds than Los Angeles, Chicago and New York (where I live).

Listen, this went on lots longer than I promised but I just wanted to tell you <u>my</u> thoughts. I surely respect your own feelings, which are perhaps, different than mine.

All my best wishes,

Mrs. Audrey Ewing
Toyota, Inc.
N. Main
Muskogee, Oklahoma 74401

HGB/rc

The boss on this particular account wasn't being allowed to say all the wonderful things that should be <u>said</u> about their product.

October 18, 1993

Dear Tina,

I loved having lunch with you and can't seem to get out of my mind that you are the brilliant management supervisor who isn't allowed to say all the things—to put it mildly—that could be said for your wonderful product, JOHNSON & JOHNSON K-Y Jelly. I understand about conservative clients because I used to have them when I was an advertising copywriter; I also run into <u>wild</u> conservatism when we happen to show a bare breast. I don't even do that anymore, even in the most innocent and elegant way, or we get taken off the newsstand in the Winn-Dixie supermarket chain. Tina, I can't help thinking (fantasizing?) how wonderful it would be to say some of the things that are really exciting and useful about your clients' product. Since old copywriters never get it out of their system, I've just jotted down a couple of thoughts it would be wonderful to get in your clients' advertising. I get very aggravated when I think how much K-Y Jelly really <u>does</u> mean to lovemaking, how many millions of people it helps, and they won't let you <u>say</u> so! Tina, if there ever <u>is</u> a "breakthrough," I want to work on the headlines and copy, okay?

Your busybody friend,

Ms. Tina McDermott
V.P. Management Supervisor
LINTAS
Dag Hammarskjöld Plaza
New York, New York 10017

HGB/rc

IDEAS FOR K-Y JELLY ADVERTISING COPY

For some (perfectly nice!) people, sex always seems to be accompanied by a little apprehension! Make the experience easy, comfortable, romantic with K-Y Jelly.

Sex is more beautiful, comfortable, memorable when it's easy for him to be inside you.

Let K-Y Jelly banish tension, enhance your lovemaking.

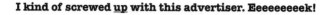 **I kind of screwed up with this advertiser. Eeeeeeeeek!**

June 9, 1993

Dear Mr. Tuchler,

Thank you for your letter regarding Cosmo's article, "We All Lie, Cheat, and Steal a Little . . . When Is a Little Too Much?" in our May issue. You are certainly correct in catching us in a discrepancy error—the copy ("Sweet'n Low") not matching the illustration (a model swiping Equal) . . . we should have used the generic term "sweetener" in the text.

As for our illustration, we were trying to convey a situation most of our readers could relate to—unfortunately, as staffers and friends have revealed to me, sophisticated girls <u>do</u> steal packets of sweeteners even from the most chic restaurants! We consider this quite minor on the "moral weakness" scale.

Certainly, though, I'm sorry if using Equal packets in the photo has caused you dismay—this was unintentional. I am personally addicted to Equal and use many packets a day. I hope you'll accept my apologies.

All my best wishes,

Mr. David B. Tuchler
Director, Equal Marketing
The NutraSweet Company
Lake Cook Road
Deerfield, Illinois 60015-5239

HGB:ss

My favorite suggestion to an advertiser of all time, and they never picked up on it. I'm still going to sell this one one day.

March 30, 1992

Dear Rob,

Rob, would you consider running this idea by your creative people some day . . . provided <u>you</u> think it has any merit.

It has nothing to do with Cosmo . . . just a campaign I would love to see Smirnoff do because it's different and fresh . . . and <u>might</u> sell vodka.

In print ads across a no-seam white background <u>spread</u> a man would be lying on his stomach—very bronzed—in swim trunks and a beautiful girl would be standing beside him—or possibly on her knees—giving him a rub-down with Smirnoff. The headline would be HIGH TIME FOR SMIRNOFF or JUST RIGHT FOR A SUMMER DAY . . . THE SMIRNOFF RUB-DOWN.

She might have the bottle in her hands.

Does this sound too awful? It really <u>isn't</u>! I used to do that with a friend when I was a single girl and it's really quite delightful. The vodka is cool. You stop and drink some if you want to. After all, the alcohol rub-down is a longtime reality and it might as well be with Smirnoff <u>vodka</u>.

Okay, if you decide it isn't for you, I'll go quietly! If you want me to sell it to your creative people, I'll be glad to! Repeat: it doesn't have to go into Cosmo. I just made my living so many years being a copywriter, it's hard to break people of the habit!

All my best wishes,

Mr. Rob McKinley
McCann-Erickson Worldwide
Third Avenue
New York, New York 10017

March 21, 2002

Terry dear,

Thank you for showing me the advertising campaign from Saatchi and Saatchi, one ad of which has already run. To put it mildly, I'm <u>horrified</u>! The ad that has run looks like a vagina surrounded by pubic hair . . . have we lost our <u>minds</u>?! The second, which I understand <u>hasn't</u> yet run and is cancelled, looks like a penis, albeit a pastel shade. The woman with the hair in her face is obviously having an orgasm. Let me stop . . . you didn't ask for a critique since, mercifully, the last three ads in the campaign have been cancelled. Saatchi did the first wonderful television campaign for Cosmo in the U.K. when we launched. Through the years I have had such respect for Saatchi and Saatchi and I'm sure they will think of something worthy of them and us <u>now</u>. I think everybody <u>knows</u> that Cosmopolitan is a magazine that appeals to the sensuous nature of its reader but she also has a few other interests in life than sex. Perhaps those don't need to be stressed in an advertising campaign and I don't know what theme you and the agency will eventually close in on but there is plenty of material to work with because the Cosmo girl <u>is</u> multifaceted. I deeply appreciate your showing me this campaign even if I'm still nauseated and going out for a breath of air.

Mr. Terry Mansfield
The National Magazine Company Limited
National Magazine House
Broadwick Street
London, W1V 2BP England

HGB:ss

This was our first Turkish editor, and she wasn't producing <u>Cosmo</u>, eventually had to go.

April 14, 1994

Dear Elif,

You and I don't know each other and I'm looking forward to our getting acquainted. We will do that when Cosmo has a conference of international editors this October. Elif, I'm not the one who decides what to put in your magazine—the editor is <u>the</u> sole judge—but I really feel we can't <u>do</u> what you are doing. Ecran Arikli I think would not have made an agreement with the Hearst Corporation, who own Cosmo, if they wanted the magazine to be something totally different from the Cosmopolitan that we publish—otherwise they would just have started a new magazine without bothering with us. What I am getting at is that the cover is totally unacceptable! If you want to do your own magazine, that is one thing, but if you want to edit Cosmo, then we simply don't use men on the cover let alone one with his pants open—there! May I go on? The naked girl with one hand on her crotch and one on her bosom is also pretty strong for us.

What is the girl with the whip on pages 84 and 85—it looks very sado-masochistic, a subject we might deal with but never in such a glamorous way. That would also go for the girl with the chains around her neck on page 87—if I've got my pages right. (It would be nice to see some page numbers a little <u>often</u>. The last one I saw was on page 80.) I think this is 93 but not sure. Anyway, the blonde girl is too "raunchy" for us—definitely not a Cosmo girl.

Our women are sexy and gorgeous but they don't look like girls from a burlesque show.

Next we get on to the men's section with the man looking like a vampire in striped pajamas. On the next spread we have a man with a snake crawling on his face and opposite him a man fondling his crotch.

Elif, really, this isn't the right direction to go in everybody's opinion who has anything to do with the magazine. Naturally, I haven't polled everybody in the entire world but I don't need to—Cosmo has a specific format and although each international editor has her own ideas about what goes in the book, I don't think they would be along the lines of your particular presentation. As I mentioned, you don't have any page numbers so I can't tell you where we are but opposite the Clinique photograph—pale blue jar on white page, we have a really disagreeable girl again—naked and sad. Then we get to the special men's supplement. Another man with his pants undone on the cover, then we get to the penis on page 7 and the raunchy girl holding her breasts on page 10.

Elif, I don't think we could go on like this. Do you wish to edit Cosmo or do we try to find another publisher in Turkey? I don't quite know what to do next. Perhaps you will tell me.

All my best wishes,

Ms. Elif Dagistanli
Turkey Cosmo
Bir Numara Yayincilik A.S.
Sabah Gazetesi Medya Plaza
Gunesli Ikitelli
Istanbul, Turkey

HGB/rc

July 28, 1998

Dear Hugo,

We are still basking in the glow of our wonderful launch of Cosmopolitan in Beijing when you were the host of the world to David and me. The wonderful portfolio of pictures that you put together for us we look at every week if not every <u>day</u> . . . that was a very memorable launch party and we have the photographs to prove it! Both of us love the pure silk Mandarin coats that you had made for us. . . . comes fall I'm wearing mine to some very spiffy New York social events over a black evening dress (more than you want to know?). We are so proud of our new magazine and expect it to be more and more successful as the years go by. I know it will with you as the leader. Please give my best wishes to Yan Luo . . . another dynamo!

Love to you both,

Mr. Hugo X. Shong
Managing Director IDG
Tower B.
COFCO Plaza
Jianguomennei Dajie
Beijing, P.R.C.

HGB:ss

This letter explains price structure for U.S. models used on the cover of an international edition, also payment for articles.

February 11, 1993

Dear Terry,

It was good to talk to you today. Regarding the models on the covers of U.S. Cosmo, we pay them a flat rate of $500 plus agency commission. We are then free to give the U.S. cover shot to any other edition which would like it without paying an additional fee. The model agencies in this country made a bit of a fuss a couple of years ago but we got them stopped with this rationale (a fairly accurate one): being on the cover of Cosmo is the greatest thing that can happen to a model aside from a billion dollar contract with a cosmetic company. The Cosmo covers have traditionally been acknowledged as the epitome of glamour and female gorgeousness and I don't think there has ever been a model we wanted whom we couldn't photograph. We had to go to the mat with Cindy Crawford and one other famous model but we really meant it—if they were going to start charging extra for use on the international editions, we would simply manage to find other models. In addition, we pointed out that the people who use these covers—Greece, Turkey, Holland—simply do not have big amounts of money to spend. They operate on a total shoestring and getting extra money for the model simply is not feasible. For all material inside the book, as I mentioned, we pay a 20% additional "bonus" if the material is used in one or any number of international editions. We can chat further.

Best,

Mr. Terry Mansfield
National Magazine Company

HGB/rc

I work for a wonderful company, the Hearst Corporation, and occasionally I want to tell one of the bosses something wonderful he or she has done. Of course, in the last letter in this chapter I've given them hell about one of their magazines!

August 26, 1996

Dear Frank,

The Frank Bennack magic was working all over the place at New York Hospital! I'm sure you got me the Stavros Niarchos suite and I hate to tell you this but it <u>does</u> make a difference. As you know, it's a wrap-around view of the East River downtown and it just makes you <u>feel</u> better when you look out the window. If you didn't personally intervene, and I think you did, at least the Hearst contributions must have weighed heavily because I was treated like Princess Fergie, Princess Di and the Queen Mother put <u>together</u>!

Your flowers were gorgeous . . . the biggest, most scrumptious bouquet of any but that's just the way you do things.

Frank, I'm fine! Everything went exceedingly well. We did what we had to do, I'm home, and every day you feel a little bit better. I appreciated your call just before I went in—the happiest I've been since then was getting home this afternoon (Saturday) to all my manuscripts. I'll see you or talk to you soon.

Deepest thanks
and love,

Mr. Frank A. Bennack, Jr.
The Hearst Corporation
Eighth Avenue
New York, New York 10019

HGB/rc

November 1, 1991

Luella dear,

Are you deranged?! Five pounds of the most wicked, wanton fudge I have ever seen or tasted. Actually brilliant is more like it because I <u>am</u> tipping the scales at 98 pounds with both my nightgown and wristwatch on and I can actually <u>eat</u> this wickedness (starting right this minute). I love my prezzie, enjoyed our chat so much . . . you were dear to call.

Much love . . .
all my thanks,

Mrs. Frank Bennack
Logan Road
New Canaan, Connecticut 06840

HGB/rc

May 6, 1997

Jack dear,

You and your company are always so generous with me about expense regarding my car or anything <u>else</u>. Is it you who looks over my phone bills? For the last eight weeks I have been calling Shawnee, Oklahoma, every single day because my beloved sister, not an easy life—she has been in a wheelchair for sixty years, having been felled by polio when she was a teenager—has been in the hospital trying to recover from pneumonia, which I don't think she is going to do. More than you want to know about Helen Brown's rationale about making so many phone calls at company expense but I wanted you to <u>know</u> what I have been up to. I've seen those phone bills from employees who have racked up hundreds of calls to one number and I even used to go and talk to some of them about the overboard situation. This won't go on forever! I'll stop if you get seriously irritated.

Best,

Mr. Jack Rohan
Controllers Office
West 55th Street
New York, New York 10019

HGB:ss

October 18, 1990

Dear Veronica and Randy,

I just wanted you to know what a contribution you made to November Cosmo. When we were coming back on your private plane from Lyford Key, the plane stopped someplace in Florida, I believe, and all our luggage was inspected by a nice doggie. I thought that was such an interesting proposition—that dogs were used to sniff out cocaine—that I came home and suggested we do a story. This one is "first person," or "first-<u>doggie</u>" and we think it came out remarkably well (page 152). I expect to get some more story ideas the next time we're together and I hope that will be soon.

Love,

Mr. and Mrs. Randolph A. Hearst
East 66th Street
New York, New York 10021

HGB:/rc

TO - Frank A. Bennack Jr.,Cathie Black   January 7, 1998

FROM - Helen Brown

SUBJECT - <u>HARPER'S BAZAAR</u>

Make it a magazine of fashion for the <u>consumer</u> - inspire and help

her with wardrobe at same time be respected by fashion industry ...

I'm certain we can do both! From secretary to princess, women <u>love</u>

clothes...this hasn't changed, just gets <u>more</u> so, although the

clothes we <u>fancy</u> change. Whereas GLAMOUR, MADEMOISELLE and, to a

certain extent, VOGUE, have diminished fashion pages to emphasize other

things, we would concentrate hard on clothes, like the fabulous French

L'OFFICIEL used to do. Cover beauty, of course...beauty and fashion

allied, a little decor - one spiffy home per month - news of designers

themselves (Armani, Valentino, Lauren, Donna Karen) - feature clothes

on celebrities at parties - but lots of gorgeous pages of fashion for

<u>my</u> life (affluent spender) - plus updating a wardrobe, caring for

(Duchess of Windsor had her own dry-cleaning plant), storing winter/summer,

travel clothes, giving to charity for tax write-off...a magazine - gorgeous,

gorgeous! - to undulge me in this important area of my life...after all, I do

C O S M O P O L I T A N
INTERNATIONAL EDITIONS

TO -

FROM -

SUBJECT -

put something on my body every day of my life and care about it!

THE HEARST CORPORATION

TWELVE

Dear Staff

As mentioned in the intro to this book, an editor who once worked at Cosmo told St. Martin's Press that my staff saved memos I wrote them. She was right. Some people did save every single one, like forever, possibly because I followed my own advice about putting only good things in writing—bad news I delivered in person. Here's a sample of the fan mail.

MEMO FROM

COSMOPOLITAN

959 EIGHTH AVENUE, NEW YORK, NEW YORK 10019 (212) 649-2222

August 7, 1990

Bobbie	Mallen	Diane	Irene	Susan K.
Nancy	Lisa S.	Sue B.	Gail	Betty
Pat	Sandy	Andrea	Suzanne	Ramona
Barrie	Leslie	Jill	Joanne	Mary Margaret
Larry	Elizabeth	Susie	Lisa F.	Susan S.

Dear Staff,

You have gone <u>beyond</u> anything I could have dreamed in your
analysis of the Cosmo Girl, what is going on in her life, what
might be expected in the future. The material is so <u>interesting</u>
I read it like a novel. And this year there seemed to be fewer
opposite viewpoints—you <u>all</u> pretty much think she is more
idealistic in job wants, men aren't doing housework, Cosmo
girls haven't given up sex—just more careful, etc. etc. The
point isn't that you often <u>agree</u>—the point is that this took a
lot of work on your part and is <u>totally invaluable to me</u>.
Advertisers gobble it up and it helps <u>me</u> know the Cosmo Girl
reader as nothing else could.

<u>All</u> my thanks,

HELEN GURLEY BROWN
EDITOR

Friday, Sept. 27

Dear Staff,

Except for Guy, Diane, Barbara Ann, Mallen, Sue Schreibman,
Linda Shahanian, Myra, Abelardo, Pat, Susan Kenny, ~~Conrad~~ Carol,
Susan Korones, Nancy Mattia, Sara, Virginia, Mark, Kelly
and ~~Don~~ Baskerville (some of whom came in and stayed
one hour, some of whom came after the sun came out, but
~~nevertheless~~ coming in is coming in)

you are ALL PANTYWAISTS!

Do you believe everything you hear on television?
Did it not occur to you the networks have had nothing
to promote recently except A.I.D.S.?

The buses ran. The subways ran. The taxis ran.
The Argonaut Building and the Hearst Corporation
were not officially closed (it was left up to
individuals).

Please deliver your editor from another week with
Yom Kippur and a fakey hurricane in the same week.
          (this is New York, not Long Island)

HB

** Known as The Yom Kippur Open

MEMO FROM
COSMOPOLITAN
224 WEST 57th STREET, NEW YORK, NEW YORK 10019 (212) 262-7916.

Dear Staff,

Tomorrow, Tuesday, May 24th, as a special favor, do you think you could be in or near your office—or in or near somebody else's—at about 12:15 noon.

Claeys Bahrenburg is going to take me to lunch and I'm going to ask him to walk around the office with me before that. I want him to see how crowded we really are!

Shall we bring in "fillers"? No, I don't think it's necessary! It won't be the first time I've pointed out that we need more space and, one of these days, I hope it will be the last.

Many thanks,

COSMOPOLITAN

—————————————————Helen Gurley Brown—

To all the girls at Cosmo:

This isn't a very big deal, but if anyone
is working late and doesn't have time to
go home before a date, please feel free to
use the shower (which looks like combat
equipment at Okinawa in World War II) in
my new john. Have to bring your own towel -
that's what I'm going to do.   Please don't
NOT take advantage of this (outstanding)
offer because I do mean it.

Second offer: Why don't we use the new
conference room (which you have to be a contor-
tionist to confer in if there are more than
ten of you) to have LUNCH in between, say,
noon and 2:30. Editors are going to be sending
writers in there to work during other hours.

Helen

THE HEARST CORPORATION

Larry Mitchell was the very helpful photography buyer for <u>Cosmo</u> at the time I needed to be a vamp.

HELEN GURLEY BROWN

December 19, 1988

Dear Larry,

The Theda Bara costume was a great success. . . . Kim got me a headband with clusters of grapes and I was a slinky, authentic <u>vamp</u> . . . thanks to your help. I was naughty to ask you to get out pictures—and keep several of them—because it ties up your time <u>and</u> costs Cosmo money. If I am going to bang down on everyone else to be careful about money, I shouldn't be the ring-leader with personal requests. You were wonderful and I won't do that again. Here's the last Theda batch of photos to return. (Do you believe somebody came as Salome in thousands of veils with the HEAD (gigantic!) of John the Baptist on a tray, which she borrowed from the New York City Ballet?! I mean I thought I was very hot stuff until <u>she</u> came in with everything but drum rolls!)

Larry, the wine is a passalong—given to me at Cosmo sales conference—but hope you can use.

Love,

COSMOPOLITAN

―――――――――Helen Gurley Brown―

February 20, 2001

Irene,

You're probably getting bored hearing from me but I just re-read TRAVELS IN HIS EROGENOUS ZONES for a Hard Copy interview—Drew is doing a wonderful job with our centerfold as was never done with any of the previous ones—and your copy is simply <u>wonderful</u>. Television is acting as though we went out to find the perfect male nude body and I have to explain that he is almost an <u>adjunct</u> to what the words are saying. I don't quite go so far as to say it could have been <u>any</u> male nude body but anybody sensible realizes that it is what we <u>say</u> on those two pages that will make a difference in somebody's life if she pays attention. I'm going to say that nobody reading that copy—sophisticated or unsophisticated, Cosmo reader or otherwise—could not get something from the instructions and you didn't even know how good you were being. There!

COSMOPOLITAN

—————————————Helen Gurley Brown—

Bonnie,

That is a wonderful blurb for CELLULITE—I love "Tricks for Trashing, Burning, Hiding Cottage Cheese."

Andrea,

You have taken my breath away with your contributions to
GOOD GIRL/BAD GIRL round-up. they are so darling . . . every
single one is usable and perfect. i love good girls pack their
toothbrush; bad girls pack their diaphragm, good girls own
only one credit card and rarely use it; bad girls own only one
bra and rarely use it. etc.etc.etc. I like <u>all</u> of them! everybody
contributed nice things but i'm only writing you, susan and
lisa notes . . . yours were outstanding.

COSMOPOLITAN

—————————————Helen Gurley Brown—

September 5, 1999

Felicia

you are always so GOOD about my requests for product.

Ron Perelman is coming to dinner wednesday night 9/28—
don't know whether I can get Revlon reeled back in or not!

do you suppose you could LOAN me 2 or 3 revlon fragrances—
cologne, spritz, toilet water or whatever. i would put them in
the guest bathroom so he can see we use revlon products! only
fragrance i think—wouldnt have occasion to have anything
else out on a shelf.

i <u>will</u> return them for your "files"—many many thanks

COSMOPOLITAN

Helen Gurley Brown, Editor • 224 West 57th Street, New York, New York, 10019, (212) 649-3555

September 5, 1982

Dear Ellen,

Peter Levine must be the family <u>comic</u>! Mommy, indeed, did <u>not</u> start at Cosmo as a messenger—she started at the top and then went <u>over</u> it! Ellen, when I planned to go over to your table at that super Italian restaurant in the Village, I waited too late and you were gone. Ed Ney, who I have a crush on and who is head of Young & Rubicam, was taking us to dinner and I hung on his every word just a touch too <u>long</u>. David will love hearing that he looked "handsome and well rested." I miss you badly, that never stops, but, would you believe, I really do <u>glory</u> in your success (not to be said of any other editor at any other magazine!!). See you soon?

Love,

Ms. Ellen Levine
Woman's Day
Broadway
New York, New York 10036

HGB/ilm

Donna Lagani was and is <u>Cosmo</u>'s dynamo publisher . . . nobody brings in business like this one. Donna let me hold Baby Joey in my arms when he was only three weeks old, and I had never held a baby before. Very trusting!

MEMO FROM

COSMOPOLITAN

959 EIGHTH AVENUE, NEW YORK, NEW YORK 10019 (212) 649-2222

June 25, 1987

pussycat dear,

a tiny token from thailand. we'd never have GOT to amanpuri if you hadn't kept pushing . . . what a PLACE!!! We weren't traded up to a villa—must be something in your smile (we KNOW you are used to turning strong men weak, especially if they have ad budgets, but the hotel director apparently couldn't help himself <u>either</u>). The tree-house we HAD was delicious and what a heavenly little Thai respite . . . we'll compare notes.

Did Joey like the baby shower? How could he not since he was the baby it <u>happened</u> for. EVERYBODY is happy about <u>Joey</u>!

Love,

Abelardo Menendez was a class art director, discovered by our head art director, Linda Cox. Alas, Abelardo was HIV positive, had AIDS, and didn't live very long after this letter was written.

May 21, 1991

Abelardo dear,

I miss you—dreadfully—and that doesn't even begin to describe it! I think about you not only every day but many different times during each day.

You are part of my life and always will be. I wouldn't be who I am or where I am—whatever and wherever <u>that</u> is—without you! I know you have battled and are battling very hard your particular illness and I still have faith that it can be bested. I'm sending some special newly minted four-leaf clovers from my sister's house in Oklahoma, said to be very potent!

> All my love forever
> and ever—call me
> up if you feel like it,

Mr. Abelardo Menendez
Perry Street #1-A
New York, New York 10014

HGB/rc

COSMOPOLITAN

October 14, 1991

Dear Susie,

It is an honorable thing to offer to give blood for a friend. What
you did—after your blood turned out to be somebody <u>else's</u>
type!—was even serious-er. You got the bank filled up for me
with <u>other</u> people's blood . . . which is just as nice—or nicer—
than other people's <u>money</u>! I'd be dead before I even <u>got</u> to the
hospital without you.

Love,

COSMOPOLITAN

Helen Gurley Brown

Ramona

Thanks for typing
these long-
WINDED

letters!

I do
appreciate

THE HEARST CORPORATION

COSMOPOLITAN

Helen Gurley Brown

Roses are red
Violets are blue

Ramona is
a genius

But what _else_
is new??!!!

THE HEARST CORPORATION

Dear Susie —

If you
are _this_
← color

We will all Be _this_
Color

With envy

But if you are
this color

You have over done
it !!

Welcome
home

COSMOPOLITAN

—————————————Helen Gurley Brown—

Ramona, Susie

if anyone ever interviews you for a book about me, I want you to

1. negotiate for an <u>insanely</u> high price. tell them you don't blabber for peanuts!

2. explain that tho we recycle (a president's wife doesn't <u>begin</u> to get the free samples of a magazine editor), we always trade <u>up</u>. The recycled present is better than what we would have given had we gone out and <u>bought</u>.

<u>got</u> that?

good!

THIRTEEN

I'm Pissed!

An almost sacred letter-writing rule for me is that you don't criticize or complain in writing . . . do it in person or on the phone. Written words hurt people . . . how many stabs of pain do you want to deliver in what could be a permanent form? I have completely abandoned that conviction at times, however, to <u>write</u> agitation/irritation. Those complaining letters are here. My biggest "complainers" have to do with the perception that somebody has hurt my husband. This little group of "how could you <u>do</u> that's" is here, too.

This man and his wife were my close friends—<u>close</u>. For twenty years Annie and I chatted on the phone virtually every Saturday morning, lots of times in between, but her husband became convinced I didn't come through for him and has never forgiven me. I haven't asked him to . . . I didn't do anything <u>wrong</u>!

April 26, 2002

Herb dear,

Will you go one more round with me? I wouldn't be shocked if you said no—I can be boring—but I <u>hope</u> you will read this letter. It distresses me that you are still mad at me for my not having contributed to Rick Lazio's campaign when he was running for U.S. Senator. I tried to explain at the time that it wasn't the money—though I can be cheap. It was the fact that I was supporting Hillary Clinton <u>totally</u>. I know you despise her but I think she is smart and capable and deserved a chance at being Senator. I think I believed in her just <u>about</u> as much as you did in Rick Lazio although, unlike you, I never tried to help with funding. Herb, you've gone through this with me before but I just can't understand that you don't understand that you don't send money to try to defeat the very person you are seriously rooting for! In terms of I <u>owed</u> you, that is as accurate as it gets but, Herb, a not big-deal contribution to your candidate couldn't make up in any <u>way</u> for the incredible week-ends you provided David and me at West Hampton, summer after summer. They were all <u>magical</u> and it would sure take more than a campaign contribution to your friend for us to get even. The caviar festivals haven't been bad either! Herb, I tried to do what I <u>could</u> as we went along. Annie thought she would like some kind of job for a while, not in decorating or fashion but in an office of some kind. I did call up people and try, landed her a couple of pippypoo places that weren't worthy of what she had to offer but I did <u>try</u> because that's what she felt she wanted. Ann wound up getting one of the people an interview with

Grace Kelly, which made her the best talent booker of the century. Herb, I also got a job for someone you sent me, Liz Fisher. I don't think she meant a great deal to you—step-daughter of somebody you knew—maybe he was on your board . . . anyway, he asked for help with Liz. I think you asked yourself, whom do I know who might help and my name came up. She got the job, which I'm not always able to do.

Herb, by now you probably <u>have</u> stopped reading but I'm upset that <u>you're</u> upset because yours and Ann's friendship means so much to me. Mercifully, I don't think your anger with me spilled over to David and I'm grateful for that. He's nuts about you and he sent a contribution to you for Lazio. I believe you took us to dinner at Swifty's close to his birthday last year, gave him a present, and that made him happy . . . mustn't be mad at David. Maybe you'll think of something I can do to get back on your good side short of supporting the <u>next</u> person who runs against Hillary. I hope so.

Bestest,

Mr. Herbert J. Siegel
East 72nd Street
New York, New York 10021

HGB:ss

I miss this close friend—a lot! In this case she did something I didn't like, never asked to be forgiven or I might have. Takes guts to stay mad at somebody with whom you've been really close.

May 3, 2002

Lizzie dear,

You and I write each other letters. I've always liked that, enjoyed writing almost as much as receiving. Here is my latest.

Lizzie, as you know, I was deeply distressed that you wrote such an unhappy account of THE SWEET SMELL OF SUCCESS. Nobody can fuss at you for not liking it. As I mentioned when I saw you the other night, we like or hate with our gut and nobody can rearrange those feelings. I just didn't think, hating it, you needed to write. Lizzie, I don't believe that anyone at the paper requires you to do or not do something in your column—I don't think there is such a person who says you must run it, kill it, revise it, whatever. I don't think you would work for that newspaper if there were such a provision. My take is that you simply wanted to write your opinion of the play. That certainly sounds honorable but, in this case, you needed to consider whether or not you were killing a friendship. I don't know why that play is so important in my life. David has done numerous terrible movies and I have been the first one to say so. It's just that in this stage of our lives, with his having worked on this project for over eight years and finally got it to Broadway, it was/is important. Repeat: it didn't hurt deeply that you didn't like it . . . there are others who feel the same way along with the others who applauded. The point is that you wrote, for public consumption, a really scurrilous account and I thought, for friendship-sake, maybe you didn't need to do that. Mostly you don't write hateful . . . you are a lover. Something in this particular property has offended or distressed you and that's allowed. What I wish hadn't been allowed was your wish or need to write the hateful words overrode what those words might do to a long time friend. Lizzie, the books are so uneven. You have <u>always</u> given more, given <u>everything</u> to help somebody's cause. . . . I won't even begin to <u>try</u> to mention the projects of mine you have applauded and complimented. I sometimes think you didn't even write about the new editors of Cosmo, whatever they might be up to, because you thought that would perhaps be disloyal. Whatever, Lizzie, I will never get delineated or express deep enough thanks for <u>everything</u> you have done. This is a new development in our lives. I thought you could have resisted writing the diatribe no matter how much you despised the play. You made a different decision. Unfortunately, I don't think we can ever go back to the way we were and that takes courage to say and <u>do</u>.

Ms. Liz Smith
East 38th Street Apt. 26-A
New York, New York 10016

HGB:ss

When it was announced I would be leaving <u>Cosmo</u> as editor in chief, <u>The New York Times</u> ran a major story, some of it not accurate!

COSMOPOLITAN

Helen Gurley Brown, Editor-In-Chief International Editions

January 22, 1997

Dear Tim,

I think you are a shit! I don't mind what anybody says in terms of his own opinion but when you say "the new editor's task will be to freshen a magazine whose relevance has waned over the last two decades since the end of the Sexual Revolution," how unrelevant can you be when for the last sixteen years, including 1996, you were still the biggest selling magazine at college campus bookstores and the sixth biggest newsstand seller of all magazines published plus how unrelevant are you if twenty-nine international editions plus six new ones which will come aboard this year, want to use your format.

"Brown has been criticized for keeping issues like AIDS and sexual harassment off the pages of Cosmo." We never <u>did</u> that....they have been <u>on</u> the pages, we just didn't take the outlook embraced by others but they were there.

"No centerfolds." We haven't had a centerfold since 1990, seven years ago, except for one special last centerfold in the February issue because we were doing something of a retrospective. Do you ever check <u>facts</u> before you start writing? Repeat - <u>we</u> couldn't be canceling centerfolds because we canceled them ourselves seven years ago?

Some of the things you got right. Saying (inaccurately) that Cosmo
was no longer relevant pissed me off.

Sincerely,

Mr. Tim Whitmire
New York Bureau
City Desk
Rockefeller Plaza
New York, New York 10020

HGB:ss

COSMOPOLITAN

Helen Gurley Brown, Editor-In-Chief

February 17, 1999

Kate dear,

Are you a crazygirl or something?

Do you want me to go to Frank Bennack? <u>He</u> would see me . . . the door is always open.

What I had in mind is showing you <u>three</u> places in U.S. Cosmo—only three among dozens/hundreds of fabulous photos/features that are in direct opposition to things I tell the international editors . . . constantly.

To be truthful, I didn't have so much in mind your explaining to me why you <u>do</u> them, but me explaining to <u>you</u> why possibly we shouldn't! I'll give you one example: pages 225, 231 I can't READ the reverse type (white on brown). I have most of the editors stopped with the reverse type—they used to do pages and pages—but what is the use of having words in the magazine you can't <u>read</u>? U.S. Cosmo is their bible prototype. If <u>you</u> do it, it must be okay but by me this particular thing <u>isn't</u> okay. And there are 2 other things—only 2 in the whole book—I marked dozens of pages to tell you how <u>good</u> you are, not that you don't already know.

Kate, Frank gave me two whole years to work with Bonnie. He put it in writing. If/when—and only then—you think she is ready, he said, she gets the job. Obviously it didn't/couldn't take two years. I never ever consulted with Bonnie about anything after that except once: same situation as this one with you. She was using lots of OUT OF FOCUS photos. I simply said to her that out of focus wasn't as clear, sharp and lovely as The Real Thing, in my opinion, and I tried to get international editors not to do it. She quit and they quit— maybe they quit first.

Kate, my job with international editors isn't just some "make busy" thing management came up with for me, tho that is the kind of thing they would do. We take a ton of money from overseas and it will get moreso as those magazines grow . . . hard to grow (circulation-wise) in the U.S. but Turkey, Greece, Argentina, Beijing, blah blah blah are wide open.

After you met with me, if you so deigned (and I literally meant ten minutes), you could say to me, "Helen, I don't agree . . . we're going to keep doing it my way." (just those 3 things are all we're talking about) and I would have said "fine. I just wanted to explain."

I guess I'm sort of aghast that you would refuse a meeting. If I wanted to talk about the laundry, politesse would indicate that you'd see me. Your magazine is fabulous, there would be no way I could or should advise you at this point but your manners have gone out to sea! I can't get a ten-minute appointment with Kate for a worthy cause? I think your management would think it was funny. I certainly do.

Airlines and hotels do so many things right I like to tell them in writing. Occasionally, however, they get something wrong, and I think should also be told.

May 18, 1994

Dear Mr. Wolf,

I hope you won't think I'm pretentious for telling you this is the most smashing advertisement for an airline that I have ever seen. Usually everything shouts and screams and says way too much. I haven't been <u>on</u> an United Airlines flight for about 8 years! Coming from a country weekend at the Hearst ranch in Northern California, David, my husband, and I plopped on the United Airlines flight from San Francisco to Los Angeles. I took off my shoes and was barefoot. A man across the aisle took deep offense at that and asked the stewardess to have me put my shoes back on. I said I wasn't in the mood to do that. The stewardess finally said I would have to leave the airplane unless I put my shoes on, which I would have been happy to do except we had people waiting for us for dinner in Los Angeles and I didn't want to put my husband through the ordeal of doing everything alone. The man across the aisle may have been mortally offended by my bare feet (they were very pretty, clean, manicured, etc.) but I was mortally offended by United Airlines' attitude and neither David nor I have ever set foot on another United flight though we both get around the world once or twice a year and take frequent trips to the coast.

Why am I telling you this? Absolutely no reason at all. Pure indulgence!

All my best wishes,

Mr. Stephen Wolf
CEO
United Airlines
Chicago, Illinois 60666

October 19, 1999

Dear Mr. Blauvelt,

I am probably the only person in the world who will ever ask you about this, but does the air conditioning <u>have</u> to be so frigid in the Waldorf-Astoria ballroom, even in winter? I can understand a little bit in summer though I am usually icy cold. In June, July, August and even September and April perhaps things have to be kept chilled so nobody gets into a fever but today it's miserable, rainy, not <u>that</u> warm and I had to go get my raincoat from the cloakroom to wrap up because the ballroom had a gale blowing through. It is generally <u>always</u> that way. I know you are just trying to keep people comfortable but I've even heard <u>men</u> comment about the frostiness of the place when possibly it isn't <u>absolutely</u> necessary 365 days a year. Would you think about this? Some of us ladies are not wearing our long woolies but, as I said, even the men were commenting today.

> Respectively . . . I've spent a
> million happy nights in the
> ballroom,

Mr. James Blauvelt
Banquet Manager
Waldorf-Astoria Hotel
Park Avenue
New York, New York 10022

HGB:ss

September 21, 1992

Dear Walter,

You wouldn't have wanted to be around here Friday night when I tried to dry off the wet spinach leaves—it took about a roll of paper towels, half an hour of hissing and cursing . . . not pleasant! Walter, the spinach shouldn't be <u>wet</u> when it goes into salads; also if you have some left in the package, it deteriorates more quickly if it has been dampened down. We're doing fine with the parsley and romaine . . . now if we could just send dry spinach leaves, that would be wonderful!

Love and cheers,

Mr. Walter Oliver
Regent Food
Third Avenue
New York, New York 10028

HGB/rc*

༚༚ ༚༚ ༚༚

Addressee of the letter on the next page was the owner-publisher of <u>The New York Times</u> . . . I went right to the top! Did me no good whatever. Subject of complaint now has a bigger job than ever at the <u>Times</u> and—do we care?—he and his wife, Alex Witchel, are best friends of David and mine—we see each other as often as we can.

November 17, 1989

Dear Punch,

This isn't the kind of letter you would ever want to read - though I hope you don't stop reading! - or that I would ever write because why bother....people don't <u>read</u> angry letters! (<u>I</u> don't).

This one isn't angry...it's <u>heartbroken</u>.

May I add my voice to those of others who think Frank Rich is a totally irresponsible <u>prick</u>....(and I usually use that language only in <u>bed</u>).

By writing an unmitigated wall-to-wall, beginning-to-end scurrilous review of A FEW GOOD MEN, which opened at the Music Box Theatre Wednesday night, he has almost without question prevented a Broadway run. Theatre goers take Frank Rich seriously. If he says a play is bad, they just don't buy tickets.

Bad movie reviews don't matter. Moviegoers don't read reviews. With books it doesn't matter either. People read what pleases them regardless of a review. With plays, it matters. Nobody is going to plunk down $100 for two tickets to a play if Frank Rich hates it - and the play can't stay open long enough (the producers

can't afford to keep it open) for word of mouth
to do the trick if there are no lines at the
box-office - because they read Rich.

So why not take Frank Rich seriously - he is
a serious reviewer.

Because he is also a hater - not of everything -
but many times of what might be popular. (I don't
think this morning's review of Gypsy counts. He said
going in it was his favorite musical; it has a track
record of 31 years)

A FEW GOOD MEN played for a month at Kennedy
Center in Washington to sold-out audiences. They
got on their feet every single night for the so-called
standing ovation. President and Mrs. Bush joined in
one night.

At previews in New York same thing happened.
On opening night it was cacophonous - not one single
person wasn't on his feet and the cheering went on and
on. Punch, I'm not an idiot - standing ovations aren't
the review but they tell you something.

This play is good - a good crowd-pleasing play.
Such cynics (and realists) as Bernie Jacobs, Jerry
Schoenfeld, Jay Presson Allen, Lewis Allen, Robert
Whitehead, Roger Stevens and my husband all decided
the week of the previews it had a real chance - because
they were getting nothing but raves from attendees.

Katharine Hepburn was in the standing ovation group
at one of the previews.

And now, thanks to Rich, these things will
happen:

1. 21 actors will be out of work

2. So will stagehands, lighting, make-up
    people, etc, etc.

3. A promising, maybe brilliant, playwright
    Aaron Sorkin - will probably stop writing
    plays and write movies because if this one
    doesn't work - with all the approbation
    from audiences - why bother.

4. New York audiences will be denied something
    good. The only original new play on Broadway.

Punch, I am personally involved...for sure.
My husband is one of the producers and I've seen the
play five times but, as a play-going addict, I know it's
good and that opinion has nothing to do with my husband.
I just don't understand the New York Times keeping a
reviewer who spoils and despoils so many things. David
Hare (in Variety) says "The Times is pleased with the
enormous power wielded by Frank Rich." What a thing
to be pleased about! I think you are better than that.

All my best wishes,

Mr. Arthur O. Sulzberger
The New York Times
West 43rd Street
New York, New York 10036

HGB:ss

Dear Harrington's,

I give up . . . how <u>do</u> you open a can of Harrington's pure Vermont Maple Syrup?! We have tried everything but a stick of dynamite! A metal beer can opener doesn't do it. Apparently you can't <u>unscrew</u> the top . . . our arms are out of the sockets from trying. A metal corkscrew that can get into a bottle of wine will only penetrate <u>cork</u>, not metal. Possibly we can turn the can upside down and open it with an electric can opener but you then wouldn't be able to store the syrup because the unopenable opening on top sticks out and you couldn't leave the can upside down the rest of its life. I am really discouraged. Some thoughtful (I <u>think</u>!) person sent me two cans of what looks like a wonderful treat. My husband is an addicted pancake enthusiast but we are both going nuts trying to penetrate what <u>might</u> be a treasure. Help!

All my best wishes,

Harrington's of Vermont
Richmond, Vermont 05477

HGB:ss

COSMOPOLITAN

Helen Gurley Brown, Editor-In-Chief

July 29, 1996

Dear Phillip:

It was a pleasure to have dinner with you and Jan last week. She's charming—I suspected <u>beforehand</u>—as are you. My take: you are unpretentious, talented (to put it mildly), attractive, funny—you even let me impute to Mel Gibson everything that's been happening to Pierce Brosnan this past year—having a baby with the environmental reporter of the Today Show, widower raising three children alone, etc., etc. Very tolerant! (I'd cross-filed information!)

Phillip, all that being <u>true</u> plus I am an admirer (as I told you, PATRIOT GAMES is on a laser disc in my office to watch when I exercise after lunch—very small disc collection—PATRIOT just happens to be one of my favorites)—so how can <u>that</u> director be the one who attacked David so viciously, inaccurately, last Saturday?

Phillip, the item in Variety is as innocent as it gets . . . ask someone other than Mace. David wasn't saying that he, alone (brilliantly), was bringing THE SAINT in a million dollars under budget. When Army Archerd called from L.A., he said he'd heard the picture was <u>over</u> budget and David said no, you were <u>under</u> budget. I was in the room and heard—it only went on five minutes. At the end David said be sure to mention Mace Neufeld and, after they'd hung up, I said why . . . Mace Neufeld hasn't been real friendly to you. David said, "because Mace gets his feelings hurt and I wanted him to do that." Phillip, the idea that it could <u>not</u> be the director and the crew who kept a movie on or under budget wouldn't occur to anybody but the lowest-grade amateur and it wouldn't occur to David in a thousand million years to take credit from <u>you</u>. He is <u>thrilled</u> to be working with you—or was until you cut him to pieces—has never had anything but the highest praise for you and I have listened to him carrying on about you to everybody at Paramount plus a few dozen others. As for <u>me</u> taking credit for anything on THE SAINT, are you <u>crazy</u>?! Army—a friend—asked David how I was and David said I was in London with him. Phillip, I am as uninvolved as it <u>gets</u> in somebody's movies. David doesn't let me read scripts because he says I have no judgment. I didn't come to the set of THE SAINT because he said I had no business there. To read something evil into Army Archerd's perfectly benign little paragraph bespeaks something <u>weird</u>. Maybe the writing wasn't as clear as it should have been but did Mace steam you up? Are you that easily <u>steamed</u>? I know you have been in pre-production and principal photography for a year and a half and the weight of a major movie rests with you but I needn't remind you David has been working on THE SAINT for over three years—most of that time <u>with</u> you—and I don't think he has ever consciously given you a bad time. How could you have hurt him so deeply with your diatribe?

Did David suggest I write this letter? Is the Pope Jewish? He would <u>kill</u> me if he knew I were writing but write I will. The Mace Neufeld situation has been an unusual one from the beginning but I believe it was David who approved bringing him to THE SAINT (I think he had approval of any additional producer who came aboard) there had to be <u>some</u> arrangement since David couldn't be with you on location all the time and you didn't want to work only with a line producer. No problem. David has never gainsaid it was the right thing to do and it isn't <u>my</u> problem why Mace isn't friendly. It <u>is</u> my problem that you excoriated my husband in front of the whole crew and his peers . . .

I don't think you <u>had</u> a better friend than David in the entire industry. How can you turn on him?

Phillip, why this letter . . . a real busy-body letter from a <u>wife</u>?! It's because you have hurt and wronged somebody deeply for no reason I can glean and I think you are a <u>shit</u>!

Sincerely,

Mr. Phillip Noyce
℅ The Saint
Pinewood Studios
Iver Heath, Bucks
SLO ONH England

December 14, 1992

Dear Rob,

I've now seen A FEW GOOD MEN four times and can write my letter.

I think it's the best movie I've ever seen. I truly do. I should have written after the _first_ screening before everybody got on the bandwagon!

So this is what a courtroom looks like?! So _this_ is what a director does! It really is hard for a civilian to recognize just What is Going On because of a director any more than you can understand how an orchestra gets conducted if you don't play something. In this case I guess the director did _everything_! Let's just say A FEW GOOD MEN was a good play and you have turned it into a masterpiece.

Thank you for letting _me_ have a screening . . . the only _real_ perk of sleeping with a producer, I've always thought . . . I can buy my _own_ mink.

Rob, when you are giving credit to people for contributions to A FEW GOOD MEN (as you graciously did at the charity premiere) don't forget David. This is obviously a who-asked-_her_ suggestion from a _wife_, but while you were mentioning your associate, Andrew Scheibman, and the Castle Rock people without whom _nothing_ would have been possible, as you pointed out, I thought to myself it wouldn't have hurt Rob Reiner to mention David. David thinks you are the most gifted person he has ever worked with—has nothing but praise and says you have been impeccable with him. He would _kill_ me if he knew I were writing this but, Rob, the agony, money, sweat, dedication and _time_ (nearly four years) that went into _getting_ A FEW GOOD MEN to you are kind of staggering. David nurtured AFGM from that first scruffy reading on upper Broadway on an icy winter night early in 1989, worked closely with Aaron on both play and later screenplay (not that Aaron needs a mentor, but David _did_ help), got producers for the play, put in personal money _twice_ (once for advertising when the show was about to close because Frank Rich gave it a review. I tried to get Punch Sulzberger to _fire_ him but going to bosses never works. As you probably know, Liz Smith's and

Katharine Hepburn's support, plus the advertising, after the bum review (which <u>counts</u> in the theatre, as you know), pretty much kept the play alive until word of mouth did it. David was at the University of Virginia during <u>those</u> weeks, often at Kennedy Center during <u>those</u> weeks. Cast changes in New York while fighting off puerile suggestions from another producer's wife (not Jay Presson Allen) who had the clout to make the whole thing disappear if they didn't get her stopped—David dealt with <u>that</u>. Then there was that <u>other</u> icy night—this time at Claridges in February 1990—when Mike Medavoy called to say Tri-Star was putting the property on turnaround. Knowing what David had gone through already <u>I</u> was planning to <u>jump</u> but window too low, and I would only have got maimed, not killed. David said, "Are you some kind of <u>idiot</u>?! There never was a property like this . . . we'll get somebody better." And he did. So, Rob, I won't worry about you at the Academy Awards because contractually David will be <u>with</u> you but just don't forget there wouldn't <u>be</u> any Academy Awards but for A. your genius, B. David's nurturing the property for such a long time. So <u>there</u>!

Love and cheers

Mr. Rob Reiner
Castle Rock Entertainment
N. Maple Drive
Beverly Hills, California 90210

HGB/rc

March 19, 2002

Mr. Howell Raines
New York Times
(FYI—This is the fax I sent to New York Times <u>LETTERS COLUMN</u>)

Power is heady right? Presupposes people have to do as we say or not do as we say. I'm just wondering . . . is Ben Brantley, drama critic of the world's arguably most important newspaper, the New York Times, powerful enough to keep people away from the recently opened Broadway musical the <u>Sweet Smell of Success</u> with his vicious, vengeful March 15 review? ("A recipe for a benzadrine cocktail," "You're likely to find yourself counting the moments until dawn"). Possibly. Well, I might just point out that people who have seen the show already are crazy about it . . . Regis Philbin, Joel Siegel, Nora Ephron, Pat Collins, Stanley Donen, Elaine May, etc. and many more, that the house, pre-Brantley and from word of mouth has been packed night after night with enthusiasts. I'm one of the packees . . . have seen the show nine times so far—seven previews in Chicago, first preview and opening night in New York. At each of these performances—truth—people have been on their feet cheering at the end of the show. I showed so often because of being married to one of the producers, David Brown, but let me assure you when David does a clinker movie (who could get <u>through The Island, Canadian Bacon</u> and a couple of others), I'm the first and loudest complainer. Perhaps Brantley's years in the Paris bureau of Women's Wear Daily gave him a low boredom threshold . . . how many handbag, shoe collections and transitional sportswear can you examine without yawns setting in? Maybe he's getting his revenge by trashing one of the best musicals anybody could ever hope to see. Hope you got it out of your system, Ben. I'll be going back to see the <u>Sweet Smell of Success</u> for the tenth time next week.

FAX 456 0417   May 11, 1998

      Kathie

Dear ~~Betty~~ Lee,

        We are a naughty girl to badmouth something
we haven't <u>seen</u>, as in DEEP IMPACT, especially if the
"something" is David's movie which he worked on for
22 years!   I did invite you to a screening (last Friday)
and you wouldn't have had to pay the $8.00 but I
didn't imagine you could come ...I know you can't
do everything people want you to. Pussycat,
sometimes the public is <u>right.</u>   If they go to
something, it's because it's <u>good.</u>   As Gene Shalit
said, "this isn't a nitwit volcano movie."   It's
very moving and <u>non</u>-violent and most of the people
at my screening cried toward the end...real actual
tears. Frank Gifford is mentioned by the astronauts
up in space. So...perhaps you'll see the movie
<u>sometime.</u>   It is full of the most wonderful children
you've ever seen- <u>no</u>, not in bad situations but just
belonging to some of the families the story is about...
so <u>there!</u>   David is in Rio de Janeiro this morning
                (DEEP IMPACT)
- what else - <u>promotiong!</u> - and will (mercifully!) have
missed his favorite person diss-ing his movie.

           Love,

FOURTEEN

Thank You for Having Me on the Show

I still can't believe I've been on so many television shows . . . entertaining isn't what I do for a living, but being a television guest, plus a little hard work at your day job, is what makes you famous, and I've enjoyed that. The people in these letters and lots of others I <u>owe</u>. For two and a half years I was on <u>Good Morning America</u> every Friday morning. When it was over, I didn't write . . . I sent David Hartman and Sandy Hill flowers.

Because Robert Dolce, booker on <u>The Tonight Show</u>, liked me and I was willing to appear with guest hosts, not just Johnny Carson, I wound up being in the top ten most used guests on the show. Dolce has a pile of my letters a foot deep.

June 13, 1974

Bob dear,

That was such a lovely pussycat call. I really did feel I didn't do very well, and it meant <u>everything</u> to have you say it wasn't so. Other people I <u>sort</u> of trust—but not like you—also said they enjoyed the show, so I guess it was a happy event after all. Just know that your friendship and support mean everything to me and I hope we'll be together for a long time (I still have junior high school buddies so it's rather dangerous to get <u>involved</u> with me!). Let me know what's happening in your life when you think I <u>should</u> know. Meanwhile, hold a happy thought that David's mechanical shark can <u>swim</u> . . . they know he's okay on dry land, but now they have to put him in the <u>ocean</u> . . . and let's all plan to have a splendid summer.

Love,

Mr. Robert Dolce
THE TONIGHT SHOW
W. Alameda Ave.
Burbank, California 91505

HGB/pm

COSMOPOLITAN

Helen Gurley Brown, Editor · 224 West 57th Street, New York, New York, 10019, (212) 649-3555

April 20, 1978

Dear Robert,

I think "our performance" wasn't <u>bad</u> . . . since I'm not a comedienne, if I can give somebody straight lines so <u>they</u> can be funny, it's really the <u>best</u>. I used to think Don Rickles was a monster when he first started performing at Slate Brothers on La Cienega Blvd. 20 years ago—so insulting! Then about 10 years ago, I heard him as a dais guest at testimonial dinners and he put everybody else <u>away</u> . . . they were so boring and he's so irreverent and fresh. I still like him enormously . . . he's very gentle with me and makes the most out of any little tiny offering. That's what you do, too!

All my thanks, much love,

Mr. Robert Dolce
THE TONIGHT SHOW
W. Alameda Avenue
Burbank, CA 91505

HGB/pmq

July 14, 1993

Dear Joan,

I just watched "our show" and I thought we were all <u>wonderful</u>, particularly <u>you</u> (this was the show with Linda Ellerbee and Deborah Norville and they're okay <u>too</u> but you and me talking about men and image and facelifts and sex . . . how can a show possibly get any better?!) Don't worry, I know who makes it all happen and you just do it better all the time.

Much love
and thanks,

Ms. Joan Rivers
Columbia Broadcasting System
West 57th Street
New York, New York 10019

HGB/rc

February 16, 2000

Geraldo dear,

I had the loveliest time being one of your guests last Monday night when we talked about Hillary. A few of the others knew considerably more than I did about the background of this election but you gave me equal time and listened hard and seriously . . . one of your special lovely traits. Geraldo, you know I have admired you wildly since you were just a puppy and you have grown up to be a wonderful full-blooded best-of-show Westminster <u>winner</u>! I heard from people all over the country about the show . . . you must have a big audience or something! All my thanks. . . .

Love and hugs,

Mr. Geraldo Rivera
Fletcher Avenue
Fort Lee, New Jersey 07024

HGB:ss

August 16, 1994

Roger dear,

That was wonderful! I have never <u>had</u> a better interview and we know there have been a few. Why is that? Because you <u>listen</u> and you are so <u>lively</u> and I love the quiz—about whether something is or isn't sexual harassment and regarding my own life—how much did one depend on sex? In these 32 years nobody has ever asked me that—<u>ever</u>—and it is a fabulous question . . . only <u>you</u>! I am glad we are such long time friends and I plan to make it even longer, okay? Congratulations on your tremendous success with CNBC and now Channel 56.

Love and cheers,

Mr. Roger Ailes, President
CNBC
America's Talking
Fletcher Avenue
Fort Lee, New Jersey 07024

HGB:ss

Dear Wendy,

Is there anybody in the <u>world</u> who doesn't watch Larry King? I think I have heard from <u>everybody</u>, including a bunch of people I ran into in Paris last week . . . strangers who would stop me in a restaurant . . . I absolutely loved it! Having a whole hour with Larry is about as good as it gets . . . he is always so good to me and sells so much product (whatever you are hustling at the moment). Thanks for making my visit so happy . . . the plane tickets and the limo pick up worked gorgeously, too.

All my best wishes,

Ms. Wendy Walker Whitworth
Vice President
Senior Executive Producer
CNN America, Inc.
The CNN Building
First Street, N.E.
Washington, D.C. 20002

HB:ss

July 12, 1994

Dear Marlo and Phil,

David has already written about Phil's being inducted into the Hall of Fame but I want to say also how deserved the honor and how graciously you accepted. Marlo, your introduction was inspired and it was charming to hear that you had flirted shamelessly . . . <u>we</u> all noted and self-awareness doesn't hurt. Phil, yours is the show others—so <u>many</u> others—aspire to but no one ever gets there.

I know you did a rerun of our March '93 show this past week and I must have heard from a hundred people—I found that thrilling. Just keep doing what you're doing forever and ever. <u>You</u> may get weary but no one else ever will <u>watching</u>.

Love and cheers,

Mr. and Mrs. Phil Donahue
Fifth Avenue
New York, New York 10021

HGB/rc

November 15, 1993

Dear Shoshanah,

You had asked for a recipe that might be cooked on ROBIN LEACH TALKING FOOD when I do the show Friday, December 3rd. This is going to be more material than you want to plow <u>through</u> but we start with the fact that I don't really <u>cook</u>! I do desperately simple things for David, my husband, but you couldn't really call them <u>recipes</u>. If it is anything as complicated as stuffed peppers or tomato sauce for pasta, the housekeeper cooks it and <u>leaves</u> it for me. So what we have here (on pink paper) are terrific recipes from a Cosmo editor. If you like any of them, you could use one of them and say it was mine—I have no guilt! Or we could tell the truth and say it comes from a Cosmo editor I trust.

On the small white cards are recipes that I <u>have</u> used in the past—they actually come from my single-girl days (the name of the girlfriend who gave them to me is next to the title). They all work like gangbusters and if you prefer one of them because it is <u>authentic,</u> then we will choose one of those.

Shoshanah, the restaurants that David and I frequent the most and love and adore are:

    The Russian Tea Room
    Le Cirque
    The Four Seasons
    Elaine's
    Syrena—an exquisite Japanese restaurant at 11 East 53rd Street

Please call me if you have questions. I'm so looking forward to the show.

        All my best wishes,

Ms. Shoshanah Wolfson
ROBIN LEACH TALKING FOOD
West 33rd Street
New York, New York 10001

HGB/rc

FIFTEEN

Worthy Causes

Philanthropy is big business in this country. Once when I walked home from a lecture with the anthropologist Margaret Mead—we lived in the same building—she explained that while most governments take care of their countries' needy—adequately or poorly—in the United States women have assumed that role, chairing fund-raisers and hustling hard. We all get notices in the mail asking us to buy tables or, at least, tickets, possibly to be on a committee or lend our name. To a few you say yes, but likely you have your own causes for which you are working hard. For years mine has been the National Abortion Rights (pro-choice) Action League. I never had an abortion, but some of my girlfriends did before they were legal, and we don't want to go <u>there</u> again. I don't raise money for NARAL but do kick in financially, attend major functions. Once in a while I hustle for a different cause, at the same time frequently saying no to friends on the money-raising trail.

October 4, 1990

Dear John,

I'm not holding a marker of yours and how am I going to get you to do this?!

Would you consider seeing these two people to chat for 15 minutes?

Kate Michelman, Executive Director, National Abortion Rights Action League

Ann McGuiness, Development Director

Kate and Ann are pretty, charming, smart and represent a <u>very</u> good cause.

70% of the people in this country are in favor of women having a right to choose abortion (Pro-Choice).

Yet the opposite side (Pro-Life) are so vocal, nasty, well-organized and financially endowed they are chipping away at this precious right, so hard fought for and won nearly 18 years ago in the landmark Supreme Court decision, Roe vs. Wade.

The Webster case, decided by the Supreme Court in July '89, opened the door for <u>states</u> to make the decision about bringing a fetus to term; i.e., the court gave the states back the power to restrict a woman's right to choice.

As the days go on, it seems the most effective way of securing this right is through the political and legislative process. Examples: Jesse Helms needs to be defeated, so does Bob Martinez, running for re-election in Florida, the first governor to call a legislature session after the Webster Bill passed so that the Florida women could be <u>denied</u> choice! Tom Harkin of Iowa should be returned to the U.S. Senate; he is being challenged by a rabid anti-choice candidate.

What in the world does all this have to do with you?

There possibly (<u>probably!</u>) are causes closer to your heart. Well, I am asking if Kate and Ann can come to talk to you because I know you love and respect women (to put it mildly) and this is one of the most <u>basic</u> issues concerning women. How <u>can</u> we have once been so enlightened and now be slipping back again?! The girls (if I may call them that!) would just like to tell you about some of the work they are doing toward trying to elect <u>pro-choice</u> candidates (even if they <u>aren't</u> in our state).

Will they ask for money? I don't think it's <u>that</u> specifically they have in mind, though you never know! They have just asked me to ask you for an appointment because you are important and influential and they want to present their cause. John, people "pick on you" because you are wealthy but also because you are the most <u>generous</u> and tender-hearted of people.

They will telephone you for a possible appointment and I hope you'll say yes. Whatever the decision I do appreciate your reading this letter.

All my best wishes,

Mr. John Kluge
Metromedia
East 67th Street
New York, New York 10021

HGB/rc

January 22, 1998

Dear Frank,

BACK TO THE FUTURE is one of your most brilliant columns.
I remember before Roe v. Wade—we used to stretch one of my
roommates between two twin beds and pile luggage on her tummy to
try to get the baby not to happen. We could have killed her. . . .
Mercifully our "solution" never got near a miscarriage. I'm just
thankful a <u>few</u> brilliant people like you are on the right side (and can
write good!) because there are a lot of creeps out there trying to gum
things up. Thank goodness so many hundreds of thousands of
people will see this.

Love and cheers,

Mr. Frank Rich
New York Times
West 43rd Street
New York, New York 10036

HGB:ss

March 16, 1999

Dear Bob,

Your BUSH V. BLACKMUN column this Sunday is the most wonderful thing I ever read! Lots of people like me haven't been able to figure out <u>where</u> George W. Bush came down on choice and you have made it very clear—he's against it and "if you don't want to overturn Roe v. Wade, your heart's not right!" My husband got so excited about this column (an <u>ancient</u> feminist . . . from about 1940 on), he read it out loud to me while I was exercising. Thrilled you also mentioned Kate Michelman, who is one of the <u>best</u>. Thanks for putting everything in place . . . I'm sending this column out like my Christmas card, as though nobody else read the New York Times!

All my best wishes,

Mr. Bob Herbert
New York Times
Op Ed Page
West 43rd Street
New York, New York 10036

HGB:ss

June 1, 1992

Dear Mike,

Your segment on population control was <u>brilliant</u>! I've been wondering and fussing and fretting and <u>agonizing</u> that nobody has wanted to connect abortion or the lack of information <u>about</u> with the cataclysmic growth of the world's population and George Bush's connection with the dilemma . . . it seems only you have the brains or courage to do such a splendid thing on the biggest/best television show in the world. That was really a thriller.

With great admiration,

Mr. Mike Wallace
60 Minutes
CBS
West 57th Street
New York, New York 10019

HGB/rc

Years ago I started helping a friend, board member of the Hospital for Special Surgery, find entertainers for their big fund-raising dinner, usually by fax and phone call to their representatives. Conquests have included Tony Bennett, Rosemary Clooney, Betty Buckley, Nell Carter, and lots of others. This letter was a special request for the evening.

May 5, 2001

Marvin dear,

Here it comes . . . the no good deed goes unpunished letter.

Monday, June 24th, is Patricia Mosbacher's birthday and everybody at Hospital for Special Surgery is wondering if you might come to the gala dinner that night—you've entertained before and helped us hundreds of times with others—to sing Happy Birthday to Patricia. You wish people Happy Birthday better than anybody because you do it in the manner of Mozart and several other estimable composers. That's all you would need to do—just sit at the piano and play your genius rendition of Happy Birthday, that's it. Of course, getting to the Waldorf to <u>play</u> is a lot of work but I am trying to make this sound "easy." Marvin, I know you are also entertaining at a major cancer dinner within the next three weeks and you just may not feel like taking on another assignment but how can I resist asking. Maybe you'll drop me a note or telephone as to whether the Happy Birthday greeting might be possible. You've done so <u>much</u>, people might <u>almost</u> be willing to let you off the hook if you're up to <u>there</u> but we might <u>not</u> . . . a posse might be sent or goodness knows <u>what</u>. I'll so look forward to hearing.

Love and Cheers,

Mr. Marvin Hamlisch
Park Avenue
Apt. 6-S
New York, New York 10028

HGB:ss

October 1, 1991

Dear Joy and Regis,

I know you can't go to <u>everything</u> though you try to help your friends. Could I get you to come to <u>this</u> (it isn't a "cause" but everything takes energy).

> Event: 60th Anniversary Celebration of the Whitney Museum
>
> Place: Whitney Museum—945 Madison Avenue
>
> Date: Wednesday, October 30
>
> Time: 7:30 p.m.

The evening is to honor all the Whitneys who created the museum plus Brendan Gill.

Joy, Regis, this is a little different from other events in that the <u>place</u> is different—plus a different kind of people <u>go</u> to these things—mostly collectors, celebrities, painters (Jasper Johns, Robert Rauschenberg, James Rosenquist were at the last one), and the evenings are kind of glitzy and spiffy but fun. Leonard Lauder is the president of the Museum. David and I have a table and these are people who will be with us: Morley Safer (he paints), Norman Mailer and Norris Church (she paints), Tony Bennett (he paints) and <u>you</u> (I hope) because you are both good at everything. This is black tie—formal invitation will arrive later. You could leave <u>early</u> . . . Just stay <u>part</u> of the time.

Will you call me. Thanks, pussycats.

Love,

Mr. and Mrs. Regis Philbin
Park Avenue
New York, New York 10021

HGB/rc

October 11, 1991

Dear Joy and Regis,

I am so absolutely thrilled you can do this.

The other guests at our table are: Jane and Morley Safer, Norris Church and Norman Mailer, Tony Bennett and Susan Crow, June and Bryant Gumbel. We'll have fun.

Love,

Mr. and Mrs. Regis Philbin
Park Avenue
New York, New York 10021

HGB/rc

©© ©© ©©

November 1, 1991

Regis dear,

You are the absolute, unequivocal, World Class <u>best</u>!! The damn weather report knocked out the first few minutes of Regis and Kathie Lee this morning but I got to see the showing of the famous Regis portraits done at the Whitney dinner last night—fabulous! You not only <u>attend</u> these health-threatening big events but do wonderful things to help the Cause. Regis, the Whitney Museum and my bosses at Hearst will be ecstatic . . . I'm getting a tape for them. Meanwhile, the important thing is that you even <u>almost</u> had a good time.

Love and cheers . . .
see you soon,

January 15, 2002

Muffie Dear,

You are and Sherrell are always so supportive of anything that David or I are involved with—I think you shelled out thousands of dollars when David was made a New York Living Landmark—you even came to dinner with lots of other things to do. . . . .that touched David (and me) very much. Muffie, alas, we can't attend the Daisy Soros gala April 22—it looks gala indeed. Beverly Sills is <u>always</u> worth honoring. Muffie, I've sent a check for a thousand dollars, just as a token of support for Muffie, to the Special Events Department at Lincoln Center. Don't abandon us, even though we aren't doing something you would like. You must absolutely keep us on Muffie's list for whatever occasion.

                              Love to you and Sherrell,

Mrs. Muffie Potter Aston
Park Avenue
New York, New York 10021

HGB:ss

Coco dear,

You are so good to write David and me a personal note about the Steel Pier evening benefiting the Society of Memorial Sloan-Kettering Cancer Center. We'll be in Bangkok that week opening a Thai edition of Cosmo. Coco, that doesn't mean one couldn't participate financially in helping Sloan-Kettering but we have such a kind of out-of-control charity list right now, I don't think we can add something. We <u>have</u> from time to time contributed to Sloan-Kettering, particularly Evelyn Lauder's work. We always love to hear from you—I know it is going to be a fabulous evening.

Best,

Mrs. Coco Kopelman
The Society of Memorial Sloan-Kettering Cancer Society
Riverside Drive, Suite 14-O-E
New York, New York 10023

HGB:ss

November 6, 2001

Dear Caryn—may I call you that?

Thank you so much for the invitation to the New York Women's Agenda Star Breakfast, December 4th. I don't know whether to tell you the truth or to tell you something a little more palatable—I guess I'll go for the truth because it usually gets around anyway. Caryn, I don't <u>do</u> breakfast ever, ever, ever. If I were to make an exception, it would have been to attend a Mike Bloomberg breakfast last week, also at 7:30 a.m.—I am a passionate supporter. I can stay up all night but don't think I have ever been to a breakfast in all these hundreds of years. My husband and I feel we <u>are</u> friends of Prager and Fenton. Jeremy Steinberg is an absolute peach (we'd better not tell him I said that . . . he might think it sounds too sappy) and has so far kept us out of the slammer every year. I don't even think he <u>cheats</u> when doing our tax returns, he just tries to be fair to everybody, especially <u>us</u>. Caryn, I hope we get to meet someday. Sorry I won't be at the breakfast—I know it will be gala.

All my best wishes,

Ms. Caryn Schatz
Prager and Fenton
Third Avenue
New York, New York 10017

HGB:ss

February 27, 2001

Mathilde dear,

I have so much respect for you in so many areas, not the least being that you <u>ask</u> for what you need and want and not infrequently it happens! Mathilde, I <u>don't</u> think I am the one to wear the new AIDS ribbon at the Academy Awards. I have never been an active supporter in your cause, while respecting all the people who <u>are</u>, and I don't think I want to participate in this particular way. It would be first-time involvement for me and simply not a move I am comfortable with. You are right to ask and we won't discuss whether I am right or wrong to have declined.

All my best wishes,

Mathilde Krim, Ph.D.
Founding Chairman and
Chairman of the Board
AmFAR
Wilshire Boulevard, Suite 3025
Los Angeles, CA. 90036

Smith College isn't exactly a charity, but they have all my papers in the Sophia Smith Library, and I'm establishing a journalism chair there after I'm gone.

August 6, 2001

Dear Carol—may I call you that?

Everyone is excited about your appointment to the Presidency of Smith College . . . do I have the right office designation? I'm not an alumnae—I didn't <u>go</u> to college—but Smith was good enough to ask for my papers for the Sophia Smith Collection and I've been happy to send along through the years. I visited the library a couple of years ago . . . Ruth Simmons was good enough to put me up at her house . . . at least I <u>think</u> that's where I was. Carol, I'm sure the college has chosen a <u>brilliant</u> new leader. The University of California at Berkeley is a giant—and respected—institution and they probably had to do some prying to get you loose. I will surely look forward to your new adventure. Smith is in my will in a fairly major way (I have no children) in that we are establishing an HGB Scholarship for an African American or Hispanic student in journalism. Carol, if you are ever in New York for fifteen minutes, please come by and say hello. Ruth used to do that and I would adore to see you. My office, at the Hearst Corporation, is <u>fairly</u> midtown (57th and 8th Avenue) and I will just expect to see you on the doorstep someday. Meanwhile, congratulations and <u>all</u> my best wishes.

Ms. Carol Tecla Christ
Office of the President
Smith College
Northampton, Massachusetts 01063

HGB:ss

SIXTEEN

Deepest Sympathy

We all write "sorry he's gone" letters, sometimes sorry <u>she's</u> gone, though the weaker sex (are they kidding?!) tends to stay around longer. I could have included lots more letters in this category, alas, but these are typical.

December 29, 1992

Courtney dear,

I can't believe Steve isn't with us—he was one of the most dynamic forces God—or whoever creates things—ever put on the earth—wasn't he astonishing? The life force inside your beloved husband was like none I've ever seen in any other person and it touched us all again and again. I did write to him once or twice about the gratitude I felt for things he did for David—he took David and Dick Zanuck into Warner Communications, not once but <u>twice</u> when they needed a home. He was always uncritical, backed them totally. Those stories are legion, of course . . . people Steve helped but never asked <u>anything</u> in return. Courtney, his illness was so prolonged and intense one can only imagine what you have been going through these past years. I know you brought him <u>everything</u> in the way of solace and advice. And you brought him a beautiful new child to enrich his life. Nicole must be a wonderful little girl—that combination of genes could only produce a prodigy (and a beauty)! Courtney, I am so fond of you. I'm sending my deepest sympathy and I hope you'll stay in my life and be my wonderful friend as you have always been.

Much love,

Mrs. Steven J. Ross
East 71st Street
New York, New York 10021

HGB/rc

Dear Carol,

Poor baby . . . your beloved Carrie has gone somewhere else. One can only <u>imagine</u> the pain you suffered the many months that she was ill and that's just <u>yesterday's</u> pain . . . now we have today. Carol, I have heard you speak so lovingly of your daughters and I know you loved and helped this one in every possible way. Pussycat, she's peaceful now and you will go on being <u>you</u> . . . helping and reassuring and brightening the lives of <u>millions</u> of people.

Deepest sympathy. . . .
All my love,

Ms. Carol Burnett
Spoleto Drive
Pacific Palisades, CA. 90272

HGB:ss

Berney Geis published <u>Sex and the Single Girl</u>. His wife got her bathrobe sleeve caught in the flame of their gas stove one morning when making tea and burned to death. Does it get any worse?

March 31, 1999

Berney dear,

Some things are unimaginable and almost not dealable with. How could such a tragic thing have happened. . . . I know you must go over and over again the things that should have been done or not done to prevent such a tragedy. Sweetie, all I can do is send my deepest sympathy. I was very fond of your wife and respected her beautiful brain and talent as well as her being a First Rate Person. We have Picasso hanging in our den because she introduced us to Harry Abrams and we got a little art into our lives. I guess I actually met him at your apartment a year or two earlier but Darlene took care of the art acquisition. Berney, I'm grieving deeply for you and sending all my love and deepest sympathy.

Mr. Bernard Geis
York Avenue
Apt. 31-F
New York, New York 10021

HGB:ss

Yes, maybe it does get worse. This couple's son was murdered.

September 10, 1997

Dear Barbara and Jerry,

I usually can write letters—it's what I <u>do</u>—but was so horrified by what happened to Jonathan I just couldn't think of anything adequate to say. I <u>still</u> can't, although I know you must be grieving deeply and inconsolably. I didn't know him but he must have been such a fine young man. . . . I don't think I've ever heard more eloquent tributes from everyone who <u>did</u> know him and for students to absolutely worship a teacher is pretty unusual. He obviously had the <u>best</u> parents and, with your influence, was able to influence <u>other</u> people's lives just as his parents have. I know how much good work you both do for so many people who need help. I was always reassured when <u>you</u> participated heavily in Literacy Volunteers. I never get to see you but am sending my love and sympathy at this very late date. I know your son must have been proud of <u>you</u>.

Sincerely,

Mr. and Mrs. Gerald Levin
Warner Communications
Rockefeller Plaza, 29th Floor
New York, New York 10019

HGB:ss

Lally's mother, Katharine Graham, was owner and publisher of The Washington Post, first publication to expose Watergate.

July 27, 2001

Lally dear,

It must have sunk in by now how much people loved and respected your mother. . . . I don't think I have ever <u>seen</u> tributes like the ones which poured in. I always felt she might have made <u>you</u> more a part of her publishing world but that is A. none of my business B. your <u>own</u> world is one of achievement and recognition. I always wanted you to write lots more for Cosmo than you ever could. Lally, I <u>am</u> sending deepest sympathy. Whoever one's mother is/was, there is nobody else <u>like</u> and the grieving is inevitable. I am glad you are in my life and I want to keep it that way.

Much love,

Mrs. Lally Weymouth
East 79th Street
New York, New York 10021

HGB:ss

This girl's father, Ted Ashley, was a leading Hollywood agent for many years, then head of Warner Brothers Studio.

September 9, 2002

Fran dear,

You said I <u>couldn't</u> (mustn't and shouldn't and <u>don't</u>!) but I have to just do a special testimonial to your wonderful father. For me he was special because as big as he got, he never <u>took</u> it big. . . . always fun, approachable and the friend he had always been. Once when we were on an airplane together, going to the first screening of SOUND OF MUSIC in Minneapolis, he gossiped with me about one or two of his clients and how outrageous they were—Rex Harrison was one. I only mention this to illustrate his unstuffiness. I was on the floor of the airplane laughing . . . maybe he felt my response was worth the indiscretion and, of course, I never <u>did</u> squeal. Where did we first meet? It seems to me it was <u>before</u> Ashley Famous but, whatever, I just wanted to tell you I adored him and miss him <u>now</u>.

Love,

Ms. Fran Curtis
Rogers and Cowan
Fifth Avenue
New York, New York 10019

HGB:ss

Robert Wagner was mayor of New York City for eleven years.

February 15, 1991

Dear Phyllis,

You will have heard from everyone and everyone will try to say The Right Thing. He was, of course, a prince and the interesting (not surprising but wonderful) thing is that <u>everybody</u> agrees. You can't get the tiniest dissent from <u>anyone</u>. What I want to say is how fabulous it is he found <u>you</u> and you made him so happy these past important years. Thank goodness there were that <u>many</u>. I remember your wedding day when you were in that pretty beige lace and chiffon dress—was it Bill Blass? You were such a beautiful bride and he looked so happy with you. Well, that was a prophetic look because he has probably been the <u>happiest</u> of his life with you. It was a wonderful merger and now comes life by yourself only you aren't <u>totally</u> because so many people love and adore <u>you</u> and want you close forever and ever. David and I are certainly two of those.

I am sending my <u>deepest</u> sympathy and will check up on you soon.

Love,

Mrs. Robert Wagner
East 62nd Street
New York, New York 10021

HGB/rc

April 19, 2001

Cindy dear,

I didn't know your mother and sometimes I think I don't know <u>you</u> anymore. We see each other so seldom but I was touched by the story in the New York Post. You were a wonderful child and, while you give your mother credit for <u>everything</u>, there aren't so many who would be devoted and attentive to her all of her life, including the last ten difficult years. Don't you ever do anything scruffy? I don't <u>think</u> so! I am sending deepest sympathy.

Love,

Ms. Cindy Adams
Park Avenue
New York, New York 10022

HGB:ss

November 11, 1993

Dear Walter,

I can't believe your mommy isn't with us anymore—I can see her in her bright red dress sitting on the couch at your Christmas party kind of holding court but nicely . . . I loved <u>talking</u> to her—she was kind of sparkly. Well we all know you were a <u>wonderful</u> son; now you're an orphan and that will make you sad for a little while. You did everything <u>right</u> on her behalf and that's why she lived so long. David's in Toronto right now on a movie location but we are both sending deepest sympathy.

Love,

Mr. Walter Cronkite
East 84th Street
New York, New York 10028

HGB/rc

August 15, 1994

Ernest dear,

The first time I ever laid eyes on Jackie was at your swimming pool one sultry summer night. David had scared me half to death getting ready for the occasion because you were his best friends and he wanted me (without much hope) to make a good impression. I don't know whether that ever happened on <u>my</u> behalf but, as far as she was concerned, I thought she was the sexiest, freshest, most different from other people's wives person I had ever met. She was in a swimsuit, very tan and truly the life of her own party—which never didn't happen at any party she ever gave. She also was nice to me. I remember her calling you "babe" and I thought that was a lovely nickname for a husband. The years went on and we got to be what I consider <u>close</u> friends although we didn't see each other too often. Ernest, there is nobody like <u>anybody</u> else but, in her case, she seemed more different than others. For one thing she was always fresh and honest, qualities you don't run into in so-called Hollywood wives or anywhere else! You simply knew what you were getting from her was the true truth—she never dissembled—yet her enthusiasms and admiration for things in people she really liked were boundless. We know she worked, at something professional, when other Hollywood wives didn't and was successful in doing so all those years. I think her joy in dance was a manifestation of her joy in life.

Sure, she had aggravations and, I presume, rocky times although I don't think I ever knew about them and nothing compared to her illness but she was somehow always ebullient and enthusiastic about life itself—she liked great food and good writing and French oceansides and good friends . . . she was, in a word, non-<u>prissy</u> or uppity . . . she was the real thing.

I don't know what you are going through—no one ever knows on behalf of someone else—but, within your great sadness, I hope there are moments of sheer joy in the knowledge of what you gave her and how loyal you were to her. You gave her the means to travel and look at the world—even if you were not always <u>there</u> as in Africa and, I believe Russia—not to mention the two sons and the life <u>style</u>. I guess she is one of the few people I know who ever took advantage of her own swimming pool but that was reflected in her very well shaped and controlled body. I'm rambling . . . I wish there were something I could do to cheer you along but cheer isn't what happens right after the loss of someone that much a part of you. I'm sending my deepest sympathy—she was my friend and I will miss her a whole lot.

Much love,

p.s. You and Jackie took us to dinner the night David and I got married—at Perino's. Then I think we went to a strip joint. I always felt if you both hadn't <u>approved,</u> I never would have got him. You must stay close to David—he needs you.

Mr. Ernest Lehman
Chenault Street
West Los Angeles, California 90049

HGB/ss

Austin's mother, Austine, a southern charmer, was married to his father, William R. Hearst, the original press lord's son, one of my bosses.

July 2, 1991

Dear Austin,

When I first met your mother I thought she was the most elegant creature I had ever encountered and I never changed my mind. Along with elegant, she was also a class act but then you already know that. Every encounter I ever had with her I felt she was <u>totally</u> interested in the other person and she simply bowled me over. Through the years, she was totally wonderful with <u>me</u> . . . enthusiastic and appreciative and, from the first hour, made me feel part of your extended family. Austin, I know how she doted on you and Will . . . she would feel her very finest legacy is the two wonderful sons she gave to the world and you <u>did</u> turn out well! Your remarks at her funeral were just wonderful. I'm sending my deepest sympathy. It isn't going to be as wonderful a world without her but she made it a lot better while she was here.

Love,

Mr. Austin Hearst
Hearst Entertainment Distribution
E. 45th Street
New York, New York 10017

HGB/rc

SEVENTEEN

Dear Elizabeth, Aleta, and Helen

Elizabeth Jessup was my childhood friend in Little Rock beginning in 1932, when both of us were age ten. Now, at eighty-one and eighty-two, we talk to each other frequently (she in Little Rock). Elizabeth is another who saved <u>all</u> my letters, written through the years after Mother, Mary, and I moved away from Little Rock to Los Angeles in 1936. I borrowed the collection—a shoe box full of crinkly, yellowing pages, mercifully mostly typed (after I learned how in 1940), to look through for this book. Deep affection is here. Elizabeth and I almost sound like lovers, except both of us were relentlessly boy crazy and they for <u>her</u>. It's a wonder the friendship survived, but I forgave her for being gorgeous and more popular than me because I treasured her. Our nicknames for each other were Kitten (mine) and Sassafras and Buzzie (hers).

Here are a few letters I managed to smooth out and keep from disintegrating in my hands so they could go to the printer. Aleta was Elizabeth's mother and Helen is Elizabeth's daughter, my god-child.

I'm just starting in, sweet—no rhyme or reason or greeting, because I'm afraid something will interrupt me before I get it all off my chest. Two post-cards left me in an aching frenzy to write to you, but no address and it had to keep somehow. I think I miss you almost more than anyone I know, Buzzie. It isn't very logical—there are other people I have more in common with now I suppose—Buzzie, we're almost as different as two girls can be—we really are, but it's always you I want to drag off to my woodland trail and kidnap for a couple of days while I just talk the daylights out of you.

First, Sassy, I'm not sure I believe in God. I'm sure I'm more of an Agnostic than I am a Christian. I still say my prayers at night, because I can't bear to give that up—if it's only the summing up of all I want to accomplish and improve the next day—whether Anyone hears it or not, I say my prayers. But outside of that, Buzzie, it gets to seem more like believing in Santa Clause every day. I have no right to discuss authenticity of the Bible—I haven't read it in so long, or enough of it when I did read it to have authority to condemn it, but I believe that dictates of conscience can be as forceful. When you really come down to it, we haven't a proof in the world—it's all just in our imagination, and we have no more right to say that our beliefs about God are right than the ancient Greeks who worshiped gods of nature. We are doing exactly what they did—trying to explain and give reason for that which we do not understand. We don't know why we're here, or where we'll go, so we strive to clarify the reason for our existence by creating a God to worship. I'd shock anybody to death if I so much as intimated my thoughts, I'm sure. But it almost obsesses me—I keep wondering what on earth will happen to me if I stop believing in God entirely.

I've decided that you grew up about three years before I did, Sassy—I keep finding out things that intuition (for lack of a better word) tells me you knew a long time ago. Every man is something to be coquettish and charming for, and every girl is just another someone like yourself who would just as soon cut your throat as to look at you, is my latest inhibition. Modified just a little bit. It's hard for girls to be truly superb friends—it's much easier to keep a boy for a friend year in, year out than a girl. Yesterday I almost decided that the people who were the sweetest and friendliest and most congenial were just the ones who were scared to death to be any other way! Isn't that absurd? To say that the people who come the nearest to being angels are scaredy-cats? And yet, I think lots of them would like maybe just once in a while to whale away and tell somebody to go to the devil! Course what I'm really doing is trying to justify myself for developing a Scarlett temperament! But I do get to thinking more like her all the time.

Buzzie, we now want different things in life, but it's partly because we've recently lived different lives. Dear old environment again. I've always been mercenary—if I'd been beautiful I might be a gold digger, but I'd rather die than be poor all my life. I have a hideous, disgusting, but sincere ambition to have a great deal of money someday, and I probably shall and not be any happier with it. It's going to be fun to watch us get what we think we want.

Heaven only knows what we'll do with me in Los Angeles in August—the four boys I've kept up with or who have kept up with me are going to be vacationing I think, so I shall just see if I can't persuade you to have a whole slew of parlour dates so I can absorb valuable pointers like a sponge. Gosh, do I need em?

> Yours, Buzzie—because you're a captivating little angel and devil rolled into one—and I love you—because you're 'so different from the rest' and you love me too.

October 3, 1940

Buzzie, dear—

There aren't words to tell you how sick I feel about this marathon of not writing. If you were anyone else, I'd say—"I've been busy" but because you're you, that's really the only thing I can say anyway. Buzzie, I never knew what studying was— really haven't studied since I left Pulaski Heights Junior High, and here all of a sudden I am confronted with homework in seven subjects every night—I simply don't do it. I struggle with three one night, and four the next and not to mention an hour or so of transcribing shorthand notes every afternoon. When I don't study, I'm _going_. Staying home is a privilege it seems.

I wish I could tell you all about every single thing I've done, because it's all been as colorful and extraordinary as an American novel. Last year seems so remote and unreal—have I said all this before? Because I can't resist, I'll thumbnail synopsis part of it—

Saturday night Pat and I dated two boys from Stanford who were the smoothest people I've seen this side of Richard Greene—however we took in every bar within walking distance of the Biltmore and Mark proceeded to get intoxicated—quite wholeheartedly. We were on our way to Errol Carrol's when he stared acting like a savage. To say that I was absolutely helpless is to say that rain is wet. I couldn't do a thing, Buzzie—I never realized before that a girl might actually be taken advantage of against her will—it's so entirely possible. If you'd like to think you'd rather be a stone wall than a girl sometime, just get kissed and kissed and kissed against your will and be utterly powerless to do anything about it! I struggled, and fought, and buried my head in my fur collar and everything but ate the stuff. I pleaded and begged and hedged, and so eventually—I simply screamed to the top of my lungs and had hysteria. I laughed and cried and the tears, streamed down my cheeks until I wondered if I were going mad. That surprised him so that he only became sulky and ungracious and of course still disgustingly drunk about the whole thing. I scrubbed my face and brushed my teeth for fifteen minutes.

If I stay up any longer you'll be responsible for subjecting the people at Woodbury tomorrow to a slaphappy Gurley, and you wouldn't do that, would you?

I'm keeping your last letter, Buzzie—it was sweet as anything you've ever said or written, and thank your daddy for his lovely missive too—it was exactly like him.

And if you want to take turn about is f.p. don't write me for a year, but if you want to make me happy, do make it soon.

With all my love,

Helen

August 4, 1942

Buzzie, darling,

I've been planning to wire you for three days, but decided I couldn't say enough in a wire, so here's an airmail.

I might just as well try to get to Russia for the opening of the second front as to be there on September 8th or 9th—you see, Baby, the trip is expensive enough these days, but I'd have to take at least two weeks off from work without pay, which I just can't do.

For several months, anyway, I've known in the back of my mind that you'd be really coming down that aisle, and I've known all the time that I just had to be there somehow—and yet here it is, just a little more than a month—and there isn't a single way out. The night I opened your letter, I woke up the whole house, and we sat around at 2:30 a.m. trying to figure out some way I could do it. Everybody's willing to sacrifice this—do without that—and generally hold down the fort until I come home, but all of that only adds up to a partial part of what I'll need. Baby, I get goose liver green to think of anyone else being maid of honor—I would have been happy just to be a flower girl, or hold the champaigne [sic] glasses at your reception or even just wash them—and then you had to give me top billing, and make it twice as hard for me to say no.

I've never even imagined your getting married without my being there to beam at and cry on—you—but if you're going to, I'll just have to perform those duties at some slight distance.

Please—please send me every single detail of it—if you have time then before, and if not sometime afterwards, clippings, samples, etc. Who are your bridesmaids and what are they wearing, and oh, just everything else.

I love you very much. I'm proud as an Easter bunny and thank you for the glow you've given me.

Kitten

COSMOPOLITAN

Helen Gurley Brown, Editor • 224 West 57th Street, New York, New York, 10019, (212) 649-3555

July 11, 1988

Dear Elizabeth,

How nice to have a letter from you and that's
interesting that I was there in a dream. I
think I'm okay but it's pleasurable to be
checked up on. I used to dream about you to
the point of absurdity for about twenty years
in Los Angeles and, of course, I still do sometimes.
How wonderful that you have a condo at Gulf Shores.
I know that surf and that weather must be the
best there is. Sweet that you took your new grand-
child and his parents for an early visit . . . I
know they appreciated that. I'll tell David about
TIME AND AGAIN by Jack Finney. He is always
looking for ideas. Elizabeth, I remember the
Beer Barrel Polka on the Santa Monica pier just
as clearly as yesterday! We repeated it at
Lakeside Country Club a month or two later when
I came to visit you and they happened to be
playing it in that large room of the rebuilt
clubhouse. Otto Brawley was there and I don't
think thought we were wonderful with our mad
dance. We're just back from northern California --
a terrific retreat among the tall pines and Douglas
firs. It's called Wyntoon and was built by W.R.
Hearst for Marion Davies -- her own little private
Bavarian village. It is almost indescribable --
the cottages are painted with fairy tales --
Goldie Locks and the Three Bears, etc. etc. but

as we thought we were

COSMOPOLITAN IS A PUBLICATION OF HEARST MAGAZINES, A DIVISION OF THE HEARST CORPORATION

by old German masters so it really isn't
corny. My big moment (though it took actually
about 45 minutes) was coming down the McCloud
River -- not very wide but it rushes along
madly over lots of rocks and rills -- on my
fanny in an innertube from a logging truck.
About a mile and a half and I never had so
much fun. I didn't capsize until the very end
so I feel successful -- and still here, thank
God!

             Much love . . . let me hear from you,

             H

Ms. Elizabeth Bilheimer
North Woodrow
Little Rock, Arkansas   72205

HGB/rc

Now it's forty-six years later, and there were many letters in between—I've spared you!

September 30, 1997

Elizabeth dear,

You were so good to call after Mary died last week. Somehow I wanted you to know about it. She was never in yours and my life together very much but she certainly heard a lot about you from <u>me</u> through the years and, as I've told you, I'm so <u>deeply</u> grateful for what you did for her with the LRHS news reports, seeing that her class ring and other memorabilia are in the exhibit and what you personally did to bring Niloak pottery back into her life. We always knew you were a pussycat. Had a wonderful long letter from my godchild. . . . she brought me up to date on all her children, we both glory that her father is doing so well health-wise and she says you are enjoying yourselves. . . . I <u>knew</u> that! You gave me a real prezzie when you gave me her for a godchild. Hope to get my husband home from California in a week or so—am taking him to Budapest to open Cosmo in Hungary. Seems appropriate. Some Hungarian exports (the Gabor sisters) have done very well with men and even had careers of sorts. Your birthday is soon . . . I'm always relieved because it brings you closer to my <u>age</u>! It's always wonderful to hear from you.

Love,

Mrs. Roy Bilheimer
North Woodrow
Little Rock, Arkansas 72205

HGB:ss

August 29, 2001

Elizabeth dear,

You can't imagine how happy I was to hear from you . . . except for the unhappy news about your back problem and the skin cancer removal that left the slightly raised eyebrow and a scalp that isn't feeling lively. Maybe those conditions have got better. I had skin cancer on my face dug out with a <u>trowel</u>—several trowels—a few years ago because California girls spend all day Saturday and all day Sunday all summer <u>long</u> at the beach and do <u>almost</u> irreparable damage. Not to change the subject and talk about <u>me</u>, with my grizzly acne in eleventh and twelfth grade in high school, they put me under an x-ray machine on Saturday afternoon and left me there five minutes at a time . . . that's what they <u>did</u> in those days. So much permanent damage was done in the chin area, dermatologists now wonder that I <u>have</u> one. Oh well, we go to the best people and that's what <u>you</u> have done. I would tend to trust Steno, and Indian doctors are some of the best we <u>have</u> in this country. Honey, I don't get up at six a.m. to do my exercise but I <u>do</u> it everyday—forty minutes right out of bed in the morning, another forty minutes after lunch. I hate every single minute and dread these two sessions every single day but think the results are probably worthwhile. An hour in the swimming pool is a major investment but I'll bet it's helping. Elizabeth, I can see you as a thirteen-year-old swimmer, so much better than me . . . I think you could even swim a hundred yards to get an important merit badge. Okay, the six a.m. sounds <u>almost</u> intolerable but I hate what I'm doing just as much two hours later . . . there!

Elizabeth, I'm so glad to have your new address and phone number. I'm always telephoning at the wrong time to actually <u>find</u> you but one of these days. Back to the Conditions. . . . <u>two</u> blood transfusions for a low hemoglobin? An attack of fire ants that caused a major fall? I'm impressed (not happily) but probably those two "gruesomes" have got better. As somebody said, old age is <u>not</u> for sissies though I never acknowledge to myself that I am over thirty-seven. Whatever is wrong with me I always think they have the wrong <u>person</u> . . . as far as I am concerned, that would even be <u>more</u>

true for you . . . I never knew a healthier or more active young person. You made the finals for a track meet—I think that is what they were called—were on an Over and Under team . . . I didn't make the cut. Since you were always <u>prettier</u> than anybody, I felt you shouldn't have been quite so athletically blessed.

Elizabeth, I will plan to come and see you one of these days or you will come and see me. I'm kind of traveled-to-pieces right this minute but next year that will go away. Loved Charles Allbright's column about the poem . . . charming. Wonder if he is any kin to Madeleine Allbright . . . maybe her last name has just one <u>L</u>. She is kind of a super person and, I'm sure, so is her namesake.

Love and hugs and thanks for such a lengthy, satisfying letter,

Mrs. Elizabeth Bilheimer
Chenal Parkway #7034
Little Rock, Arkansas 72211

HGB:ss

Elizabeth's mother was good to me, her daughter's friend, when I was a little girl in Little Rock. She was one hundred when I wrote her this reminiscing letter.

December 31, 1991

Dear Aleta,

I certainly was all puffed up because you wrote to me twice this year—I <u>loved</u> your letters. Aleta, you are going to indulge me and let me tell you one more remembrance of my pleasurable times with you—and there were so <u>many</u>! After my father died, when I was 10, things were a little—and what do I mean a <u>little</u>?!—sad around my house. I'm sure my mother felt utterly overwhelmed and frantic. I don't think we were left very much insurance money, women didn't have jobs in those days and she worried about her two youngish daughters. Add to that a somewhat <u>normally</u> depressed outlook—though I'm sure she was utterly different when she was younger—let's just say things never seemed very happy at my house though Cleo gave us everything she had and lived through Mary and me. Anyway, to get to the point, when I came to <u>your</u> house there was always laughter and fun and certainly <u>music</u>, not to mention wonderful things to eat! I want to recall just this one evening for you if I haven't before; it was midwinter, before Christmas, and you let Elizabeth have some of her young friends over for dinner, then the girls spent the night. I would say there were perhaps twelve of us altogether. I sat at the card table with Morris and Allen Hilzeim on whom I had a tremendous crush. It was the most delicious evening. I <u>think</u> we went to a movie though I also have a recollection of <u>possibly</u> going swimming in a heated pool at the Y. The only reason I think of swimming is that I remember you were going <u>with</u> us and I remarked to myself the wonder of anybody's <u>mother</u> going swimming! Whatever, the dinner-party aspect of the evening was so glamorous . . . mostly kids just did things in the daytime—<u>you</u> made it all happen! I can remember Elizabeth's bedroom almost as easily as my own bedroom right this minute. The bed was against the south wall, your bedroom was across the hall, Elizabeth's doll house was the best in the business . . . it had not skimpy baby doll furniture but things you could really pick up and get the good out of. Wonder what happened to that doll house.

Aleta, we are beginning still another year and I will expect to keep track of you during it.

Much love,

Ms. Aleta Jessup
Presbyterian Village
Brookside
Little Rock, Arkansas 72205

EIGHTEEN

Dear Cleo and Mary

Talk about people who saved <u>letters</u>! Mother saved every letter I ever wrote her and, since we lived thousands of miles apart from 1947 until she died in 1980, and since I wrote <u>every</u> working day (close to a typewriter, no big deal), the letters accumulated. A large canvas suitcase containing letters I haven't had a chance to go through—I can either go through or get this book to the publisher—sits in the apartment. Probably nothing more interesting there than here. My sister, Mary, in a wheelchair from 1937 (legs paralyzed, polio before the Salk vaccine) until she went bye-bye in 1997 (sixty-one <u>years</u>????) was also written to. These two were my motivation to do as well as I did in life. We needed the money, but they were also believers and encouragers.

COSMOPOLITAN

———Helen Gurley Brown———

mary dear,

i had this fantasy last night - not a dream, just

thinking to myself - about what kind of life you

would have had if you <u>hadn't</u> had polio...whom

would you have married? where would you have

worked? what city - and would you have had children?

my "conjecture" is that you would have stayed in

los angeles - w e ALL would - after all, we s tayed

two years after your illness ...i think you would

have graduated from woodbury, got a super job

and lived THERE. now...there is every possiblity

the alcoholism would have surface ANYWAY i suppose...

but you'd be all through that by now. i got so

carried away i couldnt stop thinking of the whole

thing...not sadly but just INTERESTEDLY...my

life would have been altogether different if i

hadnt met ruth schandorf through a silly clubthing

i belonged to at woodbury college - i was program

COSMOPOLITAN

chairman of the alumnae group - asked a vogue

editor to speak to a meeting, she said glamour

- their sister publication - was starting a career

council with young career women - i then went to

THOSE meetings - met ruth and later she introduced

me to david which madepossible the book and cosmo -

it could all have been so DIFFERENT! dont know whether

better or worse...worse i think! anyway, my dear,

you must tell me what you think you might have done -

you DO have this lovely brain and i think you would

have had a smashing job somewhere - altho i'm

alwao afraid you would have done the traditional

thing of marrying and having kids and not USED the

brain.

        so!

COSMOPOLITAN

Well, we had a SLIGHTLY happier bulletin

this morning...there was a press screening of macarth*er*

last night and SOME people liked it...we'll just

hope for the best. I heard it wasn't good but

THESE people said it was perfectly fine...

maybe it's someplace in between and won't

embarrass anyone!

i drove out to the country today to have

lunch...that was SO pleasant...i didnt drive, of

course...i may NEVER drive again though i used to

consider myself a GOOD driver...the leafy trees,

flowers...newyork is quite beautiful in the countryside

- a bit like the south, NOT like california. i really

loved seeing YOUR yard, front and back, mary...

so green and verdant. i guess there IS some soil

in you and maybe even a little in me! hope

your tree lives but if it doesn't we'll

plant another!

all my love,

HELEN GURLEY BROWN

April 24, 1966

Mary dear,

Your friend Michael Drury had the most smashing idea.
I told her there weren't enough hours or fingers to
make pincushions for the hilton hotel chain and she said
she'd been thinking of something else you could do to make
a lot of money and decided you should write a book.

Now don't go away...it's a <u>wonderful</u> idea.

There definitely is a story in you...starting with
the afternoon we were playing bingo and going on from
there. You can talk about <u>everything</u>, including
your experiences in the orthopaedic hospital, on hope
street, growing up in a wheel chair, all the funny things
and sad things, descent into alcoholism, ascent into
A.A. - marrying, rehab, etc.etc.etc.

Now, you can write under a pen name if you like.
The point of this is you could make a lot of money,
you would find it very rewarding once you got into it
and, perhaps most important of all, as Michael points
out, you could <u>help</u> some people. She says she feels
you have something to say to people - to <u>her</u> -and I
think you do too.

Now this isn't the insurmountable task it sounds like...
you just take one step at a time.

The first is to write downe every last experience you
think should be included...<u>everything</u>....just a few

words about each to get it in your mind. Or maybe some of
them will be complete chapter headings. In other words,
no writing - just see what ought to go in.

You would eventually have a list of a hundred perhaps -
or more.

Now...this is the point about this. If you did the
preliminary writing - just like a letter almost -
I could probably take it over eventually and whip it
into shape as they say. I know quite a bit about it at this
point.

That wouldn't be doing you a favor but actually be something
I would enjoy.   When I finish my cookbook I'm not sure
what the next book will be. I've been trying to think
of a novel plot - or plot for a novel - but nothing has
seemed quite natural...not a shoo-in like sex and the
single girl (sex and the office was never a natural either).

Now, strangely enough, this _is_ a natural! You would make
a _wonderful_ story - you _are_ a wonderful story. The way
you tell is whether or not you think of more ideas than
you can get down on paper and I already can and I'm not
even _you_....all the experiences at the orthopaedic and
your operation where they pounded on you....and of course
a complete run-down on finding out your legs _weren't_ coming
back - and all the adjusting.

I tell you, Mary Alford, this is a _natural_!

Now, my idea is that it should be not lugubrious but
written rather lightly and even funnily. The pathos will
come through and the inspiration and the helping other
people just by telling the truth...it doesn't have to
be an important literary document.

Listen, Mary dear, you're going to break my heart if
you say no to this. What you would write after putting
down the lists and lists of things to include would be
a diary...a long diary. Sweetiepie, you will get to
enjoy it....it will be like a catharsis or psychoanalysis

after the first miserable ten pages when you think
you're going to die because you're so self-conscious.
Just kepp plugging along anyway. The important thing is
to get it <u>down</u>...I'll fix up the rest. I rewrite every day
of my life now.

Remember, no one ever has to know it's you if your
prefer not to be known...but it <u>is</u> a way to make money
beyond youry wildest dreams if it clicks at <u>all</u>.

I'm holding my breath...gad this is an inspiration!

It will only work if you are very very honest and
talk about being in love when it didn't work
and being jealous if you ever were - and about your
cats being your family some of the time
and - well <u>I</u> can send you a list of a hundred incicents
that ought to go in just from my knowing you.
Eventually everything would be put into shape chronologically.

Time to go to bed.

         All my love,

February 10, 1969

Mother dear,

It was nice to hear from you yesterday . . . in the middle of
our blizzard! It's stopped blizzarding so now the snow is just
stacked up but not melting very fast. I must say it's
gorgeous . . . last night when we went out—the snow had just
stopped and no scooping or shovelling had started—the world
was like a wonderland. We had a car and driver and I felt like
a russian empress passing silently along the snowy streets
while the black huddled peasants were all walking! Actually
everybody looked dark against the snow and walking was the
only way to get there unless you hired a car. (20th fox pays
thank goodness). Today we had another one bring us to work
and will have one to take us home. I really get a kick out of
new york and its weather—the heat, the fine, bright days and
especially the snow. I left the kittycats out last night—their
kitchen seemed too frosty and i dont like to leave the gas on
for fear of suffocating them. well brownie was fine—he slept
like a slab of butter—but samantha was feeling just too
affectionate and she would climb on top of my back if i were on
my stomach or stomach if i were on my back . . . probably
liked the heating pad . . . and she practically had to be unstuck
like adhesive tape. Plus all the purring. Quite touching but
sleep-killing.

You were very nice to call me up and I always appreciate it.
Your bad weather and our bad weather will be over one of
these days. Meanwhile, it's nice not to have a cold or flu or
anything crumby!

all my love,

June 15, 1975

Cleo and Mary dear,

Thank goodness the CRAZINESS will soon be over—with newyears' eve—and we can all get back to normal! I'm not used to going out at night and it is about to KILL me!

We're going to one more show tonight—the one with liza minnelli . . . IT'S lousy but <u>she's</u> good—and then we dont have to whoosh around <u>any</u> more.

I thought you would approve of the white dress i just bought (picture attached)—it didn't cost the price in the ad—i got it on 7th avenue—but it <u>is</u> beautiful and old-fashioned looking—ivory silk chiffon. I have so MANY pretty clothes—I'm afraid I'm getting WORSE instead of better! Every so often i give some to the arthritis foundation and take a tax write-off—which only convinces me all OVER again I have too many!

i hope you're getting enough to EAT.

all my love,

COSMOPOLITAN

—————————————————Helen Gurley Brown—

june 12, 1973

Cleo dear,

It's too BUSY around here but that's because I had a 3 hour
lunch and having not got <u>in</u> until 11 o'clock that obviously
took some HOURS out of the day! Cosmo is going well, indeed,
and that is a happy bulletin. They're increasing the print order
the next few months and we'll see how many more copies we
can sell. The more copies we sell, the more money I make so I
<u>like</u> increasing the print order!

I made strawberry yogurt on my yogurt machine yesterday
and it's DELICIOUS! It's so simple—just heat a quart of milk in
a saucepan, let it cool, add a tablespoon of yogurt (it's like
sourcream or heavy cream) bought in a STORE, put the
containers in a heater overnight and presto, you have yogurt! i
dont think you've ever had any but you <u>might</u> like it . . . i may
make some sometime when we're all back at Mary's. I know
she's planning on your visiting this summer and i'll plan to
come along, too.

all my love,

June 10, 1974

Cleo dear,

Wonderful to talk to you yesterday. You
sounded great.

Mary says their tornado warnings have calmed
down now and I hope you're having smooth
weather also. Ours is SUMMER - 90 degrees -
but I just love it and couldn't be happier.

The lady who's collecting all the papers
for Smith College came to see me today -
they take up about 16 feet of space she tells
me and i'm going to go up there and VISIT them
some day! I thought they might throw something
out but they kept every last grocery list I
believe. I'm so happy I'm there. She says lots
of people wont part with their papers EARLY
but I'd rather have them there than moldering away
in a trunk.

Am getting ready to have some cottage cheese
and pears - that's what I live on in the daytime
but at night I get to have something more
interesting!

all my love,

Hi!... what's new?

6/11/74

Dear Cleo,

It's such a beautiful June clear day . . . maybe the BEST time of year. I went to the florist this morning and ordered some flowers for deserving cosmo people—the office pays for them. A big bunch of yellow and white daisies for an assistant art director . . . he's just had a big fight with his lover (another boy) and is about to throw himself out the window. Love! I can REMEMBER what it was like to feel that way and felt he needed to be cheered. Then I got two pots of yellow chrysanthemums—bright yellow gold—contained in a basket and sent them to our decorating editor. She has fixed up <u>my</u> office with all kinds of plants and seemed to deserve plants of her own. Lots of people do nice things for me all year, Cleo . . . makes life very frisky and nice.

Hope you don't mind this bel air stationery. i happen to have lots left over and thought i would use it up.

the company gave me a beautiful new olivetti portable typewriter. haven't really used it yet but it will be nice to have all my life. had been using david's—which i swear writes in SPANISH . . . and which is pretty tired and weary at this point. now we can retire it. it IS the typewriter my books were typed on so i'm rather sentimental about it.

Hope you're just fine, love. You <u>sounded</u> fine, Sunday.

All my love,

March 29, 1975

Mary dear,

It's a cold winter day—just before Good Friday—on which to be thinking <u>Easter</u> thoughts . . . it looks as though it's going to <u>snow</u> . . . but I have a bunch of beautiful pink tulips on my desk . . . and a sister who is a beautiful pink tulip all year <u>long</u>.

It's <u>nice</u> to have a sister, Mary . . . it must be awful not to have one! Who else could understand your <u>parents</u> the way sisters do . . . or travel through all the childhood adventures. Why do I think ours were <u>special</u>? They really <u>do</u> seem kind of yummy to me sometimes—the games of kick-the-can, playing tarzan and jane in a big tree in the Gustafson's yard, the hundreds of hours of movies shared with other gaping (hypnotized) little friends, rubber gun season, paper dolls, dolls, dollhouses, jacks—long summer nights of game-playing out of doors. It was just nifty and I'm glad we were both there to do it together.

You have more guts, courage, integrity and all the other good qualities than any human being I know . . . you are really <u>something</u>! And then there's all the love in your soul for your house, and friends, and husband and mother and sister . . . I'm sure we rank up there with the love for your <u>animals</u>! Well I am blessed to be blessed with such a sister and I love you among the top two or three of all things <u>too</u>. We will stay close and keep on being sisterly the rest of our lives.

COSMOPOLITAN

—————————————**Helen Gurley Brown**—

7/13/76

Mother and mary dear,

This time last week we were cooking our potroast, mary, and splendid it <u>was</u>!

Do you realize I ate up a whole HEAD of romaine lettuce thanks to your fabulous salad dressing. usually it turns to garbage right in the <u>ice</u> box (the lettuce) because I can only go it about once a week!

david got home from california and it's nice to have him around the house. he's noisy but companionable! he's also such an incurable optimist <u>that</u> doesn't hurt anything <u>either</u>.

he's so funny with the cats . . . they don't really understand him (no WONDER . . . he wakes them up when they're sound asleep to <u>play</u>!) but seem to sense they mustn't get too angry—that it won't HELP them. or maybe they secretly sense he really loves them but never really learned how to play with a cat!

i'm ready to take off for my weekly luxury—the visit to the masseur. i dont think it does much PHYSICAL good . . . just makes you feel nice. i hope you're cooking good things (which i'm sure is the case) and feeling healthy and serene.

All my love,

September 20, 1977

Dear Cleo and Mary,

Sopping wet because we're having a fall downpour—wish it were happening to YOU . . . know you need badly.

We're having a publishing tycoon at our staff meeting this afternoon—rupert murdoch who is a presslord in london and owns the newyork post now and newyork magazine. the staff wanted to visit with him and, surprisingly enough, he said yes. people are VERY vain . . . for an audience of about 15 i dont see how he can spare the time . . . i wouldn't! anyway have to bone up on his biography.

fall is here . . . with a vengeance . . . i could have managed with summer 3 more months . . . oh well!

you stay out of the rain . . .

all my love,

7/14/77

Mary and Cleo dear,

We had a "blackout" in newyork as you know when the power
went off ALL over town . . . so strange. i never cared a THING
about airconditioning though the "BLACK" was spooky . . . in
this most sophisticated city in the world not to be able to see a
THING without matches or flashlight . . . but AFTER the
electricity came back on and everything got normal i was so
thrilled with the _air_ conditioning! it was an odd interlude and
probably wont happen again for ANOTHER 12 years.

Now i must go home and feed and comfort Samantha . . . _she_
mustn't have liked the black _either_!

nobody came to the office today because the elevators weren't
working and it's one of the best days i ever HAD . . . total
quiet! i'm actually caught UP if such a thing is possible!

mary, you havent told me any books recently you'd like to
read. anything special?

all my love,

November 16, 1977

Cleo and Mary dear,

Such a beautiful newyork fall day—not cold, just nippy—i'm wearing a 20-year old pink fluffy mohair sweater—it would cost $100 today—cost plenty <u>then</u> ($35!) but it's my best color and I feel cozy. Am taking a scientist to lunch—he's so SMART but has this nice gift of being able to make DUMMIES understand complicated things like astronomy. Mary, that was once one of YOUR interests. Wish you were there to ask questions, too.

I got so fond of the Godfather after four nights I'm going to <u>miss</u> them tonight. That's television! Off to the dentist to get my toofies cleaned—gosh i am a loyal patient but STILL things fall apart! how can that be when you fed us so much good fresh milk, Cleo?!

All my love—I'm closing in
on Christmas

October 10, 1978

Dear Cleo,

It's the month of your birthday and, addressing your birthday cards, I think what a privilege to have a mother to address birthday cards to for I'm now of an age when I could not only have grandchildren but technically <u>great</u> grandchildren if everybody had started early!

Cleo, what does one say about a lifetime of love lavished on two children who may or may <u>not</u> have been worth all the sacrifice and passion attached to them? Being a passionate person and having little outlet for all your creative talents, you poured it into your children . . . our <u>gain</u>, maybe the world's loss. Who knows what you might have achieved if anyone had encouraged and guided you as so many women are helped and encouraged and guided now. We're so enlightened about women with talent, but you grew up in a family, then married a man who hadn't an <u>inkling</u> that a woman's brain could not only equal a man's, but maybe surpass it and that brain-power and creativity should be channelled into something other than <u>child</u>-raising— and, in the case of the family you grew up in—child <u>nursing</u> when you were only a child yourself. I can see you carrying your little brother or sister on one hip and joining the other children for play . . . I want to <u>weep</u> for your being burdened with child-care as a little bitty girl yourself, then, having no place else to put your talent, pouring it into your own children when you had <u>them</u>. Children always take <u>everything</u> a mother will give—and never let her come up for air; we did that with you, but I wish there had been far more outlets in your life than us . . . you drove us everywhere—me to dancing class, schoolplay rehearsals, swimming at White City (in Little Rock), shopping forrays—God, Cleo, the HOURS we spent shopping . . . I just loved it because you were always lavish . . . I remember so many happy hours at Pfeiffer and M.M. Cohen buying pretty little dresses . . . we liked those stores better than Gus Blass for <u>my</u> clothes . . . but then I was getting to where you REALLY put the time in and that was making the most beautiful little clothes for Mary and me. Perhaps it was a creative outlet for you . . . I'm sure it was . . . but we were the beneficiary . . . the beautiful <u>handwork</u>. . . . let me tell you about three or four of my favorites but there were DOZENS of others. One was pink silk shantung with a halter neck and a little jacket on top—that was my easter outfit . . . and a little brown checked taffeta dress I wore on PALM Sunday . . . imagine having TWO outfits brand new one week apart. There was a beautiful little rose cotton dress with white ruffled collars and cuffs smocked someplace around the shoulders and empire waist—and it had a sash that tied in back. Really glorious. And once you took a handkerchief and made a little triangular collar for a dress. There was the soft blue, short puffed-sleeve silk blouse that buttoned down the back you made when you and Mary were in Cheyenne one Christmas—also smocked beautifully—but that was much later. You made a lovely white long taffeta dress patterned after Claudette Colbert's evening gown in it happened one night with handmade white taffeta flowers across the front and down the deep v back . . . pretty glamorous for a 12-year-old girl! I remember my <u>first</u> evening gown, also wrought by Cleo . . . pale pink taffeta with a ruffle at the hem and sleeve and a robins-egg blue velvet sash. One of <u>the</u> most divine dresses came when I was in highschool and it practically stopped traffic . . . turquoise flowered linen—a little jumper with sexy, ruffled organdy blouse . . . you made <u>everything</u> and everything worked. You knew you were good, of course, but I'm sure you were never told often enough and virtually <u>never</u> by your children . . . what a grabby, greedy, unknowing little <u>nit</u> I was . . . i took it all TOTALLY FOR granted . . . no use saying I didn't because I <u>did</u> . . . my mother <u>sewed</u> and I had beautiful little dresses always . . . as though it were a god-decreed right! You did win a sewing contest with a sweet brown wool coat—for <u>me</u> naturally!—with soft beaver collar. I was <u>truly</u> proud of it . . . really elegant for a fourteen-year old snip.

Cleo, one could get bogged down for hours talking about the

pretty things you wrought with your pretty fingers . . . for love of us and also because you were lonely. Did anyone understand you? Your teacher, Professor Birney—maybe Leigh . . . but not altogether . . . he was too lost himself . . . and searching . . . and self-centered, though he was gentle and kind. Your brother Booker was a kindred spirit but probably didn't understand your brain . . . there were just never enough people to bring out the poetry in you, although you had good friends— mrs. amsler, mrs. engstrum, mrs. gibson—who lived near us— mrs. lyons, mamie susky (forget this spelling!) . . . Ola Stephenson in college so everything went into making a pretty home for mary and me and slipping us into beautiful dresses . . . plus encouraging any, ANY worthy endeavor in school or sunday school. Cleo, one time you helped me illustrate a bible story and I won the contest . . . a nifty basket of gumdrops . . . i was so proud . . . but it was your illustrations that did it. I'm GLAD you sent us to sunday school—and church—though you were just as free with your support (and the price to get in) to prospect theatre. after Ira died, you, feeling sorry for us, let mary and me go to the movies three or even FIVE times a week—monday, wednesday, friday—different bills each time—then saturday matinees for all those serials and westerns and sunday afternoon for the glamour movies. they didnt HURT us—except maybe dracula!— because movies were innocent then.

How always generous and indulgent you were. With the first money you earned at Sears Roebuck you bought me a little wolf jacket that was my greatest JOY . . . i wore it until it fell apart. That jacket MEANT something . . . it was like being a moviestar. For my 11th birthday you bought me a little gold expandable bracelet with locket picture—i still have it—i kept a picture of you and ira in it and i adored it . . . but that was a VERY fancy present for a mama with limited means. Christmas when I was 14 you bought binoculars at bullocks because that's what i wanted more than anything imaginable— then we went to santa anita often so i could use them. In my next to last year in highschool you bought me a LOVELY soft-pink wool dress that I wore to be one of the winners in a public speaking contest . . . and that same year—that was after Mary got polio—there were so MANY pretty things to wear—some bought, some STILL made by you—though you were a very very VERY busy girl. In grammar school my teacher told you i was gifted—or some such nonsense—miss oates was her name—and i had the lead in the mother goose play—i WAS mother goose! and you—as usual—made me a wonderful costume. The plays, cleo! and always you attended them, after having sewn me into my newest get-up (far get-uppier than anything anybody else in the production was wearing). Once there was a mother's tea at school—pulaski heights junior highschool—and I didn't invite you to it. Why? It haunts me even now. I think I was so busy <u>taking</u> everything I never had time to think how <u>anything</u> was for you, but I know that hurt your feelings and I hadn't any explanation at <u>all</u>. One summer you took me to Colorado so you could attend teachers college there but Ira plunked us right back home again—on the creek bank at osage you talked to one of your sisters about it—mary or ruth—explaining that ira didn't want you to stay there and you were crying . . . i just barely understood what THAT was all about . . . the next year he sent us off with his blessing and we stayed all summer long with aunt gladys in the mcCreary house and those people were nice to us, but again, you were toting your little girl EVERYWHERE and the times were wonderful! You took me a few times to your class at the university and I "sat in" but there was also a kiddies' arena and I was there sometimes—not often, tho . . . i didn't seem to mix too well there and mostly stayed with you. Every Sunday you took me to the downtown cafeteria—that was our day not to eat at the McCreary's—and we had pancakes with maple syrup and butter and picked up the Denver Post—then you read the comics to me . . . I LOVED it . . . we didn't have such elegant or voluminous comics in little rock. Two or three times you, Hubert, Gladys and I went up the Rocky Mountains in his open-ford and that was thrilling and scarey—SO close to the ledge—and we saw incredibly-hued rocks and a chipmunk and had a wonderful picnic. Those were happy times . . . Hubert was a smiler/laugher and fond of Gladys' sister and kid. The trains, Cleo! sometimes we slept in a berth, sometimes it wasn't a long enough trip but always you had me firmly by the hand as I took in the wonders of the station at Kansas City—the gaudiest, most exciting place i'd been in up to <u>then</u> and later at the World's Fair in Chicago I truly thought heaven had arrived. Cleo, it was a WONDERFUL thing to do for your little cat. Mary didn't want to join us; she was not KEEN to travel but I've never stopped reliving that first and second trip to the fair. You let me buy pretty things, not to mention, once again, having outfitted me in DARLING clothes . . . a scandal suit in white piped in red, another in soft blue—that was a little dress-skirt on top of jumpsuit shorts. We have photos. And the cokes we drank and frozen custard and hamburgers consumed were the best things I've <u>still</u> ever tasted.

Cleo, there was/is a sweetness about you . . . something so gentle and fine and I adored you. Later I got older and wasn't so sensible and we fought . . . still great tremendous love was always there. I didn't understand all the pain you'd suffered—physical pain when you had babies . . . they don't <u>do</u> it that way anymore!—and mental anguish because of so <u>many</u> things . . . a man who didn't think women should work or understand you at <u>all</u>, mary's getting polio, my haVING TERMINAL acne, somehow never getting to be who you really were until years later when you could go back and teach again. I am so LUCKY . . . insanely, mindlessly lucky to have had a mama who always encouraged <u>me</u> to use my brain and achieve. What would you have been, Cleo, if you had had the same chances and encouragement from <u>your</u> mother and others around you. I can see you in 1978 as an editor doing just what <u>I'm</u> doing—or maybe editing books . . . something to do with words and thoughts. You might have done research on a period of history that interested you . . . you could have

<u>written</u> about that or so many other things. You never had a chance to do all that, Pussycat, but somehow made all those things that should have happened to you happen to <u>me</u> . . . I am the total product of your love and attention. You <u>worried</u> too much about me . . . I turned out to be tough and lucky and loved . . . but your worry was always directed toward wanting the BEST, wanting <u>everything</u> for Mary and me. I could write a few dozen pages I guess about our life together . . . remember my doll house that you lovingly collected one Christmas? we put it in orange crates which were PERFECT for the purpose and I had six whole rooms—you made the doll furniture coverlets and pillows and things. And the ballets and stage shows you took me to . . . heaven! Cleo, you were a good mother. The best. If I'm something special in the world of working women now, it's because you pointed me there and David took up where you left off but that was YEARS later! Everything good for me you wanted I got. I wish I could give you everything you deserve but I give you my love and gratitude . . . <u>all</u> of it.

Happy 85th Birthday!

NINETEEN

And Almost Family

Richard Zanuck and David produced numerous movies together—
<u>The Sting</u>, <u>Jaws</u>, <u>MacArthur</u>, <u>The Verdict</u>, <u>Cocoon</u>, <u>Deep Impact</u>
and others. David was executive producer on <u>Driving Miss Daisy</u>
but left before production began as Richard and his wife, Lili, now
a producing team, produced it. Richard and his previous wife
Linda's sons are our godchildren. Alas, they don't write—not
everybody does!—but we stay in each other's lives. With his father,
Dean produced <u>Road to Perdition</u> starring Tom Hanks and Paul
Newman, last year, and it did well. Harrison is working on a production entitled THE NINTH MAN, as well as other subjects in
development. Both boys got married, and I got to attend one ceremony but couldn't attend the other.

April 5, 1993

Dear Richard,

It was such a scrumptious party. I'm sending Lili a present—hosts get <u>letters</u>! Richard, we were talking about pictures in our houses. I wanted you to know that on a table of pictures there's one of Harrison's graduation from Harvard with mommy <u>and stepmommy</u>, a really glorious picture of you and Linda and all the children and two dogs (was one of them Patton?). I think this was taken by Linda Ashley. There's a close-up portrait (color) of you and Lili, you and David getting your Thalberg. Then, moving to the wall, we have you and David with Gregory Peck in his MacArthur days, a wedding portrait of you and Lili in front of the church, you and David at the Cannes Film Festival in front of SUGARLAND EXPRESS, a huge picture of the three of you (David's in a hat), big picture of the two of you on our terrace, plus pictures of you and David with Roy Scheider, Robert Redford, Elizabeth Taylor and Richard Burton. Enough already!

Hope we'll see you soon again.

Love,

Mr. Richard Zanuck
Beverly Park
Los Angeles, California 90210

HGB/rc

April 14, 1998

Dear Dick,

Maybe the best part of the week-end was that I got to sit next to you twice at dinner and sort of catch up. I'm very fond of you, to put it mildly, and our lives <u>have</u> been twined together with a few moments of apartness, since about 1967—is that a long time or <u>what</u>?! That you are such a good friend to David, a <u>beloved</u> friend, means everything to <u>me</u> . . . he never had a satisfactory son and I think deserves you. Before I get <u>really</u> sentimental, just let me say that dinner at your house, the wedding and wedding dinner were kind of unbelievable. . . . it was a <u>beautiful</u> ceremony and no wonder we all went to pieces! My two Godsons are so beautiful I can't quite comprehend and am going to try to get into their lives one way or the other . . . we haven't been real, real close. They couldn't be as wonderful as <u>they</u> are if they didn't have you to blame it on. . . . I think they are absolutely terrific. Dean has promised to come and visit us in New York and I would absolutely adore that. Your little talk at the wedding reception was the best I've ever heard anybody <u>do</u> that kind of thing but your heart was full of love and appreciation of the occasion and of your son and it all came out. I'm so happy to have been there. Keep being the wonderful friend and person you are.

Ever so much love,

Mr. Richard D. Zanuck
Beverly Park
Beverly Hills, CA. 90210

August 30, 2000

Lili dear,

I sent a letter to Richard about the wedding which I so horrendously missed attending and there was something in that letter—in case you read—I thought might have bothered you. I think in the first paragraph I started out raving about Linda Zanuck and how gorgeous she (still) was and then I got to you a few clips later. You were as gorgeous (more?) as anybody and how you look I don't think was or ever should be an issue in your life. You are as pretty as it gets—always were and, fortunate you, that will go on. I'm disturbed about your health. . . . what a woofy thing to happen in the middle of your beautiful life. I know you must have the best people advising and taking care of you. I have so little patience for people who bring things on themselves—they smoke, they drink, they drug, they weigh three-hundred pounds (from lack of discipline) but you are so innocent. Well, sweetie, most of life is good—not that health isn't major-major. You are young and so much will just keep on getting better. See you soon.

Love,

Mrs. Richard D. Zanuck
Beverly Park
Beverly Hills, CA. 90210

HGB:ss

Lili and Richard dear,

I wouldn't want your flower bill . . . these are the most glamorous, strong, healthy and gasp-producing orchids I have ever seen on an orchid tree . . . they're <u>gorgeous</u>! Not too many people remember other people's wedding anniversaries, possibly because people don't stay married that long <u>or</u> it's enough work to commemorate Christmas and birthdays, but you are not only rememberers you are <u>lavish</u>! There never was a bouquet like the one you sent to us in Lanai last year . . . it's probably still out there on the balcony thrilling other people but the orchid plant is sumptuous. The accompanying message was heart-pleasing, too. So we've both had another anniversary . . . I'm glad the marriages and the friendship are still going so strong.

Love and hugs,

Mrs. Richard D. Zanuck
Beverly Park
Beverly Hills, CA. 90210

HGB:ss

June 12, 1991

Dear Harrison,

Hope you don't mind my mentioning you in my column this month. That really was a special night and it was wonderful to be with you and Dean and your father. Harrison, as a godmother, I surely haven't done you much <u>good</u> through the years, even when you were in school in my neighborhood. I don't know what might come up in the future—you are not the world's most outreaching, gregarious young man and I, on the other hand, am notoriously un-wonderful with children! You are not a child any longer, however, and David and I are here for whatever needs in your life might ever arise. We are both so proud to have you and Dean as our godchildren. I never wanted my <u>own</u> children but I certainly am happy to have <u>you</u> . . . how gratifying you turned out so well! Your father has been good about sending us Progress Reports—your grades have been incredible—so we <u>have</u> kept track of you. Have a wonderful summer . . . I hope I get to see you in the years ahead.

Love,

Mr. Harrison Zanuck
Beverly Park
Beverly Hills, California 90210

HGB/rc

June 17, 1998

Dear Harrison,

<u>Both</u> your letters arrived and I was so thrilled to have them—so was David. When you <u>do</u> get around to writing, you write very <u>good</u>! Your plans sound kind of exciting—a honeymoon in the Pacific Northwest—both Washington and Oregon, I understand, are lush. The air fresh and fragrant, a different world than we both live in. I'll bet your screenplay <u>works</u> . . . you know lots about that world. Good for Patricia to get a degree . . . everyone wants you to <u>have</u> one these days. David's basking in the Deep Impact aura . . . nice to have a movie people go and <u>see</u>. I just got back from Northampton Massachusetts. Smith College has my manuscripts and papers and I went to visit them (I thought I would spare you and Dean the peskiness of disposing of them—that's what children do and <u>Godchildren</u> can only be pushed around so <u>much</u>!). The papers were there with lots of other well-known ladies' papers. . . . Gloria Steinem, Betty Friedan and other pushy females. I'm half dead from schlepping my luggage on a Beechcraft 1900 that has just one seat on either side and a row of seven seats. Your father used to have Frank Sinatra's and Sammy Davis Jr.'s private plane to go to Palm Springs but the configuration was a little different! David and I are going to a dinner for Sumner Redstone this evening . . . he's being honored again and they have to fill tables . . . don't mean to be catty! It was <u>wonderful</u> to hear from you. Now that I know you <u>can</u> write (just like a grown-up and everything!) I'll expect to hear from you.

Much love to you both,

Mr. Harrison Zanuck
South Barrington—Apt. 4315
Los Angeles, CA. 90049

TWENTY

Love Letters

Weird! Being such a prolific other kind of letter writer, I never wrote many soppy little billets-doux to boyfriends. Not sure I think it's a good idea to do that, particularly if you like him better than he likes <u>you</u>. I do tuck a sort of love note into David's luggage every time he goes on a trip. They mean so much to him that he never saves any of them. But he did scrounge up two plus a poem.

Baskerville is the nickname I gave David the first month we were married and I found out how much food was required to keep him happy. No being filled up and satisfied with cottage cheese and pears like some of the opposite sex . . . he ate like a hound of the Baskervilles!

April 26, 2002

Basker dear,

This is your make-good letter from the missing one on Los Angeles trip. I can't believe I didn't do my usual Significant Letter for my Significant Other (<u>very</u> significant!)

You are my joy, <u>sometimes</u> my sadness . . . (if <u>you</u> aren't happy, there's no chance for me) my r'aison, my pleasure, my pride and my LIFE! Don't want to heap such responsibility on your big brown-bear shoulders—having somebody that mercilessly dependent on you could possibly be a <u>drag</u>—but maybe you can look at it the other way: you give somebody a reason to be glad she's <u>here</u> and glad she made such a fuss and carried on so 43 years ago you had to cave and let her carry you <u>off</u>! My reward—peripheral—is that I got carried to a beautiful castle in the sky where I spend my hours and days contentedly—gratefully and <u>happily</u>—with an outstanding big brown bear (who is also a dear little boy I get to take care of).

March 30, 2001

Bye bye baby

The thing that will keep me going is thinking about our lovely
date at the Carlyle last night . . . that's the best kind of date
there is . . . with my Basker. Come home safe soon so we can
have a Basker date again—any kind will do. I love you and am
(indescribably!) proud of you.

> XX
> Hugs & Squeezes
> (as Gene would say!)

September 25, 1993

For my husband

I wasn't exactly drowning when you met me, just wavy—
Like trying to fight World War II without a navy.

I was a little rowboat—you were a tanker
And became my mentor, soulmate, anchor.

You piloted us through blizzards and monsoons
Into magnolia fields under April moons

You made us rich, successful, famous
Asked who's made it, people would name us

I feel totally, utterly <u>blessed</u>
But wait, you have to hear the rest . . .

Ruth Schandorf said, "You'll never be bored."
She didn't mention I'd be cherished and adored!

I am the luckiest woman in the world <u>forsooth</u>
Your trying to take your sweater off in the land cruiser in Botswana
is <u>proof</u>!

Other women have men that just get by . . .
Mine has given me all the stars in the sky.

I love you, Basker.

@ @ @ @ @ @

 For eight years—eight years????—I was cuckoo about a classic Don Juan whom I would have married but he wasn't interested . . . gave me a <u>bad</u> time! The following letter to him was written after I had been contentedly married forever, twenty years after I'd last seen the D.J., in response to a letter he wrote <u>me</u>.

May 28, 1977

Sweetiepie,

Thanks for your nice letter. It made me cry!

I'm just home from London...David gets in from Los Angeles
in four or five hours...I think it's 4 in the morning
my time or something, so one is a little zonked and
emotional anyway, but I wept starting with the second
paragraph...if you could call those paragraphs!...
my god, you do write well.

It was so dear of you to write. And I consider that
a testimonial...never mind whether it's true, it seems
true enough so it doesn't have to be all the way
true. I just loved it!

Willie, we would have been a disaster married...two
years would have been the outside limit, but, jesus,
did I ever want you to marry me! (I daresay that was
quite CLEAR!)

You were naughty about girls...you really were.
I don't think you were sleeping with everybody...
maybe not with anybody (though that I doubt) but
you were "appreciating" to the point of driving me
nearly insane. You know/knew all that. Anyway,
somewhere in the middle of all that suffering I did,
these are the things I remember the most...
though there may be two or three thousand:

> 1. The first morning at the Surfrider -
>   I still have a bunch of snapshots - did you
>   ever see them...I mean the ones in the room,
>   not the ones on the beach. Do you think it
>   was the girlets?! Okay, and then spending every
>   night in that bar at Trader Vic's listening to
>   Quiet Village and drinking some kind of Hawaiian
>   cappaccino (spelling) -
>
> 2. Going to a wedding reception - you won't remember
>   this one at all - for some Knopf person and

drinking lots of champagne - I had on a black lace
dress and black picture hat...Paul Hesse took a
picture of us...it's nice...and going back to
your apartment on Wilshire Boulevard
and quietly making love, as always.

3. You barefoot, sometimes shirtless, running around
in pirate-wrap pants or cotton cords or whatever
preceded blue jeans looking incredibly
chic and insufferably sexy.

4. Mexico City/Acapulco and all the fighting and
all the loving.

(Let me interrupt to say that loving was always so simple...
wasn't it? I mean it was so simple it was like breathing)

5. Now, this one is a little hard to pin down but it
was one summer Sunday afternoon and, after breakfast,
lunch and love, we were in Hollywood for some reason -
I think perhaps we went to that Trader Vic's for
dinner and we parked on Ivar or one of those streets
between Hollywood and Sunset Boulevards and
just kissed...(this time I was wearing black
shorts and a white sleeveles shirt - sometimes clothes
help pin ~~these~~ things down though this little outfit,
like most of my L.I.'s was so corny I shouldn't
evern bring it up!) - I mean we'd made love all
day but this was just pure loving and affection
and kissing hard and long as though we'd only
just met. In Appletrees, yes.

6. That whole first week when we started being together -
from Brigadoon and, indeed, the rose in the
lapel to a lovely night when we went to Marion Davies'
old beachhouse to drink and then later in the week
when Ann - Anne? - came home and I decided this
could not be. Hah! And you sent gardenias which
are still my favorite flower.

My dear darling old friend, I could write thousands
of these...I do play them back in my mind and have
almost total recall for then...now is something else.
(Do you ever "lose" somebody's name that you know QUITE
well and gradually, perhaps over a two-day span,
painfully ~~can~~ dredge it up to absolutely prove nothing
is going bad with your brain or your memory?)

Willie, I am almost _psychotic_ on the subject of being
fifty-five. I _can't_ be...really I'm _not!_ It is
perfectly okay for _you_ to be 56...I'm sure you are more
glorious than ever, but really, a woman cannot _be_
so old. Unacceptable! I may take Samantha, my
Siamese cat - I mean she's _really_ old - 15 - and
jump off the roof. All of which is by way of saying
it r ally didn't _hurt_ to have such a lovely letter
when I got some today.

I told Red Mayer a year or so ago I'd had a note from
you or Christmas card - can't remember quite _what_ it
was, and he said, "Helen, don't start _that_ again!"
really worried I think...he is devoted to David
and to me and he could see me throwing away my
security and serenity in big bushel baskets. He
didn't understand at _all_...danger doesn't lurk...
nobody _asked_ me but Red, remembering some of my _bad_
old times (with you, my dear) was trying to be
~~xxxxxxxxx~~ wisely friendly.

We probably should _never_ see one another...we couldn't
say the things we're writing...it would undoubtedly
be _ghastly_ but know that I am grateful you happened
to me and loved me...even though I have never _ever_
suffered so much over anything as I did you...and not
all unjustifiably, you bastard! And I loved you _wildly_
and am grateful for _that_. You really _were_ worthy.
Keep the shoulders and the waistline and the verve
...they all sound marvelous. And ~~xxxx~~ live forever
so I never have to think about your not being here.

                    Love,

IN CLOSING

So, pussycat, you have struggled, scrambled, lunged, crawled—however you chose to do it—through all those letters of mine, and may I tell you how happy that makes me—we letter writers like our letters to be <u>read</u>. You have been spared a little wear and tear in that we don't have copies of <u>all</u> the letters I wrote from 1965 to 1990 because those would have been carbon copies (before computer) and were lost when <u>Cosmo</u> offices moved to a new building. I may have helped with the <u>losing</u> since I didn't imagine anyone would ever be interested in my correspondence plus I live with a man who saves everything from menus at a college reunion to postcards from childhood friends and it's tempting to counterbalance his "never-throw-it-away" with some "let's-toss-it-<u>now</u>"! Never mind, I doubt there was anything woofingly important in any of those bygone letters, and as you've seen, we have plenty of others.

Letters. I still can't explain exactly why reading the written word (as in letters, books, magazines) is more pleasing to many of us than assimilating knowledge and messages from a screen. Of course the written word doesn't replace a voice get-together, but who is the person who doesn't love slitting open the envelope and finding a personal note inside? . . . I don't know that person, do you? I've mentioned earlier you can get something you <u>want</u> from a letter, perhaps easier than an in-person or on-the-phone request, because you can ponder and work and edit and make the words more persuasive than if you just grabbed the lapels or rang up on the phone and started cajoling. I recently got Henry Kissinger to come speak at a Hearst magazine luncheon because of a good letter. It isn't that I could have got him on the phone anyway, but I was able to tell Dr. Kissinger who would be at the luncheon, why it was important for us to hear him, how much influence magazines <u>have</u> in the world, and why he ought to do it. Just one little example of letter-writing power.

I also recently wrote a parole board on behalf of the brother of a friend who ought never to have gone to prison in the first place—he was innocent—but was detained. Now his parole has come up again. I haven't heard the result of the entreaty yet but have high hopes . . . it's one of my good letters.

All right, I'll shut up right this minute so you can go get out the notepaper and start writing.

◎ ◎ ◎

ACKNOWLEDGMENTS

Special thanks to my elf Susan Schreibman, who pulled up thousands (or so it seemed) of copies of my letters from her computer so we could choose some for this book. Thanks to the friends and associates who <u>saved</u> my letters through the years (very flattering) and loaned them back to us for the book. Elizabeth Beier of St. Martin's Press, the best editor there could be, made the final cut (somewhere along the way I lost all judgment!), and I'm grateful to her boss, Sally Richardson, publisher of St. Martin's Press, for believing there could be a book in the first place. David Brown bore up pretty well during the letter selecting, being unable to see the rugs, carpet, linoleum, hardwood floors during the initial phase. He didn't contribute many of his own. How somebody who saves <u>everything</u> (earlier noted) could have jettisoned these treasures from his beloved I don't understand, but did somebody say consistency is the hobgoblin of little minds? Just thanks for getting me started <u>writing</u> books, David. We'll hope a few people have enjoyed this one.